河南省宣传思想文化战线"四个一批"人才资助项目

Comparative Career Development Education

比较职业发展教育

周倩 等 编著

郑州大学出版社

郑州

图书在版编目(CIP)数据

比较职业发展教育/周倩等编著.—郑州:郑州大学出版社,2020.7
ISBN 978-7-5645-1906-3

Ⅰ.①比… Ⅱ.①周… Ⅲ.①大学生-职业选择-比较研究-世界 Ⅳ.①G647.38

中国版本图书馆CIP数据核字(2020)第013549号

郑州大学出版社出版发行
郑州市大学路40号　　　　　　邮政编码:450052
出版人:孙保营　　　　　　　　发行电话:0371-66966070
全国新华书店经销
新乡市豫北印务有限公司印制
开本:710 mm×1 010 mm　　1/16
印张:19
字数:327千字
版次:2020年7月第1版　　　　印次:2020年7月第1次印刷

书号:ISBN 978-7-5645-1906-3　　定价:69.00元
本书如有印装质量问题,请向本社调换

河南省高等学校哲学社会科学创新团队支持计划
（2019-CXTD-09）

本书作者

周 倩　刘 莹　郭连锋
吴春苗　刘俊仁

前言

职业发展教育有多种名字,比如生涯教育、生涯发展教育、职业生涯发展教育、职业生涯规划教育等,无论何种名称,职业发展教育对于学生成长成才,对于国家未来发展都十分重要。这是由其特点所决定的:一是终身性。职业发展教育应该贯穿于人的一生。对于学生而言,职业发展教育既是一个教育过程,也是职业观念形成、稳定和成熟的过程。不同阶段应有相应的职业发展教育目标,制订科学的培养方案,选择恰当的培养方式和途径,从人的全面发展角度出发,让学生深入学习和全面掌握职业认知、就业技能乃至创业本领,树立正确的职业价值观和伦理观,增强职业生涯规划能力。二是匹配性。职业匹配理论(personality-job fit theory)认为,性格类型、兴趣与职业关系密切,兴趣是人参与活动的巨大动力,让人们感兴趣的职业,都可以提高其积极性,促使人们愉快地从事该职业。职业兴趣与性格特质之间也存在很高的相关性。职业发展教育不仅给学生传授生涯规划方面的理论知识和思想观念,而且要指导和引导学生如何参与就业竞争,以找到适合自己身心特点、兴趣并能最大限度地发挥自己潜能的职业,实现人与职业相匹配。三是过程性。职业发展教育的目标是帮助学生找到合适工作、求得职业发展、促进素质提升,提高生涯认知能力和就业能力。职业发展教育的内容涵盖自我认知、职业认知、社会认知和职业综合能力的教育和培养。可见,职业发展教育是一个有目的、有计划、有组织的促进个体生涯发展的过程,是一个由浅入深、由理论到实践的系统教育过程。

职业发展教育是一个交叉学科,综合性较强,涉及教育学、心理学、社会学、人力资源管理、创业教育等领域,集理论性、实践性、指导性等特色于一身,要求教育工作者不仅掌握有关的政策,而且具备多学科的知识,与学生所学专业相关的知识,并且具有一定的实践经验。这靠一个人、一所学校、一个部门或几个人、几所学校、几个部门的力量是无法完成的。它需要调动校内外的相关资源。具体来说，一是政府出台相关制度规定，对职业发展教育给予政策性保障。将职业发展教育作为强制性的教育内容，作为学生的必修课，前移到义务教育阶段，从小学、初中开始对学生进行系统化、正规化的职业发展教育。二是培养优秀的职业发展教育师资队伍。职业发展教育学科起步较晚，最早依托公共管理一级学科，如郑州大学2012年自主设置职业发展教育二级学科并于次年招生。因此，我国职业发展教育几乎没有专业的师资队伍。由于职业发展教育课程有其内在的规律和体系，所以需要更多的专业教师。各地、各学校也应该整合教育力量，增加和配备专业教师，并对现有职业发展教育教师进行学历提升、持续培训，提高专业化水平。三是进一步完善职业发展教育学科，增加硕士点，设置更多的博士点，培养高级专门人才。增强职业发展教育学科，还要构建学科的知识体系。目前，职业发展教育与管理、职业生涯规划与发展等方面的教材比较多，但像比较职业发展教育、中外职业发展教育史、职业发展教育原理等方面的著作缺失，没有形成科学的、系统的课程群。

美国、日本、英国等国家职业发展教育开展较好，有相关的法律明确规定学校必须对学生进行足够的职业发展教育。从政策的角度看，我国比较明确的职业发展教育虽然进行了十几年，但与这些发达国家相比，还有不少差距。譬如在日本，国家对学生的职业发展教育有立法，许多学校都将其作为必修课程。文部科学省很早就制定了适用于日本全国的职业发展教育完整框架，对小学、初中、高中、大学每个阶段的职业发展教育都做了细致安排，系统性非常强。这一框架很完备，内容深入细致，列出了职业生涯教育每个阶段，都应该开设哪些课程，掌握什么样的能力，在一些问题上甚至细化到如何具体操作。这些举措、经验，都值得我国学习和借鉴。

全书分为七章，主要介绍了职业发展教育历史变迁，美国职业发展教育，日本职业发展教育，英国职业发展教育，德国职业发展教育，国外其他国家职业发展教育和我国职业发展教育。

本书凝聚了多位参与者的辛勤劳动。各部分的负责人和执笔人如下：前言、后记，周倩；第一章，吴春苗；第二章，刘俊仁；第三章、第六章、第七章，刘莹；第四章、第五章，郭连锋。每一章的英文论文由周倩节选。硕士研究生王松洁、赵志敏、王宏、张恩铭、王艳霞，博士研究生王威丹等也做出了贡献。全书由周倩负责设计、组织并提出修改建议。

本书可供各级各类学校职业发展教育公共课教师、学生使用,也可供职业发展教育等相关学科硕士、博士研究生使用,还可作为职业发展教育教师培训用书。

对中外职业发展教育进行较为系统的比较研究,是一种尝试,面临诸多挑战,对外语水平和资料搜集能力提出很高要求。除了二手文献,还要查阅大量第一手文献。书中参考了中外研究者的论文和著作,有些地方选用的还较多,尽可能做了注释,在此表示感谢。如果有疏漏之处,还望谅解,再版时进行修改完善。限于编著时间和作者水平,书中难免有错误和不足之处,敬请读者、专家批评指正。

周　倩

2020 年 1 月

目 录

第一章 职业发展教育历史变迁 ... 1
- 第一节 职业发展教育的缘起与意义 ... 2
- 第二节 职业发展教育的理论与实践 ... 9

第二章 美国职业发展教育 ... 22
- 第一节 当代美国教育概况 ... 22
- 第二节 美国职业发展教育政策 ... 30
- 第三节 美国职业发展教育课程 ... 40
- 第四节 美国职业发展教育特色 ... 52

第三章 日本职业发展教育 ... 59
- 第一节 当代日本教育概况 ... 59
- 第二节 日本职业发展教育政策 ... 68
- 第三节 日本职业发展教育课程 ... 74
- 第四节 日本职业发展教育特色 ... 85

第四章 英国职业发展教育 ... 94
- 第一节 当代英国教育概况 ... 94
- 第二节 英国职业发展教育政策 ... 96
- 第三节 英国职业发展教育课程 ... 106
- 第四节 英国职业发展教育特色 ... 114

第五章 德国职业发展教育 ... 120
- 第一节 当代德国教育概况 ... 120
- 第二节 德国职业发展教育政策 ... 125
- 第三节 德国职业发展教育课程 ... 131

　　第四节　德国职业发展教育特色 ………………………………… 135
第六章　国外其他国家职业发展教育 ……………………………………… 148
　　第一节　澳大利亚职业发展教育 ………………………………… 148
　　第二节　加拿大职业发展教育 …………………………………… 162
　　第三节　新西兰职业发展教育 …………………………………… 170
第七章　我国职业发展教育 ………………………………………………… 182
　　第一节　我国职业发展教育的相关政策 ………………………… 182
　　第二节　我国职业发展教育课程 ………………………………… 185
　　第三节　国外职业发展教育对我国的启示 ……………………… 194
参考文献 ……………………………………………………………………… 200
附　录 ………………………………………………………………………… 204
　　附录1 ……………………………………………………………… 204
　　附录2 ……………………………………………………………… 222
　　附录3 ……………………………………………………………… 227
　　附录4 ……………………………………………………………… 233
　　附录5 ……………………………………………………………… 238
　　附录6 ……………………………………………………………… 249
　　附录7 ……………………………………………………………… 253
　　附录8 ……………………………………………………………… 268
后　记 ………………………………………………………………………… 289

第一章 职业发展教育历史变迁

本章要点：
1. 职业发展教育的内涵；
2. 职业发展教育的背景与意义；
3. 职业发展教育的主要理论及其演变。

现代社会是一个职业化的社会。职业及其发展决定人的生活质量和水平，对个人乃至社会影响巨大。伴随全球化时代、学习型社会的到来，知识信息逐渐成为促进经济发展的关键要素。职业的结构、内容和要求随着社会的发展变化，也在不断地变化。个体职业生涯的发展是适应社会时代要求，实现自我理想、个人社会价值的基本途径。个人的现代职业意识、职业素质以及所需要的新的知识技能必须通过不断学习才能获得和提升。因此，澳大利亚教育家康内尔（Connell，W.F.）说："现代社会非学不可，非善学不可，非终身学习不可。"终身学习已经成为现代人生活的主旋律。随着现代社会职业的不断更新、升级变化，对劳动者职业素质、核心技能、综合能力的要求越来越高，职业发展教育顺势而起。那么，职业发展教育是一种什么教育？当今世界的职业发展教育是一种什么状况？世界上不同国家对于职业发展教育都有哪些主要的理论和实践？产生了什么样的影响？对我国的职业发展教育有哪些经验和启示？本章将从职业发展教育的内涵和历史变迁开始对这些问题的探讨。

第一节 职业发展教育的缘起与意义

一、职业发展教育的内涵

职业在英文中有 vocation、job、work、occupation、career 等词汇。Vocation 一般翻译为"职业""事业",指人们从事的相对稳定的、有收入的、专门类别的并且合法的社会劳动,具有社会性、经济性、时代性、规范性、技术性等特征。职业是一定社会分工的产物,它反映了一种或多种的社会需求,是劳动获取的可以满足社会需求的一种分工角色,具有社会性特征;职业有固定的报酬,劳动者从事职业活动主要是为了获取保障生存的物质生活来源;职业随时代的需求而产生,随时代的变化而变迁,甚至消亡;职业活动不能违背国家法律、社会公德和伦理要求,为自己和他人创造物质和精神财富;每一种职业都具有自身的内在要求,如职业知识、技能、规则等。概言之,职业是人们利用专门的知识和技能,参与社会分工,为社会创造物质财富和精神财富,获取合理报酬,作为物质生活来源,并满足精神需求的相对稳定的工作。职业往往表现为人们所从事的一类相关联的具体工作 job。Work 指职业、工作时,侧重指实际的运作、操作。Occupation 表示职业时,侧重指居于或占有某个职位。Career 除了有"职业"和"事业"之意外,还翻译为"生涯"。在国外,往往使用 career development 表示"生涯规划""职业规划""生涯发展""职业发展"等,因此,career 更符合本书所指。

职业发展有广义与狭义之分。广义的职业发展,指随着社会和时代发展,社会职业形态、分工及内涵等的发展变化,包含旧有职业的衰退、消亡,新兴职业的出现和分化,以及职业本身随时代、社会等外在环境要求的发展变化,而呈现出的职业自身在社会性、经济性、规定性以及技术性等方面特征的相应变化。例如教师职业,从古代到近代再到现代,教师职业在社会地位、经济报酬、职业伦理、知识技能等方面的职业特征和职业要求所呈现的时代差异,即为广义的职业发展。狭义的职业发展,则是指社会成员个体的职业生涯发展,又称生涯发展,具体指一个人终生的职业历程,包括一个人一生中所有与职业相联系的行为与活动,以及相关的态度、价值观、愿望等连续性经历的过程。个人的职业发展是一个动态的发展过程,它不仅包含个人在职业上的成功与挫折,也包括个人在职业生涯中认知、态度、价值观、能力、职业选择等方面的发展变化。每个工作着的人都有自己的职业生涯。职业发展是个人生涯中最重要的核心组成部分。

职业发展教育,career development education,也可以称为生涯教育、生涯规划教育或职业规划教育,它是以培养具有健全人格、独立生存能力、全面发展素质的人才为目的,有计划、有组织地培养职业意识与技能,发展个体综合职业能力,促进个体职业发展,以引导个体实施职业生涯规划并落实规划为主线的综合性教育活动。职业发展教育也有广义概念和狭义概念。广义职业发展教育指由社会企事业单位、劳动服务部门、教育培训机构等社会机构开展的职业发展教育,一般指与职业发展相关的咨询与培训。狭义职业发展教育指学校根据国家政策指导和经济社会发展开设实施的职业发展课程与指导。按照教育对象不同,职业发展教育可以分为小学生职业发展教育、初中生职业发展教育、高中生职业发展教育、大学生职业发展教育以及各类社会人员的职业发展教育等。

职业发展教育旨在增强人们职业发展的意识和能力,内容以引导个体实施生涯规划并落实规划为主线。培养职业生涯意识、职业技能,发展个体综合职业能力,实现个体的职业发展,促进个人全面发展是职业发展教育的根本任务。全程性、全员性、实践性、系统性是职业发展教育的基本特征;包括职业规划、职业咨询与心理测评、择业指导、就业辅导、创新创业教育等一系列有助于个体职业发展的内容体系为职业发展教育的实施工具。

大学生职业发展教育是高校在国家政策指导下,根据经济社会发展的要求,有目的有计划地对大学生进行职业生涯意识、职业知识和技能、综合职业能力培养的素质教育实践活动,既包括教育教学活动,也包括咨询、指导、技能训练、社会实践和服务等活动。高校职业发展教育的目的在于帮助大学生认知和沟通专业与职业、职业与事业及其关系,帮助他们了解工作、职业以及社会职业对人才的要求,培养他们的职业规划与生涯发展意识,强化他们在就业中的主体意识,从而在求职择业中能够进行合理的职业定位,顺利进入职场或变换工作,并最终达到人职匹配,实现工作向职业、职业向事业的顺利转变。

二、职业发展教育的缘起

(一)工业化、信息化进程不断催生和加速社会的职业分化和更新,社会产业、职业结构、内容和要求的不断变化,对职业发展教育提出了现实需要

工业革命以来,社会产业结构发生巨大变化,尤其是现代信息产业的快速发展,生产设备和技术更新的速度越来越快,传统产业升级、社会职业的分化速度也随之加快。传统手工业被大机器生产流水线所代替,传统意义的工匠,例如制衣,其职业所需掌握的生产流程的所有工序,从设计、选料、裁剪到销售的过程,分别由专人完成,每个人都成为自己工序上的行家里手。进入信息化社会以后,专业分工又越来越被程序化的信息操控所取代。生产技术和操作方式的革新不仅带来职业分类上的变化,也带来职业自身的汰旧换新。职业分工的精细化,职业操作的程序化、信息化以及新兴职业的不断出现,不仅对社会经济、文化等造成冲击,也让人们在自由社会面对职业选择和由此带来的个人生涯发展提出前所未有的挑战。在职业发展的过程中,个体要适应现代职业要求就必须不断学习,为实现职业顺利发展创造条件。职业指导越来越被现代人所需要。

受工业革命的影响,20世纪初期,西方国家的产业结构发生了巨变。以农业、手工业为支柱产业的时代一去不复返,以工业为核心的经济体系结构逐渐稳固。伴随着工业的蓬勃发展,越来越多的工厂出现在大城市中。大型工业城市的出现,导致大量农村的劳动力,尤其是青年劳动力以及移民涌向工业城市。城市中的劳动力市场开始变得复杂而混乱。为了指导劳动力合理就业,1908年,美国帕森斯(Frank Parsons)教授在波士顿建立了职业指导局(Vocational Guidance Bureau)指导民众合理就业,标志着职业发展教育的源起。

进入21世纪,信息化时代全面到来,大数据的信息化产业异军突起,高科技、数字化、虚拟性的新兴产业特征对传统工业生产体系带来巨大挑战,新科技、新产业对传统的产业、行业运作模式带来极大冲击,对从业者观念、技能和素质提出新的时代要求。人们只有通过各种途径的职业发展教育,转变对职业的传统认知,发展和提升自己的职业技能,才能适应并满足时代浪潮所带来的社会产业结构、职业结构、内容和要求的不断变化。时代的发展,现代职业社会的迅速变化,以及随之而来对从业者要求的变化,对职业发展教育提出了现实需要。

(二)知识经济全球化时代对社会从业者的职业能力不断提出新的要求,呼唤职业发展教育

20世纪以来,西方发达国家的商业公司几乎承担了工业化时期产品的生产、销售、创新等各个方面的责任。坐落于城市中的大型公司的发展,使得劳动者从乡村向城市、甚至从一个国家、一个地区向其他国家、地区迁移。20世纪中期,发达国家的大型商业公司、企业逐渐发展成为跨国性的集团组织。跨国性企业的出现,促使许多新兴职业产生以及工业化经济在世界范围内的发展。以国家、地区为核心的区域经济逐渐向经济全球化发展转变。

伴随着知识经济全球化的发展趋势,人力资源逐渐代替了物质、自然等其他资源成为各国促进经济、社会发展的首要资源。知识社会时代,知识化的人力资源逐渐成为决定经济发展的核心因素。1990年,联合国首次提出了知识经济的概念。1996年,经济合作与发展组织(Organization for Economic Cooperation and Development,OECD)进一步将知识经济定义为"以知识为基础的经济(knowledge-based economy),是建立在知识、信息的生产、分配与使用基础上的经济"。知识经济时代,科学、技术的发展日新月异,国家对社会、社会对组织、组织对雇员的知识构成、技术能力要求越发提高。对以个体为单位的能力培养、价值体现的关注日益受到各个国家的重视和支持。职业发展教育,作为人力资源的重要培育途径,对增强个体职业发展意识,基于自我特质认知、社会职业的实际需求选择最能发挥其潜能、体现其价值的职业类型,以及提升个体综合职业能力、素质,顺利完成大学生个体由学校人向社会人的角色转型,由学校教育向职业生涯的过渡,缩短个人职业和社会发展的调适期等发挥着重要作用。当前,职业发展教育已经成为越来越多国家对经济发展不断提高的职业能力要求的重要回应,是当今世界各国越来越重视的教育理念和教育实践之一。

(三)构建现代和谐社会,促进社会稳定,需要拓宽职业发展教育的层次

失业人口是影响社会和谐稳定的一个重要因素。自从工业革命以来,

随着科学技术以及生产手段的更新,产生了大量的剩余劳动力和失业人口。世界各国都在努力通过各种措施把社会失业人口控制在一定安全范围,以保持社会的稳定和健康发展。在各种政治、经济、文化措施中,通过教育,尤其职业发展教育提高人们职业综合能力和社会适应能力,是转化剩余劳动力,扩大就业,减少社会失业的一项重要而有效的举措。越来越多的国家和政府认识到,面向社会全体大众的职业发展教育,不仅是文化教育行业在现代社会的深度发展,为社会发展培养和提供优质的人力资源,具有积极的经济意义,而且具有促进社会和谐稳定的重大政治意义。自20世纪以来,美国、日本、英国、德国等发达国家政府和组织机构纷纷投入职业发展教育的理论研究和项目开发中,并日益引起发展中国家的关注与重视。职业发展教育正越来越多地成为社会终身教育的主导部分,也越来越成为协调社会经济发展与人的自身发展之间关系的重要途径。

当前,我国高校毕业生就业难已经成为一个不争的事实。如何解决大学生的就业问题,成为社会、政府、高校、个人等多方共同关注的问题。高校职业生涯教育通过让学生认知自我、认知社会职业以及认知"人职匹配",能够很好地协助学生由学校向社会职业过渡,对于大学生就业问题的解决,颇具实效性。因而,高校职业生涯教育成为当前国内教育学、心理学、社会学等多种学科学术研究的热点。除了高校毕业生就业问题,随着我国政治、经济、文化等各方面社会改革的深入推进,大量现代社会职业分化和更新带来的社会劳动力的合理流动和安置问题,也日益凸显,亟待解决。为了满足社会经济的持续健康发展,构建和谐稳定的现代社会,职业发展教育越来越受到国家的重视。进入21世纪,在国家政策的主导下,我国的职业发展教育逐渐由以高校为主体扩展到整个社会,创业教育与指导也逐步纳入职业发展教育的体系中。并且,职业发展教育不再局限于高等教育领域,而是逐渐向高中和中小学渗透,我国职业发展教育呈现出全程性、系统性等特征。

三、职业发展教育的意义

(一)职业发展教育有助于实现个人价值与社会价值的最大化,提升个人幸福感,提高社会生产力

首先,随着经济全球一体化进程和全球金融市场的持续多次出现的动

荡,世界多元文化渗透与社会高度互联的环境下,职业人群工作、生活与转换的节奏在不断加快,人们的固定职业安全感在下降,组织发展的稳定性也在同步下降,面向未来的企业与职业同步发展趋向,使得未来发展显得比以往任何时候都更为扑朔迷离。职业发展教育可以通过加强人们的现代职业意识和职业综合能力,充分挖掘和提升个人独特的职业能力,帮助人们提高社会适应能力,最大限度地实现个人价值和社会价值,从人力资源的角度大大促进社会生产力的发展。

其次,每个人都有其独特的性格、兴趣、能力、价值观,而每一种职业也有它特定的内容与要求,并不是每一个人都能从事同一种职业、做好同一份工作,不同的工作往往适合不同特点的人去完成。一个人在从事其喜欢而又擅长的工作时,将会创造出最大化的个人价值和社会价值,并由此提升个人幸福感。职业发展教育能够帮助从业者在职业发展过程中尽快实现理想的人职匹配,从而最大限度地发挥其个人的潜能和特长,既提升个人幸福感,又促进社会生产力的提高。

(二)职业发展教育是大学生综合素质教育的新主题

自高校扩招后,加强和改进大学生素质教育受到党和政府高度关注。如何充实学生素质教育的内容,提高大学生适应社会发展需要的思想道德等综合素质教育的实效性,真正促进大学生的全面发展,职业生涯发展教育无疑是一种有效的途径。如果大学生一进校,就在学校和教师的指导下制订一个与未来职业发展相联系的大学期间的发展规划,有目标,有制约发展的因素分析,有行动方案,或许就不会有那么多大学生感叹大学生活"郁闷""空虚"和"无聊"了。实践证明,通过专业思想教育、自我探索和职业发展教育来实现思想政治教育,加强大学生素质教育,效果会更好。求学、就业、恋爱是摆在每个年轻人面前的人生课题,而由于经济转型及高等教育规模的持续扩大,求职就业正在成为青年人最关心也最难解决的问题。调查表明,大学生及广大青年迫切需要提升个人职业规划的意识、水平以及择业求职的相关知识与方法技巧。职业发展教育对大学生明确学习目标、充实学习内容、改善学习过程、提高人际交往和社会适应的意识和能力、确立积极的学习生活态度、切实提升思想品德等综合素质意义重大。

(三)职业发展教育能有效地缓解人才市场的供需矛盾,促进社会和谐

职业指导源于就业指导但不是简单的就业指导。对大学生而言,对他们进行适当的就业指导不仅重要而且必要。比如:如何进行职业定位、如何搜索就业信息、如何制作求职材料、如何应聘面试、如何签订就业协议等都是大学毕业生急需的知识技能。这些求职以及就业方面的知识技能,不仅有助于帮助大学生顺利就业,实现更好的理性就业,解决社会上出现的所谓"毕业即失业"问题,而且能对个体未来的职业发展提供必要的思想准备和方法技术指导,增强个体职业发展中的主动性和适应性。现在的就业市场还不够成熟,就业信息的渠道不够畅通,就业政策保障不够健全;还有就业观念存在滞后和偏差,包括就业中的期望值问题、一次就业定终身问题、工作职业事业相混淆问题等。职业指导不仅告诉学生如何找工作,还告诉学生如何谋职业,如何创事业,努力在毕业生与用人单位之间架起一座沟通的桥梁。通过职业指导和职业发展教育,一方面可以帮助求职者了解和掌握较为全面和准确的人才市场信息,以及未来的人才需求趋向,树立理性的职业或就业观念和预期;另一方面,能够有针对性地根据人才市场的需要和变化,为社会产业和新的职业分化发展、用人单位新的要求培养适用的合格的从业人员,有效缓解人才市场的供需矛盾,促进社会稳定发展。

职业发展教育以对教育变革与创新的不断追求和对人生终极幸福的深切关怀为基本理念,不断冲击着教育领域中长期以来形成的"职教分离"现象和由此加剧的人的单向度发展,给教育界带来了一股清新的空气。因此,继美国之后,英国、德国、瑞典、加拿大、澳大利亚、日本、俄罗斯等各国纷纷立法,积极开展职业发展教育。职业发展教育的设想一经提出,立即得到政府、企业、社区、教育研究机构等多方的关注和大力支持,并在全球很多国家形成轰轰烈烈的教育改革运动,受到学生以及社会各界的广泛好评,促进了就学和就业率的上升及社会秩序的稳定。

目前,我国对职业发展教育的关注度正在逐渐提高,党和政府已经深刻认识到开展职业发展教育的重要性,尤其已经把对大学生的职业发展教育作为提高高等教育质量、落实大学生就业、和谐社会生活、促进社会经济发展的重要途径。高校陆续将职业规划课纳入必修课或者选修课。2007年,国务院办公厅下发《关于切实做好2007年普通高等学校毕业生就业工作的通知》,教育部、人事部、劳动保障部印发《关于积极做好2008年普通高等学校毕业生就业工作的通知》,要求进一步提升高校就业指导服务水平,提高广大毕业生的就业能力,"将就业指导课程纳入教学计划"。2007年12月28日,教育部办公厅印发《大学生职业发展与就业指导课程教学要求》的通知,2012年8月1日,又印发《普通本科学校创业教育教学基本要求(试行)》的通知,规定本科高校必须将"创业基础"课纳入必修。同时,高校组织的各种就业、创业等职业发展教育的实践创新和竞赛活动,也得到了扎实有效的推动,受到社会各界的广泛关注。职业发展教育对广大高校毕业生顺利进入职业社会,缓解人才市场供需矛盾,促进社会和谐正在发挥越来越显著的效应。

第二节 职业发展教育的理论与实践

职业发展教育作为就业指导工作与职业指导教育的延伸和发展,主要包括职业生涯规划教育、职业心理测评与职业咨询、求职择业指导、创业教育等内容。作为一种专门的社会服务工作和研究课题,职业发展教育最早起源于美国。20世纪初,在第一次工业革命引发美国主体产业结构变革的影响下,职业指导得到了美国联邦政府的关注和支持,随即职业发展教育迅速在社会和高等学校中推广开来,对美国现代社会发展产生了极大推动和影响。受其影响和启发,英国、德国、日本等一些发达国家的职业发展教育也取得了长足的发展。借鉴美国等发达国家职业发展教育的经验,对建立适合我国国情的本土化职业发展教育理论体系和具有实际效能的职业发展教育实践体系,具有积极的意义。

职业发展教育自20世纪初期在美国出现以来,至今已有一百多年历史。其发展可以分为三个主要的阶段,即20世纪初到20世纪40年代末,职业指导的主导阶段;20世纪50、60年代,职业指导向生涯辅导的过渡阶段;20世纪70年代至今,职业生涯教育为主导的阶段。[1]

---

[1] 陈禹.人力资源开发背景下美国高校职业生涯教育研究[D].东北师范大学博士毕业论文,2011年。

一、20世纪初到20世纪40年代末:职业指导阶段

早期的职业发展教育也叫职业指导或就业指导。1894年,美国加州工艺学校就有人推行就业指导。20世纪初,刚刚经历过工业革命的美国,移民大量涌入,为了减缓社会矛盾,美国的弗兰克·帕森斯(Frank Parsons)首先使用了"就业指导"的概念,专门研究了就业指导的问题,并于1909年《选择职业》(Choosing a Vocation)一书提出了一个全新的观点,即人与职业相匹配是职业选择的关键。"人职匹配"的职业指导理念,告诉人们不仅仅是"找工作",还要"选择职业"。帕森斯设计出很多问卷,帮助人们认知自我和职业匹配。同时,提出了以"人职匹配"职业指导理念为核心的职业指导运动,在波士顿建立了职业局,以指导移民、青年劳动力等不同类型的民众合理就业。帕森斯在职业发展教育方面做出了开创性巨大贡献,被誉为"职业指导之父"。

帕森斯基于对职业指导的含义、方式、效果等多方面的关注,提出了认知自我、认知职业、进而在其基础上进行两者有效匹配的职业类型选择模式,为指导个体合理选择职业提供了依据。1910年,波士顿召开第一次全美职业指导会议(National Conference on Vocational Guidance),这次会议,为职业指导在全美的普及奠定了基础,对职业指导在美国的发展起到了积极的推进作用。哈佛大学的教授保罗(Paul H. Hanus)在会议记录中写道:"全美有45个城市派出了工商界、教育界、社会学界等代表上百人参加会议,纽约、芝加哥、底特律等大城市尤为重视。很明显,系统化的职业指导引起了全国的关注。"[1] 1913年全美职业指导协会(National Association of Vocational Guidance, NAVG)的成立,标志着职业指导在美国的全面开展。

伴随着职业指导深入开展,教育与职业指导逐步融合起来。1916年,哈佛大学首次为学生开设职业指导课程。美国联邦政府在1917年颁布的斯密斯-休斯法案(Smith-Hughes Act)指出,要大力发展与职业指导相关的教育,并为其开展提供专门的基金。在政府的关注与协助下,职业指导逐渐成为美国教育体系的附属部分。20世纪20年代,职业心理测验开始在美国高校职业指导中得到广泛应用。帕森斯的人职匹配理念主要地应用在20世纪

---

[1] Hanus, Paul H. Vocational Guidance and Public Education[J]. School Review, 1911(19): 51-55.

20年代的美国学校教育中,通过智力测验、心理测试等途径对学生个体进行职业指导。这成为那个时代美国高校中职业指导开展的重要特征。同时,美国高校开始普遍出现专门的职业指导课程。

20世纪30年代初,美国爆发了大规模的金融危机,失业率大幅上升。在众多问题中,就业问题的解决成为重中之重。为了解决青少年的就业问题,1936年在联邦政府的支持下,美国大范围开展了"国家青年管理项目"(National Youth Administration,NYA),通过加大学校教育中职业技能培训比重、促进职业指导有效开展等手段,开阔学生对职业类型的认知,提高学生的就业能力,使学生获得更为丰富、有效的职业技能,从而适应当前的社会状况。1937年,全美职业指导协会(NAVG)向美国教育部提出,应该对美国的青少年开展终身性的职业指导。这一提议得到了联邦政府的关注和回应。美国联邦政府在1938年底提出了职业信息及指导服务项目(Occupation Information and Guidance Service),并将其划分到职业教育部门,由1936年颁布的乔治迪恩法案(George Dean Act)提供资金支持。伴随着这一项目的深入,美国教育部指出,职业指导应贯穿于学校教育的整个过程中。职业信息与指导服务项目的实施,标志着美国政府对学校中的职业指导和职业发展教育的重视和需求。

从20世纪初期到20世纪40年代末期,帕森斯的人职匹配理念一直是美国各级教育机构开展职业指导的主导理念。职业指导逐渐渗透到美国整个学校教育体系中。为了促进大学生就业,在高校中广泛、深入开展的职业指导,越发受到政府、社会、民众的重视。在联邦政府的资金、政策支持下,美国高校中的职业指导逐渐形成了以帕森斯人职匹配理念为核心指导思想的专业化体系。尽管20世纪50年代以来,生涯发展理论已经替代了人职匹配理论成为美国高校开展职业生涯的核心指导理论,但是在当前美国高校的职业生涯发展辅导和咨询中,强调学生个体基于自我认知和社会职业认知,进行充分、有效匹配进而合理选择职业类型,仍是指导学生选择、确定职业生涯发展方向的重要依据。帕森斯的人职匹配职业指导理论对美国以及其他发达国家高校职业生涯教育的开展仍具有积极的影响作用。

二、20世纪50、60年代:职业指导向生涯辅导的转化阶段

二战后,人力资源素质的开发、管理和应用对经济发展的促进作用开始

受到美国联邦政府关注。学校教育中加大了职业指导的力度,以提高毕业生的工作技能,满足经济发展需求。当时的美国,几乎各级公立、私立学校都为职业发展教育的开展设立了专门机构,并有资金支持。在这样的时代背景下,美国学校中以帕森斯人职匹配理念为核心的职业指导逐渐式微。为了适应社会职业对人的需求变化,提高人的职业知识、能力,促进个体对职业的合理选择,20世纪50年代,产生了多种新的职业指导理论。

1942年,心理学家罗杰斯(Carl Ransom Rogers)在心理咨询领域中提出了"以当事人为中心"的心理咨询与治疗方法,主张在咨询领域中,遵循不主动、不判断、不指导的非指导性的技术路线和原则,充分尊重当事人的中心地位,产生了很大影响。1951年,罗杰斯《当事人中心疗法》一书的出版,标志"非指导学派"的理论走向成熟。受其影响,就业指导开始由对职业信息的重视转向重视个人特质和个人发展,帮助的方式由"指导"向"非指导"的咨询方式发展。研究者更加关注求职者内在各种心理特质,向人性化的方向发展。职业发展教育理念开始了由职业指导向职业辅导的转变。

1951年,学者金斯伯格(Eli Ginzberg)受到"生命阶段"学说的启发,认为职业选择是一个动态的阶段积累过程,他指出:"①职业选择是一个长期的过程;②职业选择的过程越发变得不可缺少且不可逆转;③最后做出的职业选择显示了个体在职业理想与可获得的现实可能性中做出的妥协;④整个职业选择的过程由一系列起决定性作用的阶段构成。"①同年,心理学者罗伊(Anne Roe)依据心理分析理论提出了职业选择理论。罗伊认为通过强调个体早期需求的满足,父母对子女的生活经验传承可以影响个体的职业选择,家庭因素与个体的需求等级发展之间具有直接的因果关系,进而导致职业选择的发生及变化。在金斯伯格的生涯阶段划分理论的基础上,通过开展多学科的综合研究,1951年,舒伯(D.E.Super)提出了生涯发展理论,认为个体的生涯发展历程可以分为五个阶段,即成长(growth)、探知(exploration)、建立(establishment)、维持(maintenance)及衰退(decline)。对个体的生涯发展,舒伯突出"自我概念"意识,认为"自我的概念不仅仅是个

---

① Isaacson, Lee E.Career Information in Counseling and Teaching[M].Boston:Allyn and Bacon,1977.47.

体作为社会角色的重要组成部分,同时也是个体职业选择的决定性因素。"①舒伯强调职业指导是一个动态变化的发展过程,而非只是以个体的性格认知与社会职业认知为基础的静态匹配过程。舒伯生涯发展理论对美国职业生涯教育理念的发展产生了重大影响。学校中的职业发展教育,从重视专门的职业技能培养从而使学生个体符合社会职业的要求,转向以学生个体的生涯发展为核心,职业发展教育的意义不只是帮助学生找到工作,而是个体的职业生涯发展、完善,进而通过个体职业生涯的可持续性发展,发挥个体的人作为可利用社会资源的价值。

1959年,约翰斯·霍普金斯大学教授约翰·霍兰德(John Holland)出版了其著作《职业选择理论》。在书中,他提出通过对个体个性与职业类型进行分类,进而分析与自身职业能力相符的职业类型的职业指导理论。霍兰德的类型理论认为,通过个体的价值、技能、能力倾向等因素与适合职业环境的合理匹配,个体将会获取职业满足感。为了帮助个体选择合理的职业匹配,1970年,霍兰德制作了著名的职业性向测验量表,这一量表至今在美国、日本及我国等很多国家仍广泛使用。

20世纪60年代初期开始,美国高校中的职业指导不再被期望单纯地解决大学生就业问题,转而将大学生个体的职业生涯发展视为其重要任务。美国高校的职业指导逐渐以生涯发展理论为基础向生涯辅导过渡。伴随着美国社会向知识经济的转型,产业结构的变化要求更为先进的培训和更为正规的教育。美国政府、社会对职业发展教育越发关注。1961年,面对当时8.1%的失业率和经济的衰退,肯尼迪政府通过了《地方再发展法案》(Area Redevelopment Act),对经济开始衰退的地区提供资金援助,建立专门的职业培训机构,为失业个体提供再就业的机会,并由财政、教育和劳工部门共同组成专门委员会指导职业发展教育的开展,以提升青少年就业率,促进美国人力资源的有效开发。1962年,美国联邦政府颁布《人力开发与培训法案》(Manpower Development and Training Act, MDTA)。MDTA 针对的主要是非教育体制的职业训练与指导,通过对个体私人的职业培训、指导机构提供资金支持和政策保障,促进失业群体的就业以及对已从业人员的职业发展提

---

① Super Donald. E.Vocational Development: A Framework of Research[M].New York:Columbia University Bureau of Publication,1957.46-47.

供分析、规划服务。正如学者海尔(E.L.Herr)所述:"20世纪60年代初,很明显,失业的、甚至已被雇佣的……人们几乎都在接受职业培训,或者被教授与获取、维持职业机会相关的职业技能以实现就业的目标。"①《人力开发与培训法案》的颁布是联邦政府协助职业指导的里程碑。1963年美国政府通过了《职业教育法案》(Vocational Education Act)。在越发重视通过尖端科技促进经济发展的20世纪60年代,职业发展教育注重为雇主提供高技能的劳动力,该法案为个体寻求工作提供必要的专业职业指导、培训以适应时代的产业结构变化,具有重要的历史意义。在其基础上,1968年联邦政府又颁布了《职业教育修正法案》(Vocational Education Amendment Act),强调通过教育体系,由初等教育开始持续开展职业发展教育。

自1909年以来,帕森斯的"人职匹配"职业指导理论在40余年中一直主导着美国的职业指导。20世纪50年代初期,舒伯的生涯发展理论的诞生,强调人职匹配的职业指导逐渐被关注个体发展的生涯指导所替代,标志着职业指导理念向生涯指导理念的转变。舒伯的生涯发展理论不但是当前美国职业生涯教育的核心指导理念,而且成为多种颇具代表性生涯发展理论的基础。20世纪60年代,伴随美国一系列职业发展教育立法的颁布实施和学术研究,职业生涯教育通过课程顺利地渗透进K-12教育体系,推动了职业发展教育由职业指导向职业生涯教育全面过渡。

三、20世纪70年代至今:职业生涯教育阶段

在舒伯生涯发展理论的影响下,20世纪60年代末70年代初,美国诞生了许多与个体生涯发展相关的生涯理论。例如,霍兰德的类型学理论、克朗伯兹(John Krumboltz)的生涯决定社会学习理论、克内菲尔坎姆(Knefelkamp)和斯列皮兹(Slipitza)的生涯认知发展理论等。职业指导在美国的主导地位,逐渐被一种综合、系统、全面的教育理念——职业生涯教育所取代。美国联邦政府一直很关注职业发展与学校教育的融合,自20世纪初开始,几乎每个时代,美国政府、学界、社会等多方面对职业指导与学校教育融合都有着不同时代背景下特有的强调。20世纪70年代初期,这种强调

---

① Herr Edwin L.Vocational Guidance and Human Development [M].Boston:Houghton Mifflin Company,1974.132.

转化为国家人力资源的合理、有效开发。基于此,1970年美国联邦卫生教育福利部教育总署(American Education Agency)署长詹姆斯·艾伦(James Allen)提出"职业发展教育",英文为"career education"。1971年,其继任者西德尼·马兰(S.P.Marland)在全美中学校长年会上发表的演讲中,结合终身教育、心理学的自我认知等理论提出了职业发展教育理论。在政府和民众的支持下,这一理论很快成为20世纪70年代美国教育体系中的主要指导理论。

职业发展教育产生的原因,可以追溯到20世纪50、60年代导致美国严重失业问题的因由争论。民众的失业到底是因为经济发展缓慢从而导致的就业岗位不足,还是个体缺乏足够的职业生计能力应对雇佣的需求?美国社会学家丹尼尔·贝尔(Daniel Bell)指出:"20世纪60年代,特殊技能已经代替工作经验成为评价劳动力的首要标准。"①西德尼·马兰赞成这一观点,他认为,"美国的社会正处在一个新的变化时期,社会产业结构的变化会导致个体从事职业类型大幅、快速地改变,这种改变要求个体掌握更多种新的知识与技能以获得在变化社会中的生存能力。"②职业发展教育理论的诞生导致了美国的教育改革,西德尼·马兰指出:"所有的教育都是职业发展教育,或者应该成为职业发展教育,学校教育者必须努力让学生既可以选择能成为合格的、有用的被雇佣者,也可以选择继续进入高校接受教育深造。美国教育的总体目标就是让所有的青少年完成12年学校教育后,能够具备完成就业或继续升学的能力。"③这反映了职业发展教育理论融合学术教育与职业指导理论的教育思想。这一思想受到传统学术教育学者和专门职业技能教育学者的严厉批判。但是,职业发展教育最终获得了政府的支持。1977年,美国政府出台了《职业发展教育激励法案》(Career Education Incentive Act)以促进职业发展教育改革的开展。在20世纪70年代,美国的50个州全部在州教育局中安排了职业发展教育协调者,指导职业发展教育改革的实施。1982年联邦政府颁布了《职业训练协作法案》(Job Training Partnership Act)再次强调,通过注重职业技能培养的专业化职业发展教育,满足社会职业的需求。

20世纪80年代,经济的发展引起了社会人才需求的变化,进而导致了

---

① Bell D.The Coming of Post-industrial Society[M].New York:Basic Books,1973.49-54.
② Fuller, Jack W,Terry Whealon.Career Education: A Lifelong Process[J].Nelson Hall Inc,1979.44.
③ Marland. S. P.Career Education, Now[J].Vocational Guidance Quarterly,1972(20):188.

学生接受教育选择的变化。越来越多的学生向往接受高等学术教育,对职业发展教育项目失去了兴趣,发展势头缓慢了下来。虽然最终职业发展教育并没有以一种教育制度的形式在美国流传下来,但是职业发展教育理论对美国教育体系中职业指导的进一步完善、发展,具有深远的影响作用。1985年,起源于1913年所创办的"美国职业指导协会"(National Vocational Guidance Association,NVGA)更名为"美国职业生涯发展协会"(National Career Development Association,NCDA),隶属于"美国咨询协会"(American Counseling Association,ACA)。该协会名称从"职业指导"改为"职业生涯发展",实际上从侧面反映了职业生涯的理论以其科学性而逐渐深入人心。而后职业生涯指导运动不断推进,集高校、政府、专业协会(社会力量)三者于一体的大学生职业发展教育和体系也逐步在美国得到确立。

据统计,1982年至1990年间,美国参加"大学准备项目"(College Preparatory Program)的学生人数增加了10%左右,同一时期,有32个州的教育调查报告显示参加职业指导、职业发展教育项目的学生人数急剧下降。[①] 职业发展教育对学生吸引力的消失与学生对职业发展教育的客观需要形成了矛盾,这引起教育学者对传统职业发展教育的反思。在这样的背景下,20世纪90年代,产生了"新职业发展教育主义"教育理念,它批判了过于注重职业技能训练的传统职业发展教育,认为职业发展教育的目标应该设立为指导学生合理、有效就业以及升学指导,倡导学术教育与生涯教育的融合、以学生为核心教授普通的职业能力并设立新型的生涯教育机构如职业高中、职业发展学院,等等。在其影响下,20世纪90年代,美国开展了"从学校到职业"(school to work,STW)运动。STW运动得到联邦政府的支持,这一时期先后颁布了三项重要的法案,即1990年的帕森斯法案Ⅱ[②]、1994年的《从学校到职业机会法案》(School to Work Opportunity Act,STWOA)以及1998年的帕森斯法案Ⅲ[③]来促进STW运动的开展。STW运动,在全国范围内,面向所有学生开展,一方面通过学术教育加强稳固学生的知识基础,另一方面

---

① Gray,K.Vocationalism and the American High School:Past, Present, and Future[J].Journal of Industrial Teacher Education,Volume 33,No.2,1996.47.

② 1990年的帕森斯法案Ⅱ,即Carl D.Perkins Vocational Education and Applied Technology Education Act Amendments of 1990.

③ 1998年的帕森斯法案Ⅲ,即Carl D.Perkins Vocational-Technical Education Act Amendments of 1998.

通过实际的职业实习提升学生的工作技能与经验,将学校本位与工作本位合理结合,进而为学生由学校到职业的过渡构建有效途径。进入新世纪,伴随着政权的交接,2001年布什政府不再为STW运动提供资金支持,这宣告了STW运动的结束。然而,STW运动的教育理念却以从学校到生涯(school to career,STC)的方式传承了下来。

此外,20世纪末西方后现代主义的世界观和方法论渗入生涯规划领域,给职业发展理论带来新观点和新变化。后现代主义特征有:接纳不确定性和片断性;反对绝对唯一的真理,尊重多元事实;不要求一致性,而强调多样性和差异性;重视主观解释,而非客观经验;认为语言不仅反映事实,更能创造事实;强调创造意义等。① 这些特征与当代多变和不确定的生涯特征暗相吻合,引起许多生涯理论研究者的注意。在这些观点影响下,相继出现职业发展混沌理论、无边界职业发展理论、职业发展建构理论和职业发展咨询领域的叙事取向咨询、职业发展教练技术等生涯理论和研究。后现代职业发展理论回应了多变的社会环境和个体真实的生涯情境,对当代生涯规划辅导具有重要的指导意义。首先,后现代职业发展理论强调生涯的个体性,包容甚至提倡个体生涯发展的差异性。其次,用"混沌""复杂""动态开放""非线性发展""无边界"等描述生涯的特征,接纳生涯的不可预测和不确定性,不再一味追求规划的准确性,而是以积极的态度,对决定保持开放和弹性。再次,强调"适应"而非"匹配","职业发展的灵活性""职业发展的适应力"等强调个体应因生涯角色变化与之保持平衡的能力。最后,强调个体是职业发展的主动创造者,是自己生涯问题的专家,"意义创造"成为职业发展与生涯咨询的关键词。②

21世纪,知识经济成为美国经济的核心,对高质量人力资源的需求受到政府、社会、个体等多方面的关注。学校教育不再单纯地关注知识、技能的传授,通过协助学生个体实现终身可持续性发展、促进人力资源开发成为美国学校教育关注的核心。"从学校到生涯"的(STC)理念,以学生个体的职业发展为核心,通过教育课程的设置、职业指导咨询的开展等方式,协助学生设计职业规划及实施,完善学生个体的职为发展。伴随着信息时代的发

---

① 金树人.生涯咨询与辅导[M].北京:高等教育出版社,2007:140.
② 阮娟.后现代生涯理论及其对大学生职业发展教育的启示[J].东南学术,2016:4期.

展,计算机几乎被利用在各个领域中。在当前美国的学校中,尤其是高校中,利用计算机开展职业发展教育普遍起来。发现(DISCOVERY)和互动式指导信息系统(sigi plus)是当前在美国高校中广泛运用的计算机辅助职业发展指导工具,可以为学生提供心理测评、职业信息、在线咨询等多种职业发展指导服务,进而有效地辅助、完善职业发展教育在高校中的开展。

职业发展教育理论起源于20世纪初帕森斯提出的人职匹配职业指导理论,经过20世纪初到20世纪40年代末以职业指导为核心的阶段,20世纪50、60年代由职业指导向生涯辅导转化阶段,以及20世纪70年代以来职业发展教育三个阶段的发展变革,职业发展教育逐渐成为美国高校促进大学生合理、充分就业,完善大学生职业素质、能力,促进大学生个体职业生涯可持续性发展的有效途径,成为当前美国高校颇为关注的教育理论。这一理论有效地整合了终身教育理论,并使得大学生人力资源成为重要的潜在知识化人力资源。大学生职业生涯的健康发展对其自身和社会都具有十分重要的意义。

美国职业发展理论自诞生之日起就产生了广泛的影响,并在发达国家迅速流行起来。日本、英国、德国、澳大利亚等国积极翻译和介绍美国的职业发展教育理论和经验,各个国家基于对自身经济发展现状和未来发展展望的考虑,日益重视本国的职业发展教育。这为我国的职业发展教育提供了理论和实践借鉴。

思考题:

1. 什么是职业发展教育?
2. 简述职业发展教育产生的背景与意义。
3. 请谈谈职业发展教育的主要理论及其演变。

推荐读物:

1. 刘春生.职业教育学[M].北京:教育科学出版社,2002.

2. Herr Edwin L. Vocational Guidance and Human Development [M]. Boston:Houghton Mifflin Company,1974.

3. 罗伯特·C.里尔登,珍妮特·G.伦兹,小詹姆斯·P.桑普森,等.职业生涯发展与规划[M].3版.侯志瑾,等译.北京:中国人民大学出版社,2010.

4.黄天中.生涯体验——生涯发展与规划[M].3版.北京:高等教育出版社,2015.

国外论文导读与阅读(一):

导读:职业发展教育的世纪回顾与展望

作者:让·吉查德(Jean Guichard)

本文主要回顾了法国及欧洲职业发展教育在20世纪的发展与21世纪的展望。文章指出,早在1957年,巴黎就出版了一本定义职业发展教育原则的教科书,但职业发展教育直到25年后才在欧洲真正发展。而后法国及欧洲职业发展教育实践经历了三个重要的发展阶段,主要体现在安托万·莱昂(Antoine Léon)、肯尼思·霍伊特(Kenneth Hoyt)、唐纳德·舒普尔(Donald Super)、埃德温·赫尔(Edwin Herr)等人的贡献与魁北克省的实践。发展的原因主要在于:促进个人成功的意识形态,工业社会的快速转型、学校教育的演变及其在社会中的地位、工作组织的变化等。学校社会功能的演变,工作在个人发展中作用的变化等几个因素决定职业发展教育的未来。

职业发展教育的目的是使个人(通常是群体)能够建立一个适当的代表性框架,以应对他们遇到的学校和职业——也就是个人的转变。目前职业发展教育的社会或伦理目标,有四大共识:培养工人的灵活性;鼓励个人发展;引导学生尽可能适当地应对与培训机构中学徒分配有关的问题;鼓励社会整合。

论文还阐述了职业发展教育实践的教育目标与科学依据,不同的职业发展教育目标以及相应的设立目标的方法及其理论和模式;在职业发展教育方法评价方面,主要介绍了米歇尔·胡托(Michel Huteau 1999,2001)的研究评价理论。

对职业发展教育的展望:提出了职业发展教育在新世纪稳中求变的发展特点。职业发展教育的发展与不同环境的变化有关,特别是出现了以自我建构和个人成功为核心价值观的思想框架。不同的经济、社会或伦理目的,从培养工人的灵活性到关注减少社会不平等,尽管这些职业发展教育目

标各不相同,其科学基础也不确定,但结果却相当积极。不同的研究表明,职业发展教育应该在未来几十年内稳固并迅速发展。其发展变化,首先与学校的变化有关,其次与成人活动模式中工作作用的变化有关,最后是更多地考虑社会融合和集体发展的问题。

文章来源：

Jean Guichard. A Century of Career Education：Review and Perspectives [J].Internat. Jnl. for Educational and Vocational Guidance 1 (2001)：155-176.

国外论文导读与阅读(二)：

导读：历史视角下的职业发展及其实践

作者：埃德温·赫尔（Edwin L. Herr）

随着时间的演变,职业生涯实践的形式与实质以及其指导的对象也在发生改变。在新千年之初,本文回顾了20世纪职业生涯实践的遗产并有选择性地进一步思考那些可能在未来数十年中突出的职业发展中的理论与实践上的问题。文章从历史梳理、相关理论的发展和未来展望三个部分来论述。

作者认为职业指导首次被承认是在19世纪末期20世纪早期的美国,其发展主要与国家经济从以往的基于农业向工业革命下制造业和工业进程的加快这种转变存在直接联系。社会地位、工业化进程、城市化和移民等众多问题影响了职业指导的发展。论文将职业指导划分为两个阶段：第一个阶段是职业指导的开创时期,帕森斯被普遍认为是职业指导运动之父。早期的职业指导模式特点,应对人格尊严,将人与工作有效匹配。早期的职业指导步骤被视为一种具有实用性和人性化的方法,来帮助人们与职业结构相匹配从而维护秩序,合理的选择,使人有能力去决定可以获得的职业机会而不是被迫进入能够立即得到的职业岗位。但本阶段缺乏必要的建立在职业指导和咨询上的科学基础或理论。职业生涯发展实践虽然出现,但是职业发展理论尚未产生。第二个阶段是职业指导综合化发展时期：国家目标与职业指导。当20世纪职业发展实践展开并朝综合化发展时,一个持续的塑造其目的的主题是社会、政治和经济的影响,包括了国家政策和法规。国家目标、政策和法规都是宣扬职业和职业生涯指导质量和综合化发展的重要因素。

第二部分是从职业指导到职业发展过程以及相关理论的补充和发展。这个部分主要是从职业指导定义的变化、职业指导理论发展来探讨的。关于职业指导定义的变化,论文列举了三个阶段:第一个阶段,1937年的定义为,职业指导是帮助个体去选择一个职业,为其进入该职业做准备,并取得一定成就的过程。第二个阶段,舒珀(1951)提出并经国家职业指导协会完善后,定义职业指导为,帮助个人发展以及接受完整的充分的自己以及个人在工作世界的角色,并在现实生活中验证该理念,将其转化为现实,获得个人满足感和社会满足感的过程。第三个阶段,后来职业指导定义的焦点从集中于该选择什么,转变为选择者的特性。在这一过程中,它降低了个人与职业的匹配程度以及在特定时期及时的职业信息的重要性。相反,它强调职业选择上心理动力的天性,强调人一生职业行为发展的影响,结合了个人和职业指导的维度,提高了作为职业和教育背景相关的评价基础的个人认知和个人接受能力的重要性。

第三部分,关于职业发展的未来展望,作者认为,未来的职业发展会有以下几个方面的趋势:一是职业发展实践正成为一种世界现象;二是职业发展实践将作为个人尊严的工具;三是职业发展实践是个人灵活性的工具;四是职业顾问将会承担多样角色。

文章来源:

Herr Edwin L. Career Development and Its Practice: A Historical Perspective[J].The Career Development Quarterly(March 2001, Volume 49):196-211.

(节选的英文原文见附录1)

第二章　美国职业发展教育

本章要点：
1. 美国职业发展教育历程；
2. 美国职业发展教育政策；
3. 美国职业发展教育课程；
4. 美国职业发展教育特色。

第一节　当代美国教育概况

职业发展教育是美国整体教育系统的一个组成部分。理解美国的职业发展教育状况需要了解其教育系统，尤其是教育行政体制和学制，它们与本国职业发展教育存在着更为紧密的关系。教育行政体制决定了职业发展教育的参与主体和权力来源，学制则决定了美国职业发展教育在各个学段的不同发展目标和课程设置。因此，本节首先介绍美国的教育行政体制和学制，在此基础上介绍美国职业发展教育的历程。

一、美国教育行政体制

根据1791年美国联邦政府颁布的宪法第10条修正案的规定，"本宪法未授予合众国也未禁止各州行使之权力，皆由各州及其人民保留之"。教育即属于宪法未授予合众国且未禁止各州行使的事项，因此管理教育的权力属于各州。在长期的历史发展过程之中，美国形成了以州为主的地方分权制。1958年颁布的《国防教育法》再次确认了地方分权制，其规定："国会重申这一原则并申明，州和地方社区要控制并必须控制公立教育，并对其负有主要责任。"具体而言,在美国教育行政中,州政府负责本州的主要教育事务,州以下设学区,负责本学区的具体教育事务,联邦政府不断通过立法和拨款手段加大对各州教育的影响,从而形成了联邦、州、学区三级的教育行政体制。

1. 联邦教育行政

美国在传统上属于典型的地方分权制,联邦政府不负责领导全国的教育事务。顺应世界范围内实行地方分权制的国家纷纷加强中央政府对教育集中领导的趋势,也为了解决各个学区之间由于资源不均衡导致教育发展不均衡问题,美国也开始强化联邦政府对教育的领导。联邦政府主管教育的行政部门是1979年10月成立的联邦教育部。它有四项基本职能:制定联邦资助教育的政策,分配和监管联邦教育经费;收集和公布美国学校教育资料,资助教育科研活动并传播教育科研成果;促使全国关注重要的教育问题;禁止一切歧视,确保教育机会平等。可见,联邦教育部主要采用立法、资助、指导等宏观调控手段引导和控制教育,联邦教育部已经能够对全美国的教育发展产生实质性影响,但是基于美国长期的地方分权制传统和法律的明确规定,美国联邦政府对地方教育当局仍然没有直接的管理权,无法强制各州接受联邦政府的规定,而是各州自愿采用联邦政府的规定。美国联邦教育部的部长、副部长和各司司长首先由总统提名,并经过国会同意后进行任命。

2. 州教育行政

美国共有50个州,各州均拥有本州的教育行政权力。州的教育行政机构包括州教育委员会和州教育厅,其中州教育委员会是决策机构,真正掌握着各州的教育权力,州教育厅是执行机构,负责执行州教育委员会通过的教育法律和政策。州教育委员会的主要职能有:制定和解释本州教育政策及相关规章命令;审定本州教育预算;拟定或修订本州教育法律;收集、保存、公布本州教育资料;向州长或州议会提出年度工作报告;制定学校分类和审核标准;确定教育人员的任用标准;审批教育人员的任免等。州教育委员会的组成人数一般是10人左右,多由教育界之外的具有多元文化背景的社会人士构成,委员会成员通过州长任命和民选两条途径产生,任期一般为4~6年。州教育委员会的最高行政长官是州教育长,由州教育委员会或者州长指派。州教育厅的主要职能有:执行州教育委员会的决策;制定本州教育发展计划和实施方案;编制本州教育预算并执行预算;管理和分配来自联邦的教育经费;开展教育督导、评估、研究等。州教育厅长通常由州教育委员会

任命,也可由州长任命或民选产生,任期一般为4年。

3.学区教育行政

学区属于由州设立的地方公共团体,接受州的行政领导,是最基本的教育行政单位。学区作为管理基础教育的基层教育行政单位,直接管理学区内的一切教育事务。通过学区管理学校是美国教育行政的一个特色。美国的学区与行政区并不一定保持一致,各州的学区数量与规模也存在较大差异。例如,1977年夏威夷州全州为1个学区,而加利福尼亚州、堪萨斯州、内布拉斯加州都有1000个以上的学区。学区的教育行政机构也分为学区教育委员会和学区教育局两部分,学区教育委员会承担决策职能,学区教育局承担执行职能。学区教育委员会的主要职能有:执行各级法律和规章;制定本学区的教育方针和规定;征收教育税;建立和规定课程标准;决定教师聘任和解聘;确定入学年龄和划分儿童就学学校;任命学区督察长等。学区教育委员会委员一般是3~9人,由当地居民选举产生,任期是2~6年,委员中有一定比例的非教育行业人员。学区教育局的主要职能有:执行学区教育委员会的决策;监督、评估和指导学区内的公立中小学、幼儿园;提交年度工作报告。学区教育局的负责人为学区督学,需要具有教育专业背景,由学区教育委员会任命。

二、美国的学制

美国的教育权力主要在各州,各州根据本州的历史传统和经济发展状况设定学制,由此决定了各州的学制存在一定差异。以美国的中小学学制为例,目前美国有8(小学)—4(中学)制、6(小学)—3(初中)—3(高中)制、6(小学)—6(中学)制等多种学制组合。但是该种差异主要体现为每一个学段年限的不同,美国各州的学制总体上都包括学前教育、小学教育、中学教育和高等教育四个阶段。随着终身教育的不断发展,成人教育被作为学制中的"第五阶段"。目前,职业发展教育存在于美国学制的五个阶段之中。由于成人教育的形式多样,这里主要介绍学前教育、小学教育、中等教育和高等教育。

1.学前教育

在美国,学前教育位于学制的最底层,以3~6岁的幼儿为教育对象。学前教育的教育目标是促进幼儿身心健康,在活动中得到全面和谐发展。学前教育的实施机构主要是保育学校和幼儿园。保育学校招收3~5岁的儿童,幼儿园招收4~6岁的儿童。无论是保育学校还是幼儿园,其任务都不是简单的保育,而是促进儿童的全面成长。幼儿园附设于小学,在许多地方已被纳入正规学校教育系统,因此美国整个基础教育经常被称为"K-12",K即是幼儿园。学前教育的内容包括语言训练、音乐、图画、舞蹈、卫生习惯等。学前教育采用的教学方式是通过游戏活动开展教学,让幼儿在游戏活动中获得身心成长。

2.小学教育

小学的年限分为6年和8年,以6年居多。小学一般招收6岁的儿童,小学的教育目标是帮助学生养成良好的态度和获得基本知识与技能。小学开设的课程主要有:英语、数学、科学、外语、公民、政治、经济、艺术、社会等。小学教师采用的授课方式有包班制、科任制、协作教学制、双重进度制等。包班制指一位教师给同一个班级的学生教授所有课程,科任制指同一位教师给不同班级的学生讲授同一门专业课,协作教学制指几位教师共同合作承担同样的教学任务,双重进度制指一位教师统一讲授学术性课程,其他几位教师讲授音体美等课程。

3.中等教育

美国的中学类型多样,从层次上看,可分为"初中"和"高中",包括三三制、二四制、四年制和六年制。20世纪60年代后期,出现了介于小学和初中之间的四年制"中间学校",即招收小学五年级至初中二年级的学生。在20世纪之前,美国中学的教育目标是为升入大学做准备。进入20世纪之后,美国中学的教育目标偏向于全人教育。1913年,美国中等教育改组委员会发布了《中等教育的基本原则》报告,此报告规定了美国中等教育的七项基本原则:保持身心健康,掌握基本的学习技能,成为有效的家庭成员,为就业做准备,胜任公民职责,有价值地利用闲暇时间,讲究伦理道德。根据这七项基本原则,美国中学开设的课程也非常广泛和多样。根据杰弗里·米拉和戴维·安格斯的研究发现,美国中学开设的课程曾经在1973年达到2100门[1],可见美国中学的课程设置非常多样。美国中学课程采用必修+选修+计

---

[1] Kliebard H M.Changing course:American curriculum reform in the 20th century[M].Columbia University,2002:48.

划的设置方式。必修课程是每位学生必须选择的课程,包含了中学生必须掌握的基础知识和基本技能。美国大部分州确定的中学必修课程包括:语言艺术、数学、科学、社会研究、体育与健康等。选修课程是学生根据自己的兴趣和未来发展规划选择的课程,通过选修课程可以实现因材施教,美国中学开设的选修课程门数非常多。教育计划是为了培养学生情感意志、探究精神、创新能力而设计的综合实践活动,也可以称为活动课程。在此类课程之中,课程主题可以由学生确定,学生开展独立探索活动,教师进行指导。该类活动课程越来越受到学生的重视。① 美国中学的课程设置方式决定了美国中学课程实行学分制,明确规定学生中学毕业时要获得的学分总数量。

3.高等教育

美国的高等教育已经形成了三级结构:二年制社区学院,可授予协士(副学士)学位;四年制综合大学和专业学院,可授予学士学位;研究生院和各级专业教育,可授予硕士、博士学位。一般而言,修业年限是协士2年,学士4年,硕士1至2年,博士3至4年。社区学院兴起于19世纪末20世纪初,1922年美国社区学院协会建立,标志着社区学院在高等教育体系中的地位得以承认。社区学院的培养目标一是为继续升学(转入本科)的学生打下坚实的基础,二是面向就业开展职业发展教育和成人教育。四年制的综合大学和专业学院是美国高等教育的基本类型,综合大学和学院本科教育的培养目标是培养学术人才和各种专业人才。在本科教育方面,美国在20世纪20年代就形成了由主修课程、通识课程和选修课程构成的课程体系。通识课程保证知识的广度,使学生打好科学文化基础;主修课程保证知识的深度,使学生毕业后能直接从事某一专业工作,或为进入研究生院继续学习做好专业准备;选修课程激发学生的兴趣,发挥学生的特长。研究生院培养研究生,分硕士和博士两个层次,研究生教育为专业教育,其培养目标是培养从事基础科学和应用科学研究的专门人才。② 硕士学位课程包括一组相连贯的专业课程。博士学位课程注重让学生自由探索和表述自己的观点,注重培养学生创造重大学术成果的能力。

---

① 李其龙,张德伟.普通高中教育发展国际比较研究[M].北京:教育科学出版社,2008:54-56.
② 王天一,夏之莲,朱美玉.外国教育史[M].北京:北京师范大学出版社,2005:105-108.

三、美国职业发展教育历程

如第一章所言,职业发展教育是中国语境下的词汇,又称为职业生涯教育。职业发展教育是对个体进行职业生涯开发、提升的过程,是有目的、有计划、有组织的培养个体科学的人生观,提升个体职业生涯规划意识与能力,发展个体综合职业素养,促进个体职业生涯成功的活动,是贯通家庭、学校和职场以引导个体进行职业生涯规划为主线的综合性教育活动,主要包括人生价值教育、职业生涯规划、择业指导、创业教育和职业心理健康指导[①]。职业发展教育起源于美国。在美国职业发展教育有人称之为职业生涯教育,也被称为生计教育。在美国,职业发展教育被认为"是一种连续不断的历程,也是一种统整的教育构想,它透过生涯认知、生涯安置、生涯进步等步骤,培养学生的生涯能力;以发挥学生的天赋才能为目标,其重点放在人的全部生涯上,使个体从幼儿园到成年能逐渐形成自我引导的能力,最终结果旨在让每位学生过上适合自身特点的美满生活"[②]。可见,职业发展教育贯穿于人的一生,是一个人展现天赋才能、实现人生幸福的重要手段,因此是美国整个教育体系中的重要组成部分。但是美国的职业发展教育并不是一蹴而就的,其经历了一个发展历程,全面了解美国职业发展教育的概况需要了解美国职业发展教育的演变历程。根据美国职业发展教育内涵的变化,以一些标志性事件为界限,美国职业发展教育的演变历程可以划分为职业指导、生涯辅导和生涯教育三个时期。

1. 职业指导时期

职业指导也称为就业指导,主要解决一个人如何选择合适职业的问题。在美国,职业指导最先应用于企业,后来推广到学校,用于解决学生择业问题。1894 年,美国加州工艺学校就开始推行就业指导,帮助学生进行职业选择。随着美国经历工业革命,大量移民拥入美国,为了帮助移民就业,促进经济发展和社会稳定,职业指导问题急需研究。美国波士顿大学教授弗兰克·帕森斯(Frank Parsons)通过深入研究于 1909 年完成《选择职业》一书。在该书中,弗兰克·帕森斯教授不但首次提出"职业指导"的概念,而且系统

---

① 王献玲.职业生涯教育学[M].郑州:郑州大学出版社,2019:1-9.
② 杨迎春.美国高校职业生涯辅导研究[D].上海:华东师范大学,2006:7.

阐述了职业指导的基本内容:"①清清楚楚地了解自己,包括了解自己的能力倾向、能力、兴趣、雄心、资源及限制,以及这些特质的成因。②要明明白白地知道各种工作成功所必须具备的条件和要求、优点与缺点、待遇、就业机会与发展前途。③要实实在在地推论以上这两组事实之间的相关情形"①。弗兰克·帕森斯强调职业指导即是在了解人格特质和职业的基础上,寻求人格特质和职业匹配,这些内容即是"特质—因素论"。弗兰克·帕森斯不但明确提出了"职业指导"的概念,而且构建了职业指导的基本理论,因此标志着职业指导的正式确立。在此之后,职业指导的理论和实践都获得了长足发展。

职业指导将人格特质和职业相匹配作为研究和实践的重点,职业选择既是整个职业发展教育的起点,也是整个职业发展教育的主线,还是职业发展教育的重要内容之一。所以,职业发展教育最早诞生在美国,而美国职业发展教育最初解决的问题即是职业指导问题也就不足为奇了。职业指导阶段开始探究人格特质的分类、职业的特点、人格类别与职业的匹配,抓住了职业发展教育中的核心内容,引起了人们对职业发展教育重要性的认识,正式开启了美国职业发展教育的研究和实践之旅,是美国职业发展教育的起步期。

2.职业辅导时期

职业指导的着眼点是找到适合的工作,这就决定了职业指导的时段是职业期间,采取的手段是指导。随着职业指导实践的不断推进,对职业认识的不断深入,尤其是随着人本主义思想的出现,职业指导的局限性逐渐暴露出来。1951年,美国学者舒伯重新对"职业指导"进行了界定。职业指导是"协助个人发展并接受完整而适当的自我形象,同时发展并接受完整而适当的职业角色形象,从而在现实世界中加以体验并转化为实际的职业行为,以满足个人需要,同时也造福社会的过程"。② 可见,舒伯强调职业指导的目的是协助个人的发展,强调个人在职业发展中的主体性,实际上是从职业指导开始转变为生涯辅导。1953年,舒伯又提出了职业生涯发展理论。该理论认为,一个人的职业生涯可以划分为五个连续的阶段:成长阶段、探索阶段、确立阶段、维持阶段和衰退阶段。成长阶段是人生中的0~14岁,其任务包括了解工作的意义,并树立对工作的正确态度。探索阶段是人生中的14~25

---

① 金树人.生涯咨询与辅导[M].北京:高等教育出版社,2007:10.
② Super,Donal.E.A Theory of Vocational Development[J].American Psychologist,1953(8):186.

岁,其任务包括认知并接受职业选择信息,同时获得有关资料;了解个人兴趣和能力及其与工作机会的关系;认清与能力和兴趣相一致的工作领域和阶层;接受训练以培养技能和便于就业,或从事能实现兴趣与能力的职业。确立阶段是人生中的25~44岁,其任务包括婚姻的选择、养儿育女;从经验或训练中获得足够的工作能力;强化和改善职业地位,力求上进和升迁。维持阶段是人生中的45~64岁,其任务包括通过在职进修或在职培训以保持技能,维持已有的成就与地位;准备退休计划。衰退阶段是人生中的65岁以上,其任务包括适应退休生活;发展新角色。[①] 舒伯将职业拓展到整个生涯,采取的手段也由指导转变为了辅导,而且该种辅导是一种动态性的辅导,通过多次渐进的过程得以完成。"舒伯的生涯发展理论的提出标志着职业辅导转变为生涯辅导。生涯发展理论在职业辅导理论史上是个分水岭。至此,生涯的概念正式取代职业概念,使职业辅导成为生涯辅导的一个方面。"[②]可见,舒伯是生涯辅导阶段的代表性人物,其生涯发展理论也是职业指导和生涯辅导两个阶段的分界线。当然,在舒伯之后,一些学者对生涯发展理论进行了不断的丰富和发展。生涯辅导阶段主要解决个体如何对整个生涯进行规划的问题。生涯辅导实现了从职业到生涯的转变,为整个职业发展教育内容设计了基本的框架,为美国职业发展教育的深入开展奠基了基础,是美国职业发展教育承上启下的关键阶段,可以看作是职业发展教育的过渡时期。

3.生涯教育时期

进入20世纪70年代,随着终身教育的理念推广,美国教育界认为进行劳动准备比掌握某种劳动技术更重要。为了培养学生的职业能力,美国教育总署署长西德尼·马兰于1971年提出了生涯教育的构想。西德尼·马兰认为,生涯教育的目标是"培养个人能够创造有价值的人生,并使个人能够有意思地融入社会",生涯教育的对象是全体公民,生涯教育的时间是从幼儿至继续教育,生涯教育的性质兼备学术性与职业性,生涯教育的实施包括生涯觉察、生涯探索、生涯导向、生涯准备和生涯维持与发展五个阶段。[③] 生涯教育从教育的视角出发,对教育目标、教育对象、课程内容和实施阶段等

---

① 王建国,王献玲.大学生职业规划与就业指导教程[M].郑州:郑州大学出版社,2012:20-24.
② 杨迎春.美国高校职业生涯辅导研究[D].上海:华东师范大学,2006:6.
③ 王志强.美国生涯教育的实施及对我国的启示[J].世界教育信息,2008(3):43-44.

进行了系统的设计,力图实现学校教育与社会人才需求的结合。生涯教育的构想一经提出即受到政府的高度重视,并进入到快速的实践之中。1972年,美国总统尼克松提出,生涯教育是"由政府创办的一种最有前途的教育事业"。1974年,美国教育总署为实施生涯教育拨款6100万美元,并专门设置生涯教育署。在政府的大力支持和推动下,至20世纪70年代末,美国全国所有学区中超过一半的学区开展了生涯教育。1985年,"美国就业指导协会"更名为"美国职业生涯发展协会"。随着知识经济时代的到来和劳动分工的日趋复杂,克林顿总统于1994年签署了《学校工作机会法》,为中小学和高中后阶段的学生提供就业准备。职业生涯教育在美国获得了持续广泛的开展。职业生涯教育阶段真正将职业生涯辅导变成了职业发展教育,从面向个体转变为面向全体,按照教育的基本内容从培养目标、培养对象、课程内容和实施阶段等方面来开展职业发展活动。从严格的教育的角度而言,职业生涯教育阶段是职业发展教育的成熟时期。

第二节　美国职业发展教育政策

虽然美国管理教育的权力在各州,但是联邦政府通过各种途径尤其是制定政策对职业发展教育施加影响。与美国的教育行政体制相一致,美国职业发展教育政策主要是由联邦政府制定的政策和各州制定的政策组成,联邦政府制定的职业发展教育政策又可以分为国会制定的法律和各部制定的政策。从而,国会制定的法律、联邦政府各部制定的政策和各州制定的法规共同构成了美国职业发展教育的政策体系,保障职业发展教育的顺利开展。

一、联邦政府职业发展教育政策

联邦政府是职业发展教育的重要推动力量。推动职业发展教育的重要工具是制定政策,联邦政府在长期的职业发展教育发展过程中制定了一系列政策,对职业发展教育实施干预。

第二次世界大战之后的二十多年,美国经济实现了腾飞,教育发展也进入了黄金时期,快速发展。进入20世纪70年代,美国教育面临着内外部双重困境。在外部,美国1973年遭遇石油危机,经济衰退,失业严重,急需开展

职业发展教育,提升工人的职业能力。在内部,随着终身教育理念的普及,美国教育内容狭窄的弊端暴露,需要扩展教育的内容。为了摆脱上述困境,实现学校教育和社会对人才需求的紧密连接,美国联邦教育总署署长西德尼·马兰于1971年提出生涯教育的理念。生涯教育的理念提出之后,美国国会于1974年通过了第一个生涯教育法案——《生涯教育法》,积极用法律手段推动生涯教育的开展。《生涯教育法》强调以学校为中心开展职业发展教育,由学校设立专门的机构和人员对学生进行生涯教育,开展生涯辅导和服务工作,鼓励学生参加职业入门课程。《生涯教育法》的实施打破了学校教育和职业隔离的状况,促使学生对将来的职业进行思考,并注重培养自己的职业能力。[①]《生涯教育法》是美国各级各类学校开展职业发展教育的基本依据,其颁布和实施对于推动职业发展教育发挥了重大作用。1974年,美国将近6 000个学区开展生涯教育,占到17 000多个学区的约30%,而到20世纪70年代末期,美国50%以上的学区都开展了生涯教育。在五年左右的时间,美国开展职业生涯教育的学区增加超过20%。1975年美国通过了《生涯辅导和咨询法》,1977年美国通过了《生涯教育激励法》,这两部法律对生涯辅导与咨询、生涯教育激励进行了系统规定,从而与《生涯教育法》共同推动了生涯教育的发展。

1989年,美国职业信息协调委员会在联邦教育部的支持下制定《国家职业生涯发展指南》,该文件可以看作是教育部层级的政策,是美国各州开展职业发展教育的指导性文件。1989年发布的《国家职业生涯发展指南》包括职业发展能力框架、指导人员要求和对青年与成年人开展职业发展教育项目的指导意见三部分,对职业发展教育的能力标准和实施方式提出了总体要求。职业发展能力框架按照小学、初中、高中和成人四个阶段分别设定职业发展能力的基本要求,为不同阶段的职业发展能力提供了依据。此外,在职业发展教育的实施上注重学校、企业、社区和家庭之间的协作,通过多方联动增加职业发展教育的实施方式,提升职业发展教育的实施效果。为了应对终身学习社会对工作人员在学术、职业和生涯管理能力方面提出的更高要求,美国教育部职业与成人教育办公室于2004年对《国家职业生涯发

---

① 孟明.浅析美国职业生涯教育的特点及启示[J].广州广播电视大学学报,2009(3):9.

展指南》进行了重大修订。2004年版的《国家职业生涯发展指南》由领域、目标和指标组织指导方针构成基本框架,三个领域分别是个人社会发展、教育成就和终生学习、职业管理。美国各州均以《国家职业生涯发展指南》规定的内容为基础,根据本州的实际状况对职业发展能力框架、指导人员要求、青年与成年人开展职业发展教育项目的指导意见或者是领域、目标、指标组织指导方针进行适当修改,制定各州的职业生涯发展政策,作为本州开展职业发展教育的直接依据。在此意义上,1989年和2004年《国家职业生涯发展指南》为各州开展职业发展教育提供了指南和参考,是美国各州开展职业发展教育的重要依据,促进了美国职业发展教育的顺利开展,也使美国职业发展教育在多样性之中具有统一性。

在20世纪90年代,《学校工作机会法》是推动美国职业发展教育发展的重要政策。20世纪80年代和90年代初期,随着知识经济时代的到来和劳动分工的日趋复杂,美国的低端技术工作岗位也需要工人具有一定的决策能力和新知识、新技能,以适应工作岗位的变动性和技术性,但是美国的中小学和职业技术学校却没有培养学生如何适应低端技术工作岗位的能力。为了解决从学校教育到就业工作顺利衔接的问题,美国国会于1994年通过了《学校工作机会法》,该法的英文是"School to Work Opportunity Act",表明了该法的宗旨是实现从学校到工作的顺利过渡。该法面向中小学和高中后学生,坚持三个基本原则:"第一,面向所有人的教育,与受教育者的未来职业生涯和终身学习的关系,更加密切,更有意义。第二,家长、学生、中学及高等教育工作者、雇主、劳工代表、地方官员和其他合作伙伴都参与进来,推动地方从学校到就业体系的建立。第三,该项目给所有学生提供机会,参加一系列帮助他们确立并实现职业目标的活动,包括那些残疾学生、大学预科生和离开学校后希望进入职场的青年"[①]。《学校工作机会法》包括三项基本内容:学校本位学习、工作本位学习和连接活动。学校本位学习包括生涯探索和生涯觉察,工作本位学习包括工作训练、工作跟随、职场实习等,连接活动是学生和雇主提供的机会进行匹配,实现学校学习和工作的互动。通过学校本位学习、工作本位学习和连接活动,既培养了学生的学习能

---

① 高嵩.20世纪末美国面向就业机会的职业教育政策[J].外国问题研究,2016(12):87.

力和职业选择能力,又锻炼了学生的工作技能。《学校工作机会法》的出台和实施帮助中小学和高中后学生增强了从学校教育到工作岗位过渡的能力,使学生能够比较顺利地走上工作岗位。至此,美国职业发展教育政策的基本框架已经形成。

进入21世纪,知识经济的影响日益扩大,新兴职业不断涌现,职业生涯规划对个人发展的重要性凸显,职业发展教育开展不断深入,这些因素相互交织、互相促进,促使美国更加频繁地出台职业发展教育政策。2006年通过了《生涯和技术教育改进法》,2014年通过了《劳动力创新和机会法案》,2016年颁布了《强化21世纪生涯与技术教育法》。这些政策一方面强调学术课程和职业课程的整合,培养学生的综合能力和职业技能,应对知识经济的挑战;另一方面强调职业发展教育在实施过程中实现中小学、大学、企业、行业协会等组织的协作,建立伙伴关系,为学生掌握职业发展的经验、知识、技能和获得多样化的发展途径提供条件。这些职业发展教育政策坚持了已有政策的基本理念,结合社会经济变化进行了创新,进一步完善了美国职业发展教育的内容,使美国职业发展教育政策更加具有针对性和时效性。

为了配合上述法案的实施,美国联邦教育部、劳工部和其他部实施了一系列计划和项目,这些计划和项目也是美国联邦职业发展教育政策的重要组成部分。代表性的计划和项目包括:联邦教育部实施的"联邦工读项目""学术竞争力奖学金项目"和"国家科学与数学人才奖学金项目",联邦劳工部实施的"创业使美国腾飞项目""跨部门振兴美国航空工业特别工作组"和"总统社区就业培训拨款计划",其他部实施的"吸引学生投身公共服务事业项目""为美国而教项目"和"预备军官团项目"。通过这些项目,联邦政府为职业发展教育的实施提出要求,提供拨款,使职业发展教育法案得以落实,推动了美国职业发展教育的发展。

二、州职业发展教育政策

上述联邦的职业发展教育政策为各州开展职业发展教育提供了整体的政策依据和内容框架。然而,在分权制体制下,职业发展教育属于各州的权力范围,美国各州的职业发展教育政策是每个州开展职业发展教育的直接依据,并且不同州的职业发展教育政策具有一定差别。这里以纽约州为例,介绍州级的职业发展教育政策。

纽约州是美国经济发展良好的州之一,在充足财政拨款的支持之下,经过四十多年的职业发展教育探索,纽约州的职业发展教育已经比较成熟。《纽约规章制度》是纽约州所有政策的汇编,纽约州职业发展教育的基本内容也规定在《纽约规章制度》之中。职业发展教育的内容规定在《纽约规章制度》第八篇"教育部"之中第二章"专员条例"的"基础教育学校项目"一节,"学校的总体要求"部分规定了"职业、技术教育和艺术序列的可用性"一条,与职业发展教育相关的内容是:①所有公立学校均应为学生提供机会,让他们完成以下各领域的三至五个单元:职业发展教育、技术教育和艺术。②所有公立学校都应给学生提供在九年级开始经批准的职业和技术教育的机会。只有获专员批准的职业及技术教育课程,才可用于符合本规定所列文凭的要求。③对于1985年及以后第一次进入九年级的学生,每一项经核准的职业和技术教育系列应包括至少一个学分的职业介绍,在系列的任何时候提供。④1988年及以后初入九年级的学生,在职业技术教育学科中,应当按照经批准的三个学分系列进行组织,延长到批准的五个学分系列或者五个以上,不得扣分。⑤1988年及以后首次升入九年级的学生,在职业及技术教育方面获批准的五个学分或以上的先后次序,须使学生为就业及大专以上教育做好准备,并须令处长满意。⑥所有公立学区均应为学生提供符合技术学习标准的机会。各地区应根据本规定获得证书的具体要求,选择一项或多项选择来满足这项要求。[①]《纽约规章制度》的这一条规定对公立学校开展职业发展教育的课程设置和学分数量做出了基本要求。

此外,在《纽约规章制度》中"基础教育学校项目"一节的"幼儿园—4年级项目要求"和"5—8年级项目要求"两条中规定1—4年级和5—8年级的课程之中"生涯发展与职业学习"是必须完成的学习单元。在"高中毕业证书"部分对纽约州生涯规划和职业学习毕业证书的获取进行了详细规定。具体包括:

(1)合格的学生。①2013年7月1日开始,在2016年6月之前,学区的

---

① Reuters,Thomson. General school requirements[EB/OL]. https://govt.westlaw.com/nycrr/Document/I3652900bc22211ddb29d8bee567fca9f?viewType=FullText&originationContext=documenttoc&transitionType=CategoryPageItem&contextData=(sc.Default).

教育委员会或受托人应当和非公立学校的校长,发出一个纽约州的职业发展和职业学习毕业证书。②2016年6月开始,学区的教育委员会或受托人应当和非公立学校的校长,发出一个纽约州的职业发展和职业学习证书,只要该学生符合入门级就业高中毕业。

(2)学区或非公立学校应确保学生已经提供适当的机会获得评议或当地的高中文凭,包括为学生提供有意义的参与和发展一般课程协助学生满足国家的学习标准。

(3)学区教育委员会或受托人,或非公立学校的管理机构之前毕业证书授予职业发展和职业学习,应确保满足以下要求:

1)学区有证据表明该学生已制定、每年审查并酌情修订职业计划,以确保该学生积极从事职业探索。该计划应包括但不限于学生自我认定的职业兴趣陈述;与职业相关的优势和需求;职业目标;以及职业和技术课程,以及基于工作的学习经历,学生计划参与其中,以实现这些目标。各学区须向学生提供一份由专员编制的范本表格,用以记录学生的职业规划,或一份符合本分部要求的本地编制的表格,并在适当情况下协助学生制订其职业规划。学生的职业规划可以不限于学校提供的与职业有关的活动,也可以包括学校以外的单位提供的活动;但本分科不应被视为要求学校向学生提供职业规划中确定的具体活动。学生在其职业生涯规划中所确定的偏好和兴趣应每年进行审查,对于残疾学生,应根据本规定的相关条款,在制订学生的个性化教育计划时予以考虑。学生高中毕业时有效的职业生涯规划副本,应当保存在学生永久档案中。

2)学区有证据表明,学生展示了毕业典礼水平与职业发展和职业相关的知识和技能的研究学习标准规定的,包括但不限于职业发展,集成学习和通用基础技能;学生在9至12年级成功修毕不少于两学分的职业及技术教育课程和/或以工作为基础的学习经验。学习的数量应获得在职业和技术教育课程和/或以工作实践为基础的学习经验,这相当于单位提供的研究应包括至少54小时记录学校的监督以工作实践为基础的学习经验与职业意识、勘探和/或准备可能,但不需要,完成与学生的职业技术教育课程。为本分部的目的:职业技术教育课程意味着一个年级9~12课程或课程的职业技术教育,包括专业和综合课程经当地教育委员会批准;以工作为基础的学习经验包括但不限于:工作实习、社区服务、志愿服务、服务学习、高级项目和/或校本企业,这些经验应在符合部门指导方针的情况下,在地区的监督下提供,并记录在学生的成绩单中。①

总体而言,《纽约规章制度》规定的职业发展教育内容是纽约州开展职业发展教育的直接依据,为纽约州各个学校开展职业发展教育提供了基本要求。

当前,对纽约州职业发展教育影响更大的政策是纽约州教育部和纽约州立大学联合开发的《职业发展和职业学习资源指南与核心课程》,其功能相当于《国家职业生涯发展指南》,对纽约州各学校开展职业发展教育提出统一要求和参照。《职业发展和职业学习资源指南与核心课程》适用于幼儿园至高中(K-12),包括初级、中级和毕业级三个等级。幼儿园和小学(幼儿园~4年级)属于初级,初中(5~8年级)属于中级,高中(9~12年级)属于毕业级。根据使用说明,该核心课程包含了纽约州职业发展教育标准要求的基本内容,虽然如此,讲授达到纽约州职业发展教育标准的课程所采用的方法是无限的,任课教师或者教师团队可以独立开展课堂活动,以更好地实现纽约州职业发展教育标准。也就是说,《职业发展和职业学习资源指南与核心课程》为每一位职业发展教育教师提供了基本的参考和指南,在此基础上每一位教师可以灵活运用该指南和课程。纽约州的职业发展教育标准包括三个领域:职业发展(标准1)、综合学习(标准2)和通用基础技能(标准3a)、职业群(标准3b),其中第三个领域由通用基础技能(标准3a)和职业群(标准3b)两部分组成。职业发展教育核心课程按照职业发展教育标准设计。纽约州初级职业发展教育课程包括两部分:按照职业发展(标准1)和通用基础技能(标准3a)设计的初级核心课程,按照综合学习(标准2)设计的初级核心课程。纽约州中级职业发展教育课程也包括两部分:按照职业发展(标准1)和通用基础技能(标准3a)设计的中级核心课程,按照综合学习(标准2)设计的中级核心课程。纽约州毕业级职业发展教育课程包括三部分:按照职业发展(标准1)和通用基础技能(标准3a)设计的毕业级核心课程,按照综合学习(标准2)设计的毕业级核心课程,按照职业群(标准3b)设

---

① Reuters, Thomson. General school requirements [EB/OL]. https://govt.westlaw.com/nycrr/Document/I3652b71bc22211ddb29d8bee567fca9f?viewType=FullText&originationContext=documenttoc&transitionType=CategoryPageItem&contextData=(sc.Default).

计的毕业级核心课程。初级、中级和毕业级核心课程的基本结构相同：按照职业发展(标准1)和通用基础技能(标准3a)设计的初级、中级和毕业级核心课程均由讨论问题、基本问题和活动三部分组成，按照综合学习(标准2)设计的初级、中级和毕业级核心课程则由活动构成。按照职业群(标准3b)设计的毕业级核心课程则由综合活动构成，具体包括六个活动：商业/信息体系、健康服务、工程/技术、人力资源和公共服务、自然/农业科学、艺术/人文。

由于《职业发展和职业学习资源指南与核心课程》的具体内容众多，这里主要以初级课程为例，描述《职业发展和职业学习资源指南与核心课程》的详细内容。如前所述，纽约州初级职业发展教育课程包括两部分：按照职业发展(标准1)和通用基础技能(标准3a)设计的初级核心课程，按照综合学习(标准2)设计的初级核心课程。两部分核心课程的内容不同，按照职业发展(标准1)和通用基础技能(标准3a)设计的初级核心课程由讨论问题、基本问题和活动三部分组成，按照综合学习(标准2)设计的初级核心课程则由活动构成。按照职业发展(标准1)和通用基础技能(标准3a)设计的初级核心课程在职业发展(标准1)部分包括7个表现指标，每一个表现指标设计了2~8个讨论问题。以表现指标1为例，表现指标1是学生们开始做有助于从学校到最终进入职业选择过渡的职业规划，这个表现指标设计了3个讨论问题：什么是职业集群？在你的社区中有哪些不同的职业集群？哪个职业最能支持你的个人品质？按照职业发展(标准1)和通用基础技能(标准3a)设计的初级核心课程在通用基础技能(标准3a)部分包括基本技能、思考技能、个人品质、人际关系品质、技术、管理信息、管理资源、体系等8个方面，每一个方面设计了1~3个讨论问题。以基本技能为例，其包括三个讨论问题，分别是：为什么读、写、听、说和使用数学运算很重要？为什么基本技能对个人在职场的成功至关重要？为什么有学术能力的人有必要进入21世纪的职场？除了讨论问题之外，按照职业发展(标准1)和通用基础技能(标准3a)设计的初级核心课程与按照综合学习(标准2)设计的初级核心课程还设计了一些基本问题和活动。基本问题和活动的具体内容见表2-1[①]。

---

① Career Development Occupational Studies [EB/OL]. http://www.p12.nysed.gov/cte/cdlearn/documents/CDOS-Elem-CareerandUniversal.pdf.

表2-1 纽约州职业发展教育初级核心课程基本问题/样本活动概览

基本问题	样本活动	相关标准	备注
我是谁？	未来的我 我的档案袋	CDOS；ELA；SS； Arts CDOS	CDOS=职业发展与职业学习 ELA=英语语言艺术标准 SS=社会研究标准 Arts=艺术标准
为什么我需要学习？	学校是我的工作场所 成功的工人	CDOS；SS CDOS；ELA；SS	
我目前的学习如何为我的人生经历做准备？	工作包 学校商店	CDOS；ELA CDOS；ELA；SS	
我为什么要工作？	你被录用了吗？ 我在哪里学习？	CDOS；ELA CDOS；ELA	
我怎样才能找到成为一名高效工作者所需要的知识呢？	我是谁？ 面试	CDOS；Arts CDOS；ELA	
我需要发现自己的哪些方面，才能让我应对工作场所的变化？	我，甚至更好！ 随波逐流	CDOS；ELA CDOS；ELA	
为什么与他人互动很重要？	援助之手 友谊火车	CDOS；ELA；Arts CDOS；ELA；Arts	
如何运用知识成为21世纪成功的工作者？	职业图表职业历程时间表	CDOS；ELA CDOS；ELA；SS	

按照综合学习(标准2)设计的初级核心课程主要是将职业发展教育的内容与其他学科的内容相结合，课程内容是一系列的综合活动。活动总体设计见表2-2①。

---

① Career Development Occupational Studies[EB/OL]. http://www.p12.nysed.gov/cte/cdlearn/documents/CDOS-Elem-Integrated.pdf.

表 2-2　纽约州职业发展教育初级核心课程样本活动概览

样本活动	相关标准	备注
庆祝写作	CDOS;ELA;MST;SS;Arts	
广告分析	CDOS;ELA;MST;SS;Arts	
商业伙伴	CDOS;ELA;MST;SS;Arts	
谁是老板	CDOS;ELA;MST;SS;Arts	
广阔的运动世界	CDOS;ELA;MST;SS;Arts	
社区巴士之旅	CDOS;ELA;MST;SS;Arts	
伟大的园丁	CDOS;ELA;MST;Arts	
分数盛宴	CDOS;ELA;MST	CDOS=职业发展与职业学习
快乐绘图	CDOS;ELA;MST;SS;Arts	ELA=英语语言艺术标准
很棒的七巧板技术	CDOS;ELA;MST;SS;Arts	MST=数学、科学和技术标准
汤厨房的孩子	CDOS;ELA;MST;H/PE/FCS;SS;Arts	SS=社会研究标准 Arts=艺术标准 H/PE/FCS=健康、体育、家庭和消费科学标准
从东海岸到西海岸:我们从哪里买铅笔	CDOS;ELA;MST;SS;Arts	
家庭苹果派	CDOS;ELA;MST;SS;Arts	
世界旅行	CDOS;ELA;MST;SS;Arts	
建设我们的社区	CDOS;ELA;MST;SS;Arts	
带孩子去上班	CDOS;ELA;SS	
平坦的斯坦利去上班	CDOS;ELA;SS;Arts	

第三节 美国职业发展教育课程

哈佛大学于1909年在世界范围内最早开设了职业指导课程,加之经过生涯教育运动,美国的中小学也普遍开设职业发展教育课程,建立了从小学到大学较为完备的职业发展教育课程体系。可见,经过长时期的持续发展,职业发展教育在美国教育体系中具有重要地位,而课程是职业发展教育的核心,是职业态度和职业能力形成的载体。美国高度重视职业发展教育的课程建设,逐渐形成了体系健全、内容丰富、方式多样的职业发展教育课程框架。美国职业发展教育课程在学制上可以分为小学、初中、高中和大学四个阶段,而每一个阶段的课程又可以具体划分为课程目标、课程内容和课程实施方式等。这里主要从小学、初中、高中和大学四个阶段介绍美国的职业发展教育课程状况。

一、美国职业发展教育课程目标

课程目标是整个课程的指南和落脚点,一些学者对美国中小学的课程目标进行了深入研究。美国的赫尔与克莱默专门研究了美国高中阶段的职业发展教育课程目标,认为其应该包括三项内容:"对下一阶段教育和工作进行专门规划;工作者、消费者、休闲者、家庭成员等生活角色的价值澄清;做决策应该承担的责任与后果。"[①]该课程目标包括对生活角色的澄清、对下一阶段的规划和决策的责任与后果,不但内容全面,包括教育、工作和生活,而且内容既是对小学和初中职业发展教育目标的拓展,又是大学职业发展教育目标的基础,符合高中阶段职业发展教育的特点。学者的研究为美国中小学职业发展教育课程目标的设定提供了理论指导。在实践中,美国职业发展教育课程目标主要依据美国全国职业信息协调委员会制定的《国家职业生涯发展指南》。该指南具有权威性,规定了小学、初中、高中和成人(成人可以看作大学)的职业发展教育课程目标,是美国各州制定本州各阶

---

① Herr,E.L,&Cramer, S.H.Career Guidance and Counseling through the Lifespan(4thed)[M].New York:Harper Collins,1992:398.

段职业发展教育课程目标的基本依据。由于美国是地方分权制,教育的管辖权主要在各州,各州可以根据本州的实际状况适当添减一些指标,从而构成本州的职业发展教育课程目标。例如,路易斯安那州即在《国家职业生涯发展指南》规定的职业发展教育三个领域的目标之外,增加了生活技巧和工作伦理这一领域,从而构成路易斯安那州的职业发展教育课程目标体系。由于《国家职业生涯发展指南》规定的职业发展教育课程目标具有权威性,而且比较全面,具有较强的可操作性,这里主要介绍《国家职业生涯发展指南》规定的职业发展教育目标。

《国家职业生涯发展指南》1989年发布的,包括职业发展能力框架、指导人员要求和对青年与成年人开展职业发展教育项目的指导意见等几个部分,其中的职业发展能力框架即是职业发展教育课程目标。为了应对终身学习社会对工作人员在学术、职业和生涯管理能力方面提出的更高要求,美国教育部职业与成人教育办公室于2004年对《国家职业生涯发展指南》进行了重大修订。美国小学、初中、高中和成年人的职业发展教育课程目标也经历了重大转变。

1989年版的《国家职业生涯发展指南》明确按照小学、初中、高中和成年人四个阶段设定职业发展教育的课程目标,该课程目标分为自我认知、教育与职业发展和职业规划三个分目标,每一个分目标之下又包括若干子目标。具体的课程目标体系见表2-3。

2004年版的《国家职业生涯发展指南》由领域、目标和指标组织指导方针构成基本框架,三个领域分别是个人社会发展、教育成就和终身学习、职业管理。每一个领域之下分为若干个目标,这些目标定义了职业发展能力的广泛领域。此次没有明确按照小学、初中、高中和成年人四个阶段设定职业发展教育的课程目标。具体的课程目标体系见表2-4。

表 2-3 1989 年《国家职业生涯发展指南》规定的职业发展标准

目标	小学	初中	高中	成年人
自我认知	了解积极的自我概念的重要性；掌握与他人积极沟通的技能；意识到成长和改变的重要性	积极自我概念的影响知识；掌握与他人积极沟通的技能；了解成长和改变的重要性	理解积极的自我概念的影响；掌握与他人积极沟通的技能；理解成长与发展的影响	保持积极自我概念的技巧；保持有效行为的技巧；理解发展的变化和转变
教育与职业发展	意识到教育成果的好处；意识到工作和学习的关系；掌握理解和使用职业生涯信息的技能；意识到个人责任和良好工作习惯的重要性；了解工作与社会需求和功能的关系	懂得教育成就对职业生涯机会的影响；明白学习与工作的关系；掌握获取与运用职业生涯信息的方法；掌握寻求和获得工作所必要的技巧；了解工作如何与经济和社会的需求和功能相联系	理解学习成果与职业规划之间的关系；理解工作与学习所需积极态度之需求；搜集、评估、诠释与生涯机会有关信息的能力；准备找工作、获得工作、维持工作以及寻觅新工作的技巧；理解社会需求和运作如何影响工作的本质与结构	具备参加教育培训的技能；具备参与工作和终身学习的技能；搜集、评估、诠释与生涯机会有关信息的能力；获得工作、维持工作以及寻觅新工作的技巧；了解社会的需求和功能如何影响工作的性质和结构
职业规划	让学生理解如何做决定；意识到生活角色间的相互关系；意识到不同的职业生涯男女角色的改变；意识到职业规划的过程	做决策的技巧；理解不同生活角色之间的关系；了解具有不同职业的知识和不断变化的男性/女性角色；理解职业规划的过程	做决策的技巧；理解不同生活角色之间的关系；理解男人与女人角色上的持续变化；职业规划技巧	做决策的技巧；了解工作对个人和家庭生活的影响；理解男人与女人角色上的持续变化；转换职业的技能

表2-4　2004年《国家职业生涯发展指南》规定的职业发展标准

目标	个人社会发展领域	教育成就和终生学习领域	职业管理领域
目标1	培养对自我的理解,建立并保持积极的自我概念	达到个人和职业目标所需要的教育成就和表现水平	创建并管理一个符合你职业目标的职业规划
目标2	培养积极的人际交往能力,包括尊重多样性	参与持续终生的学习经验,以提高你在多元化和不断变化的经济中有效运作的能力	使用决策过程作为职业发展的一个组成部分
目标3	将成长和改变融入您的职业发展中		在职业规划和管理中使用准确、及时和公正的职业信息
目标4	平衡个人、休闲、社区、学习者、家庭和工作角色		掌握学术、职业和一般就业技能,以获得、创造、维持和/或促进就业
目标5			将不断变化的就业趋势、社会需求和经济条件整合到你的职业规划中

这些目标又可以具体细化为200个指标,以表征每一个目标所需要的知识和技能。可见,2004年发布的《国家职业生涯发展指南》没有再将职业发展教育课程目标具体划分到小学、初中、高中和成人的各个阶段,而是将所有的目标按照三个领域进行划分。之所以如此,该指南解释为这些指导方针、目标和指标"与个人的年龄或教育水平无关。这些指导方针、目标和指标可以作为K-Adult职业发展项目内容和评估的基础",这就是说,明确划分各个阶段应该达到的职业发展教育目标并不能准确描述每一个学生在某项目标达成上的具体状况。无论如何,两个版本中规定的职业发展教育课程目标都是美国各州开展职业发展教育的基本依据,美国各州职业发展教育的课程都是依据这些课程目标、再结合本州的具体规定而开发出来。

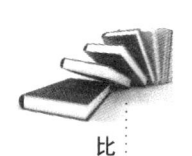

二、美国职业发展教育课程内容

职业发展教育课程目标的实现需要依赖职业发展教育课程内容的科学设计,课程内容是课程的核心。美国职业发展教育经过四十多年的发展,已经开发出内容丰富、结构合理的职业发展教育课程。由于小学、初中、高中和大学各个学段的职业发展教育课程目标不同,各个学段的职业发展教育课程内容必然不同。同时,由于美国是分权制国家,各州的职业发展教育课程内容存在一定差别,甚至在大学阶段,各个大学的职业发展教育课程内容会存在一定差别。因此,了解美国职业发展教育课程的内容,不但要明确各个学段课程内容的总体差别,而且要注意各州职业发展课程的具体差别。同时,在保持差异性的同时,美国小学、初中、高中和大学的职业发展教育课程内容也具有一些共同性的内容。总体而言,自20世纪70年代美国实施生涯教育以来,美国在中小学职业发展教育课程内容的设计时始终坚持三个基本原则:"职业生涯教育课程应面向所有的学生;职业生涯教育是一种持续性教育,自儿童早期直到中学后整个人生的历程;凡中学毕业的学生,包括中途退学者,都将掌握谋生的各种技能,以维持其个人或家庭的生活需要。"[①]简单而言,可以称为全体性、全程性和全能性原则。此三个基本原则适用于小学、初中和高中三个阶段的职业发展教育课程内容设计。在三个基本原则的指导之下,结合《国家职业生涯发展指南》规定的小学、初中和高中不同阶段的职业发展教育目标,小学、初中和高中职业发展教育课程内容具有一定的共同性内容。大学职业发展教育课程的内容也具有一定的共同性。因此,本部分首先介绍美国小学、初中、高中和大学各阶段职业发展教育的共性内容,然后选择一些代表性的州介绍其小学、初中、高中和大学职业发展教育的内容,以展现美国职业发展教育课程内容的差异性和特殊性。

（一）小学职业发展教育课程内容

正如前文所述,在美国小学阶段存在不同的学制,小学的时间也存在一定差异。这里以6年制为例进行介绍。在美国小学职业发展教育课程的共性内容方面,美国将小学阶段的职业发展教育课程目标定位为职业了解。

---

① 于珍.中小学职业生涯教育:来自美国的经验与启示[J].外国中小学教育,2008(3):53.

小学阶段职业发展教育课程包括依次递进的三项具体内容：对不同职业的初步了解、在初步了解职业的基础上加强对职业的认知、选择自己感兴趣的职业。可见，小学阶段职业发展教育的主要任务是"职业认识"。

在美国小学职业发展教育课程内容的特殊性方面，选择纽约州的小学职业发展教育课程为例。根据《职业发展和职业学习资源指南与核心课程》，小学属于初级核心课程。纽约州小学职业发展教育课程包括两部分：按照职业发展（标准1）和通用基础技能（标准3a）设计的初级核心课程，按照综合学习（标准2）设计的初级核心课程。两部分核心课程的具体内容见上述州职业发展教育政策部分。

(二) 初中职业发展教育课程内容

美国初中职业发展教育课程的共性内容方面，初中职业发展教育定位为职业探索阶段。学生需要熟悉职业的分类和"职业群"，初步选择出自己感兴趣的职业群。所谓"职业群"(career clusters)是指把一些普通的职业按照其宽泛的共同特征进行分组，将多种性质相近的职业归纳成一组或一群，以此作为课程编制的出发点和基础，目的是为了培养学生的职业意识、进行职业导向和职业探索。[①] 在美国，职业发展教育专家经过科学归类，将23 000个职业划分为15个职业群：农业和自然资源、商业和公职、通信和媒介物、建筑、消费者和家政教育、环境、美术和人文学科、卫生、公关和娱乐、制造业、航海学、销售和分配、私人服务行业、公用事业、运输。通常情况下，7~8年级职业发展教育的内容是让学生了解每一个职业群的状况，并选择出自己感兴趣的职业群。9年级职业发展教育课程的内容是让学生深入探究自己选定的职业群，同时帮助学生为进入高中做准备。

在美国初中职业发展教育课程内容的特殊性方面，这里选择得克萨斯州的初中职业发展教育课程为例。2010年，得克萨斯州制定了《中学职业生涯发展必需的知识和技能》，作为该州初中和高中开展职业发展教育的基本依据。得克萨斯州初中的职业发展教育课程包括"探索职业"和"职业入口"两门课程，分别开设于七年级和八年级。"探索职业"课程包括八项内容：培

---

① 王文槿,闫红.生涯技术教育下的美国中等职业群课程[J].中国职业技术教育,2010(25)：71-75.

养学生与职业生涯规划有关的兴趣和能力;分析自身在教育和职业生涯规划方面的兴趣和能力;分析学业和职业机会;对自身技能进行评估;认识到职业选择对个人的生活方式的影响;掌握个人理财的能力;发展有助于获得成功的各种技能;识别并探讨多个职业中的对职业生涯发展至关重要的技术技能。"职业入口"课程也包括八项内容:培养对一个或多个职业集群的兴趣;在一个或多个职业集群内探索学生感兴趣的职业途径;探索与学业相关的项目;探讨学业和事业成功所需要的专业技能;理解个人财务管理的意义,并认识到个人理财的重要性;收集并分析劳动力市场信息;探讨求职技巧;建立就业所需的专业文档。①

(三)高中职业发展教育课程内容

美国高中职业发展教育课程的共性内容方面,高中的职业发展教育定位为职业抉择阶段。高中是人生职业生涯发展的分流阶段,学生在高中毕业之后将分流进入就业、社区学院和4年制学院,因此学生在高中阶段需要在此三类职业方向中进行抉择。具体而言,准备就业的学生重点学习各种职业技能;准备升入社区学院的学生需要将学术课程和职业课程结合起来学习;准备升入4年制学院的学生需要重点学习学术性课程。高中阶段职业发展教育的课程内容是帮助学生从三类职业方向中选择自己的方向,并集中学习该方向之下的课程。②

在美国高中职业发展教育课程内容的特殊性方面,同样选择得克萨斯州的高中职业发展教育课程为例。根据得克萨斯州2010年制定的《中学职业生涯发展必需的知识和技能》,得克萨斯州高中的职业发展教育课程包括"职业准备1""职业准备2"和"问题和解决"三门课程,三门课程开设于十一年级和十二年级。"职业准备1"课程包括九项内容:使用就业技能,在高技能、高工资、高要求的职业领域获得一个入门级的工作;培养并发展在职场取得成功所需的技能;遵守职业道德,了解雇主的期望,并与不同的人交往和沟通;把学到的知识应用于工作中;在工作场所中遵守道德行为规范并承担相关法律责任;通过参加团队活动和使用人际交往技巧来达到目标;在工

---

① 贺丽,蔡敏.美国中学职业生涯教育课程设置:以得克萨斯州为例[J].世界教育信息,2014(4):31.
② 于珍.中小学职业生涯教育:来自美国的经验与启示[J].外国中小学教育,2008(3):53.

作场所应用与安全相关的技能;评估与职业生涯发展有关的工作态度和习惯;确定专业发展所必需的技能和特性。"职业准备2"课程包括十项内容:以在公司得到一个职位为标准,使用并评价自身的就业技能;发展有助于成功的先进知识和技能;遵守职业道德,对工作有期望,尊重多元文化,使用沟通技巧;在工作场所应用所学的知识和技能;了解职场中的法律责任;了解身份盗窃的危害;通过参加团队活动和使用人际交往技能来促进个人发展;了解在工作场所中与安全有关的知识和技能;为未来的教育和在高技能、高工资、高要求职业就业做准备;确定专业发展必要的技能。"问题和解决"课程包括六项内容:在自主学习中应用数学、科学、英语语言艺术和社会研究知识;使用语言和非语言的沟通技巧;遵守职业道德行为准则并承担相关法律责任;设计并开发与自身职业兴趣有关的研究项目;使用必要的技术去完成一个研究项目;对研究项目进行评估。[①]

(四)大学职业发展教育课程内容

美国大学职业发展教育课程的共性内容方面,大学的职业发展教育是学生职业发展的关键期。大学具有办学自主权,课程设置属于大学自主权的重要内容,美国大学开设的职业发展教育课程在不同学校会存在一定差别,归纳起来,美国大学职业发展教育课程包括自我评定、专业与职业探索、职业尝试、求职技能培训4个模块的内容。[②] 自我评定模块开设在大学一年级,课程目标是帮助学生进行全面深入的自我认识,任课教师通过各种量表和课程活动让学生认识自己的兴趣、性格、价值观、能力和潜能,从而让学生能够客观认识自己,为其进行职业规划奠定内部基础。专业与职业探索模块开设在大学二年级,课程目标是帮助学生客观深入地认识职业状况,学生通过学习各门专业课程、向职业咨询师咨询、与各类人员进行职业访谈等途径全面了解各类职业的特点,分析职业与自我之间的匹配程度,全面了解外部职业状况,学生能够在职业选择上做到"知己知彼"——既了解自己又了解职业世界。职业尝试模块设置在大学三年级,课程目标是让学生通过切身体验获得某些职业的认知和经验。任课教师通过安排学生参加职业实

---

① 贺丽,蔡敏.美国中学职业生涯教育课程设置:以得克萨斯州为例[J].世界教育信息,2014(4):31.

② 蔡敏.解析美国大学的职业规划课程[J].比较教育研究.2010(01):25-28.

习、开展假期实践、担任志愿者等实践活动,让学生在亲身体验中深入认识某些职业的特点,增加某些职业的实际经验。求职技能培训模块设置在大学四年级,课程目标是帮助学生掌握各种求职技能。任课教师通过课堂讲授、模拟演练等方式让学生学习以下内容:"①如何寻找符合个人职业选择的就业机会;②怎样准备自荐信和求职简历;③如何应对各种招聘面试;④怎样准备完整的求职材料;⑤怎样与职场人士建立联系和进行交流;⑥如何进行求职过程的经费开支预算"①。

在美国大学职业发展教育课程内容的特殊性方面,选择佛罗里达大学职业发展教育课程为例。佛罗里达大学的职业发展教育课程主要包括生涯规划课程、求职策略课程,具体内容见表2-5、表2-6②。

表2-5 佛罗里达大学职业发展教育课程作业及其分值

作业	要求	次数	分值
教材阅读心得	针对教材中的55个探寻职业生涯的有趣故事在WEBCT发表自己的评论和观点,思考自己处于同样环境下将如何选择,思考影响自己职业生涯的因素:金钱,权力,助人,还是充分的自由	4篇	每篇20分,共80分
个人的课程目标和职业目标	导师在布置作业之前会在课堂上详细讨论细节	1篇	30分
Kuder职业测评	使用Kuder生涯规划系统做职业测评,研究潜在的职业选择,整理个人简历,包括受教育经历和工作经历等,对简历进行评估后传在网络上,24小时内不能删除。上传的简历在截止日期前打印出来交给导师	3次	每次20分,共60分

① Maryland University Career Center. Career Planning, Internship, and Job Search Courses [EB/OL]. http://www.careercenter.umd.edu/student/courses/courses.main.asp.
② 王慧燕,卢峰.美国佛罗里达大学职业生涯规划现状及启示[J].黑龙江高教研究.2010(3):60-64.

续表 2-5

作业	要求	次数	分值
理想的个人简历	为自己的未来求职准备一份详细的个人简历,简历上的内容都是可以通过自己在大学期间的努力可以达到的,并且都将成为大学四年来的成就	1 份	30 分
就业行动计划	结合讲座、发言、前期作业和采访做出一份就业行动计划报告,为自己的长远目标设定小目标,并收集自己和外界更多的信息来明确自己的职业目标	1 份	70 分

表 2-6　佛罗里达大学职业发展教育课程具体任务和细节

任务	细节	积分
职业评估报告	写一份 3 页纸的关于自己感兴趣职业的报告。第一部分要包括职业信息如工作职责、学历、技能要求、就业前景、薪水和其他与工作相关的信息。第二部分要描述职业和自我评估的相关性(兴趣、价值观、技能、能力和职业目标等)	30
简历	简历,必须包含个人实际的过去和现在的经历,并且在接下来 6 个月内可以用的。简历必须没有差错,并且给人留下非常专业的印象。简历必须经过职业资源中心就业辅导员的指导和修改,否则 20 分将被扣除	30
信函(求职信,询问信,接受和拒绝信)	信函必须是无差错的,并且给人留下专业的印象。信函和简历一样必须经过职业资源中心就业辅导员的指导和修改,否则 20 分将被扣除	30
模拟面试报告	学生必须在 10 月 16 日至 20 日期间提出模拟面试的申请。并在面试结束后写一份 2 页纸的面试报告,内容包括:你的面试表现如何,你面试的优势是什么,存在哪些不足,如何改进以及整体印象	25

续表 2-6

任务	细节	积分
信息采访报告	采访两位自己感兴趣的职业工作者,可以是同一工作领域的,也可以是不同工作领域的,并写成报告。所有的被采访者要求有三年以上的工龄,不能采访家庭成员、同事或教师。采访后写一份 4 页纸的报告,包括:详细的工作描述和它所涉及的内容;详细说明这些采访对你的职业发展和生涯探索的影响;获得了什么新信息、思路和见解等。完整的采访联系信息,包括工作职务、地点和电话号码等制成一张名片,放在报告正文前	50
职业生涯时间轴	一个成功的求职是规划、组织和知识共同作用的结果。职业生涯时间轴要求学生把所有的信息按照时间先后整合在一起做出一个个人的求职规划。要确定你将利用的资源,需要改进哪些方面的不足,从而制成一个求职过程的时间轴。为了这份时间轴更有意义或者一目了然,时间轴可以有具体的表格,最好有日历以及其他有助于明确求职过程的材料都可以。时间轴包括你未来的目标以及你如何来实现你的目标	50
参与课堂互动		30
课堂出勤		30

三、美国职业发展教育课程实施方式

职业发展教育课程具有综合性、实践性、体验性,这决定了职业发展教育课程实施方式具有多样性。美国自 20 世纪 70 年代开展职业发展教育开始,教育部和国家教育研究发展中心就设计了一些职业发展教育课程实施方式,供各州的学校采用。各州的学校更是在此基础上积极开展职业发展教育课程实施方式的探索,从而呈现出百花齐放的样态。据统计,目前美国仅中小学校开发的职业发展教育课程实施方式就达四十多种。[1] 总体而言,美国学校通常采用的职业发展教育课程实施方式包括课程介入、教学渗透、生涯咨询、职业体验、职业讲座、模拟演练、网上支持等。当然,由于美国小

---

[1] 韩永敏,徐学莹.美国中学生涯教育探析及启示[J].教育观察,2013(7):84.

学、初中、高中和大学职业发展教育的课程目标、课程内容、课程资源和学生发展阶段存在一定差异,美国中小学和大学职业发展教育的具体某一门课程会采用不同的课程实施方式进行组合,以提高课程实施的质量和效果。

  课堂介入和教学渗透可以统称为课堂教学方式。在学校教育中,课堂教学是实现课程目标最重要的方式,也是职业发展教育课程的基本实施方式。西德尼·马兰在开展职业发展教育之初就提出,"适当有效的生涯教育,需要新的教育整合,它必须破除教育系统与社会隔离的障碍。其解决方案是:把我们的课程融于简单有力的中等教育系统中,使学生在生涯课程引导下作有力的选择"①。课堂介入偏重于对职业发展教育课程单独开设课程,系统设计职业发展教育课程的内容。教学渗透则是将职业发展教育的课程内容分散到其他课程之中,与其他课程内容相融合。前者的优点是课程内容具有系统性,便于讲解,可以安排专门的职业发展教育教师进行授课,缺点是不容易展现职业发展教育内容的具体用途,让学生产生学无所用的感觉。后者的优缺点则和前者恰好相反。目前,教学渗透受到了中小学校教师的普遍欢迎。在伊利诺伊州教育局开展的一项关于K-12学生生涯认知与发展顺序的研究中,大部分被调查的教师希望采用教学渗透方式,将职业发展教育的内容与其他课程内容相结合,从而提高职业发展教育课程实施的有效性。

  生涯咨询即主要由专门的咨询人员对学生与生涯发展相关的事务进行咨询,从而帮助学生清晰认识生涯发展中遇到的困惑。生涯咨询的人员既可以是专门的职业生涯咨询员,也可以是教师,还可以是职业生涯咨询员与教师和家长的联合。咨询的内容是与学生生涯发展相关的教育和职业规划问题,比如自己的兴趣特长鉴定、课程选择、未来学校的选择等。通过生涯咨询,不但解决了单个学生遇到的生涯发展方面的问题,而且实现了为学生提供个性化的职业生涯指导。

  职业体验是通过让学生到具体的职业环境中进行体验,以加深学生对某一具体职业的认识的课程实施方式。体验性是职业发展教育课程的重要特征。职业体验主要是组织学生参访相关的职业场所,比如医院、工厂、农

---

① 王焕勋.实用教育大词典[Z].北京:北京师范大学出版社,1995:816.

场、商店。学生除了参观某一职业工作人员的具体工作之外,还可以与工作人员或者管理人员进行座谈,了解某一职业的基本状况和咨询感兴趣的问题,在某些环节或者场景中进行"工作模拟"。通过职业体验,学生不但了解了某一职业的基本知识,而且对某些职业具有了切身体验,深入了解某一职业的工作特点,培养自己的职业情感,增长职业技能,体会自己是否喜欢或者适合某一职业。

职业讲座也可以称为教室演讲,是邀请相关职业的从业人员或者学生家长到学校为学生开展的职业生涯讲座。职业生涯教育的开展离不开社会的支持,美国特别重视利用社会资源开展职业发展教育。邀请社区某一职业的从业人员,尤其是某一职业的成功人士到学校为学生开展职业的基本状况、从业的素质要求、创业成功的经历等方面的讲座,不但可以对学生进行职业启蒙,而且可以培育学生们的职业情感。

模拟演练是在仿真环境之下通过让学生扮演相应职业角色来获得对生涯的体验或增长相关技能的课程实施方式。学常用的模拟演练包括在学校举办"招聘会"、到企业和社区扮演一定的角色。通过模拟演练,学生增强了对职业的感性体验,增加了职业发展的技能。

网上支持是通过互联网对学生学习职业发展教育课程提供课程内容、课程练习和学习资料的课程实施方式。随着互联网的普及和信息技术学习理论研究的不断深入,网上支持在中小学和大学得到越来越多的运用。美国每个州和大学都运用职业发展教育课程的网络软件,帮助学生更便捷、更个性化地学习职业发展教育课程。

第四节　美国职业发展教育特色

美国是世界上最早开展职业发展教育的国家,如果以1894年美国加州工艺学校推行就业指导为起点的话,美国开展职业发展教育已经有120多年的历史。在长期的职业发展教育过程中,美国按照职业发展教育规律,注重结合本土实际,强调职业发展教育质量,逐渐形成了自己的职业发展教育特色。

一、强有力的政策保障

美国有法治的历史传统和完善的政策体系,职业发展教育的顺利开展也离不开强有力的政策保障。在联邦层面,美国先后出台了多部与职业发展教育相关的法律。1974年出台了《生涯教育法》,1975年通过了《生涯辅导和咨询法》,1977年通过了《生涯教育激励法》,1994年通过了《从学校到工作机会法》,1998年通过了《职业和技术教育法》,2006年通过了《生涯和技术教育改进法》,2014年通过了《劳动力创新和机会法案》,2016年颁布了《强化21世纪生涯与技术教育法》,2017年实施《美国本土生涯与技术项目》。其中,《生涯教育法》《生涯辅导和咨询法》《从学校到工作机会法》等法律是专门针对职业发展教育而制定的法律。这些法律对职业发展教育的目标、模式、主体、资金等问题进行了明确规定。美国教育部也于1989年制定了《国家职业生涯发展指南》,并在2004年进行了修订,对小学、初中、高中和成人的职业发展教育目标、评价标准、课程内容等进行了详细规定。各州更是制定了数量众多的教育政策和职业发展教育专门政策保障职业发展教育的开展。例如,得克萨斯州不但制定了《得克萨斯教育法典》,对本州职业发展教育的实施进行规定,而且制定了《中学职业生涯发展必需的知识和技能》专门规范得克萨斯州中学生职业发展教育。可见,美国具有国会—各部—州三个层次、一般和专门政策相结合的政策体系规范职业发展教育,为职业发展教育的开展提供了政策依据,从而推动了职业发展教育的优质高效开展。

二、科学的课程体系

课程是开展职业发展教育的核心,美国职业发展教育开展非常成功是以科学的课程体系为基础的。美国职业发展教育课程体系的科学性表现在课程内容和课程形式两个方面。在职业发展教育课程方面,一方面从幼儿园到大学职业发展教育课程内容具有连贯性,幼儿园、小学、初中、高中和大学的内容相互贯通、依次递进,重点和难点内容在不同阶段存在交叉。这突出地表现在《国家职业生涯发展指南》规定的小学、初中和高中不同阶段的职业发展教育目标之中,每两个阶段之间的职业发展教育目标能够顺利衔接。另一方面职业发展教育课程内容具有丰富性,美国小学职业发展教育

课程内容包括培养学生的职业意识和自我意识,初中职业发展教育课程内容包括学生对职业群的深度认识和探索,高中职业发展教育课程内容包括对就业、升入社区学院或者4年制学院的选择与准备,美国大学职业发展教育课程包括自我评定、专业与职业探索、职业尝试、求职技能培训等内容,职业生涯规划和就业的内容非常充实。在职业发展教育课程的形式方面,一是职业发展课程形式具有多样性,职业发展教育课程既包括分科课程,又包括活动课程;二是课程实施方式具有多样性,中小学职业发展教育课程实施方式包括课程介入、教学渗透、生涯咨询、职业体验、职业讲座、模拟演练等,大学职业发展教育课程实施方式包括案例分析、团队训练、网上支持、阅读指导等。职业发展教育课程内容和形式的科学性有助于提升职业发展教育的质量。

三、早期的职业生涯教育

美国从一开始就注重在基础教育阶段开展职业发展教育,在1894年已经在作为中等职业学校的加州工艺学校就开展就业指导,1907年美国一所公立学校即要求教师每周给学生上一次辅导课,从而塑造学生的个性。可以说,美国具有注重开展早期职业发展教育的历史传统。随着职业发展教育开展的不断深入,美国愈加重视早期职业发展教育,并逐渐形成了早期职业发展教育的体系。1989年美国制定的《国家职业生涯发展指南》,对小学、初中和高中的职业发展教育目标、教育标准和课程内容进行了系统规定,以作为全国早期职业发展教育开展的参考。不仅如此,目前一些州已经将职业发展教育扩展到幼儿园阶段。纽约州对6~14岁的学生专门定制职业生涯发展档案包,作为职业生涯教育的基本资料而且纽约州要求对从幼儿园到高中的学生进行职业生涯规划。在职业发展教育的校外实践方面,美国联邦教育部和劳工部自1994年开展1年级至12年级学生的校外锻炼计划。小学生需要听取职业发展教育方面的讲座,并参访一些工作场所,观察职业工作的现状,加深对职业工作的认识。中学生则需要参加1~6个月的工作实习,切实增加工作经验,增长工作技能。在基础教育阶段开展职业发展教育,注重职业发展教育的早期性,保证了职业发展教育的长效性,为美国整个职业发展教育的成功奠定了坚实的基础。

四、广泛的社会支持

"生涯教育的长期性、社会性和开放性,使得这项工作需要社会各界的努力,仅仅依靠学校和教师的力量是远远不够的。"①美国职业发展教育中获得了广泛的社会支持,包括企业、社区、行业协会、学术研究机构、家长等。

首先是企业和社区。从幼儿园到大学都可以借助企业和社区开展职业发展教育,让企业和社区的人士到学校开展讲座,或者由企业和社区接待学生参访。通过企业或社区的实地参访,让学生具有从业的切身体验,帮助其进行职业生涯规划。

其次是行业协会与学术研究机构。行业协会一方面可以为从事职业发展教育工作的从业人员制定行业标准,提高职业发展教育从业人员的专业化水平,提升职业发展教育质量;另一方面,行业协会也可以创造企业、社会、协会与幼儿园、学校联系的机会,搭建幼儿园和学校开展职业发展教育的实践平台。

最后是家长。在幼儿园和中小学阶段,家长是学生的第一任教师,家长是学生进行职业生涯规划的重要的人,也是职业发展教育的重要参与者。家长不但可以到幼儿园或者中小学开展职业生涯教育的讲座,而且还可以帮助子女开展职业规划指导。

思考题:
1. 美国开展职业发展教育过程中颁布了哪些重要法律?
2. 美国职业发展教育课程内容是什么?
3. 美国职业发展教育课程如何实施?
4. 美国职业发展教育的特色是什么?
5. 美国职业发展教育对中国职业发展教育具有哪些启示?

---

① 李敏,潘晨.美国纽约州小学和初中阶段生涯教育研究[J].河北师范大学学报(教育科学版),2015(6):86.

推荐书目:

1. 戴安·萨克尼克,威廉·班达特,丽萨·若夫门.职业指导——职业生涯规划教程[M].7版.李洋,张奕,小卉,译.北京:中国劳动社会保障出版社,2005.

2. 杰弗里·H.格林豪斯,杰勒德·A.卡拉南,维罗妮卡·M.戈德谢克.职业生涯管理[M].4版.王伟,译.北京:清华大学出版社,2014.

国外论文导读与阅读(一):

导读:职业学习与发展:21世纪的社会建构主义模式

作者:芭芭拉·巴索(Barbara Bassot)

本文讨论了职业发展教育的工作模式,不同的模式产生、运行机制以及不同模式下职业发展教育的模型。在实证主义指导下,对于职业发展教育和指导的从业者来说,他们一度倾向于寻求个人和职业之间的匹配程度,在这种思路下,个人适合某项工作是基于客观现实下的"匹配"。在职业稳定,职业变化较小的背景下,人们对职业的往往"从一而终",这种匹配模式可以很好地将天赋、能力以及学识等个人条件与专业相匹配,达到个人与职业之间的平衡。对于学习者来说,尤其是面临工作选择问题的学习者来说,也更希望从实证主义的角度获取职业发展教育,即更倾向学习到如何具体地选择工作,获取工作。从建构主义来看,20世纪后半叶,在经济衰退、全球化和信息通信技术等因素的影响下,人们对终身工作的概念提出了质疑。这些变化因素使人们生活方式经历快速并且不断的变化,人们生活处于动态之中,尤其是终身学习概念的提出,如何处理终身学习和工作的关系成为人们日益关注的问题。传统的匹配模式适应不了全球化市场中不断变化的外部条件和个人职业发展的变化,人们需要成为"自己工作生活的管理者",个人建构自己的职业生涯。在建构主义模式下,本文进一步提出了桥梁模型来解释职业发展教育和工作之间的关系。在建构主义模式中,个人成为自身职业规划的制定者和参与者,更加注重职业生涯的全程性,生活和工作的处于动态稳定中。

相比较而言,实证主义指导下的匹配模型从现实出发更加注重个人和工作在已经表现出来的现实条件下的匹配,在较为稳定的环境下能够根据个人已有履历匹配出最适合的工作,这种适合是同时应用于个人需求还是工作发展的合适和稳定。但在新的市场环境和就业环境下,变化和发展成为时代的主题,建构主义相比较更适合变动的环境。本文还指出,建构主义具体来说分为建构主义和建构社会主义,区别在于前者主张个人"从内到外"建构社会和心理世界,后者则强调社会的作用。而桥梁模型的基础是两者的综合,即包含建构主义的建构社会主义。这一综合的建构主义虽然兼顾了个人和社会在建构职业发展进程中的作用,避免了忽视个人或者社会的作用,但从建构主义本身来说,强调职业规划和选择中的个体主观能动性是其与现实主义的根本区别。我们应当意识到,这一差别一方面是全球化发展进程对职业发展教育模式影响的结果,是职业发展教育模式对外部条件的适应,是职业发展教育的有益探索;另一方面我们也应注意到,基于实证主义的匹配模式依然有其不可替代的优势,尤其是在帮助出于职业探索阶段的在校受教育者而言,匹配模式能够帮助受教育者进一步了解自己已经具备的职业能力和相应的职业,弥补在校受教育者职业认知不完全的短板。确定的一点是,建构主义提醒所有和职业生涯相关的人都需要为不确定的未来做好准备。

文章来源:

Bassot B. Career learning and development: a social constructivist model for the twenty-first century[J].Int J Educ Vocat Guidance (2012) 12:32-35.

(节选的英文原文见附录2)

国外论文导读与阅读(二):
导读:我的职业影响体系:应对生涯教育面临的挑战
作者:马克·沃森(Mark Watson),玛丽·麦克马洪(Mary Mcmahon)

本文探讨了21世纪背景下如何应对职业发展教育中面临的随着社会产生的理论有待发展、理论和实践联系不密切等问题,通过建构主义理论构建了职业发展的系统理论框架(STF),并在此基础上发展了定性的职业评估工具MSCI,尝试在学校背景下,将职业发展教育的理论与实践、内容和过程相联系。职业发展教育所面临要适应21世纪青年人的职业发展需要的挑战,传统上,职业发展教育中等教育的特定阶段只局限于学科选择和职业选择,

这就规定了职业发展教育的内容。这种方式忽视了职业发展的过程性,建构主义相对于传统模式更加强调积极而非被动地参与学习。这一特点使得将建构主义应用于解决职业发展教育面临的挑战具有现实优势。此外职业发展教育面临的挑战与职业发展从业者和学生在学校环境中的作用以及职业发展教育本身的性质有关。因此,要解决职业发展教育目前的困境就需要在学校背景下,如何将建构主义应用于职业发展教育的理论与实践、内容与过程中。在建构主义的理论基础上,将建构主义与职业发展教育相结合,发展出了职业发展的系统理论框架(STF)。STF作为元理论展示了内容和过程对职业发展的影响,其中内容影响通过描述个人素质来展示个人职业发展的整体性,过程影响的描述强调了递归性、随时间变化和偶然性。STF促进了一种定性的职业评估工具MSCI的发展,通过该工具,学生可以对他们的影响系统进行连续的反思。MSCI作为一张地图,引导学生通过一个循序渐进的过程来直观地表现、阐述和反映对他们职业发展的整体影响模式。这样,有助于学生及学校职业发展从业人员更好地了解职业发展的独特性、整体性和相互联系性。

　　本文通过对建构主义在团体环境中应用的论证,弥补了以往建构主义对个人职业干预的偏颇焦点。解决了在学校环境中,职业发展教育指导者即教师如何在建构主义框架下对学生进行有效指导,而不囿于传统的"匹配模式"这一问题。从现实意义上,STF和MSCI解决了建构主义理论到职业发展教育实践的问题,在实践角度尝试解决职业发展教育新需求余职业发展教育模式不对称的问题。从理论意义上,促进了职业发展教育理论的发展,加强了理论和实践的联系。

文章来源:

Watson M, Mcmahon M. My system of career influences responding to challenges facing career education[J]. Int J Educ Vocat Guid (2006) 6:160-163.

(节选的英文原文见附录3)

第三章 日本职业发展教育

本章要点：
1. 日本职业发展教育的历程；
2. 日本不同教育阶段的职业发展教育课程；
3. 日本职业发展教育的特色。

20世纪20年代，日本教育蓬勃发展，学生人数持续增加，院校类型多元化发展。这一时期，职业发展教育以职业指导的方式首次进入日本教育史，并以惊人的速度建立起了以政府为主导的全程化的职业发展教育体系。本章立足日本教育概况，分别对日本职业发展教育的政策、课程、特色进行详细介绍。

第一节 当代日本教育概况

一、日本教育发展概况

日本现行的学校制度为六三三四制，即小学六年、初中三年、高中三年、大学四年。根据日本《教育基本法》规定，日本学校种类包括幼儿园、小学、初中、高中、中等学校、特殊学校、高等专科学校、短期大学、普通大学、专修大学等。2014年，日本的学校数以及教师与学生人数如表3-1所示。

表3-1 2014年日本学校构成及其教师与学生人数

学校种类	学校数/个	教师人数/人 合计	男教师	女教师	学生人数/人 合计	男学生	女学生
幼稚园	12 905	111 059	7 411	103 648	1 557 461	789 801	767 660
国立	49	344	44	300	5 614	2 790	2 824
公立	4 714	23 360	932	22 428	264 563	134 940	129 623
私立	8 142	87 355	6 435	80 920	1 287 284	652 071	635 213
小学校	20 852	416 475	156 600	259 875	6 600 006	3 377 471	3 222 535
国立	72	1 833	1 186	647	41 067	20 411	20 656
公立	20 558	409 753	153 039	256 714	6 481 396	3 324 063	3 157 333
私立	222	4 889	2 375	2 514	77 543	32 997	44 546
中学校	10 557	253 832	145 684	108 148	3 504 334	1 793 059	1 711 275
国立	73	1 628	1 078	550	31 220	15 719	15 501
公立	9 707	237 082	135 145	101 937	3 227 314	1 660 745	1 566 569
私立	777	15 122	9 461	5 661	245 800	116 595	129 205
高等学校	4 963	235 306	162 476	72 830	3 334 019	1 678 353	1 655 666
国立	15	575	404	171	8 613	4 450	4 163
公立	3 628	174 363	118 973	55 390	2 286 385	1 143 627	1 142 758

续表 3-1

学校种类		学校数/个	教师人数/人			学生人数/人		
			合计	男教师	女教师	合计	男学生	女学生
中等教育学校	私立	1 320	60 368	43 099	17 269	1 039 021	530 276	508 745
	国立	51	2 432	1 635	797	31 499	15 481	16 018
	公立	4	214	132	82	3 160	1 485	1 675
	私立	30	1 520	1 007	513	20 424	9 284	11 140
特别支援学校		17	698	496	202	7 915	4 712	3 203
	国立	1 096	79 280	31 214	48 066	135 617	88 278	47 339
	公立	45	1 502	711	791	3 033	1 985	1 048
	私立	1 037	77 479	30 356	47 123	131 781	85 840	45 941
高等专门学校		14	299	147	152	803	453	350
	国立	57	4 344	3 968	376	57 677	47 905	9 772
	公立	51	3 894	3 561	333	51 725	42 587	9 138
	私立	3	298	271	27	3 834	3 415	419
短期大学		3	152	136	16	2 118	1 903	215
	国立	352	8 438	4 079	4 359	136 534	15 812	120 722
		—	—	—	—	—	—	—

续表 3-1

学校种类		学校数/个	教师人数/人			学生人数/人		
			合计	男教师	女教师	合计	男学生	女学生
	公立	18	517	295	222	7 388	1 033	6 355
	私立	334	7 921	3 784	4 137	129 146	14 779	114 367
普通大学	国立	781	180 879	140 135	40 744	2 855 529	1 635 438	1 220 091
	公立	86	64 252	54 509	9 743	612 509	402 916	209 593
	私立	92	13 013	9 370	3 643	148 042	70 699	77 343
		603	103 614	76 256	27 358	2 094 978	1 161 823	933 155
专修学校		3 206	40 774	19 398	21 376	659 452	294 376	365 076
	国立	10	101	72	29	450	206	244
	公立	195	2 854	740	2 114	26 255	5 753	20 502
	私立	3 001	37 819	18 586	19 233	632 747	288 417	344 330
各种学校		1 276	8 823	5 253	3 570	121 846	64 092	57 754
	国立	—	—	—	—	—	—	—
	公立	8	47	28	19	638	211	427
	私立	1 268	8 776	5 225	3 551	121 208	63 881	57 327

资料来源：日本总务省统计局，《日本の統計》，2016年发行。

下面分别从初等教育、中等教育(前、后期中等教育)和高等教育三个层面,管窥日本教育发展的概况。

二、初等教育发展概况

日本的小学属于义务教育的前期,采取学区制,学习年限为6年。日本的义务教育起源于明治时代,而现在实施的9年义务教育制度则始于1947年。当时,日本实施了学制改革,将小学和初中规定为义务教育。随着义务教育的实施,小学的入学率迅速提高。1890年为81.5%,1905年为95.6%,1955年接近100%,实现了小学教育的普及。[①]

2014年,日本共有小学20 825所,学生人数共有674万人左右,分别就读于国立、公立和私立学校,如表3-2所示,就读于公立学校学生人数最多,其次为私立和国立。日本儿童在年满6周岁后的第一年4月,按划分的学区入学,不能跨学区就读。自1997年1月起,文部省放宽了对中小学学区的规则,采取了富有弹性的灵活政策,允许部分学生跨学区就读,满足了部分家长和孩子的愿望。另外,从表3-2可以看出,日本小学低年级学生人数少于高年级学生人数,这与日本少子化问题越来越严重有很大的关系。

表3-2　2014年日本小学学生人数(人)

年级	国立	公立	私立	合计
1年级	6 551	1 071 460	12 632	1 090 643
2年级	6 525	1 068 793	12 948	1 088 266
3年级	6 522	1 041 834	12 774	1 061 130
4年级	7 130	1 076 796	12 754	1 096 680
5年级	7 135	1 101 039	13 132	1 121 306
6年级	7 204	1 121 474	13 303	1 141 981
特殊学校	3 033	131 781	803	135 617
合计	441 00	6 613 177	78 346	6 735 623

资料来源:日本总务省统计局,《日本の統計》,2016年发行。

[①] 王玉珊.日本教育及其在经济中的作用研究[D].大连:东北财经大学,2012.

根据日本教育基本法的规定,小学阶段的教育目的是"以适应身心发展,实施初等普通教育"。小学的课程内容分为各学科、道德、特别活动及综合学习四部分。其中,各学科包括语文、社会、算数、理科、生活、音乐、美术、家庭及体育科,生活只在一、二年级开设,社会与理科只在三、四、五、六年级开设,家庭只在五、六年级开设。为了避免学习内容的重复与不足,日本文部科学省规定除算术及自然课以外,社会课以及其他课程在第三年级和第四年级设置课程目标、内容时,均采取两年连贯的方式,即各学校可以针对学生的实际情况,制订两年的课程计划,使教学更具弹性,更符合学生的需求。在道德课方面,《教育基本法》强调全体教师包括校长在内要共同协助教学,主要的目的是培养学生的道德观、明辨是非的能力以及基本礼仪。特别活动课包括班级活动、学生会活动、社团活动及学校例行活动,目的是培养学生具有团队精神,互助合作,建立良好的人际关系以及相互产生认同感。其中,社团活动只在小学纲要中被列入,属于授课时间外的活动。[①]

三、中等教育发展概况

中等教育包括前期中等教育和后期中等教育,即包括初中和高中两个阶段。二战后,日本在美国的军事占领下,接受了美国教育使节团报告书的建议,制定了初中教育制度,年限为3年,招收小学毕业生。初中同小学一样,采取学区制,不能跨学区就学。根据《教育基本法》的规定,中等教育的目的是"在小学教育的基础上,以适应学生身心发展,实施中等普通教育"。2014年,日本共有初中10 557所,初中生共有350万人左右。见表3-3。

表3-3 2014年日本初中学生人数 (人)

年级	国立	公立	私立	合计
1年级	10 370	1 068 509	81 657	1 160 536
2年级	10 414	1 076 233	82 086	1 168 733
3年级	10 436	1 082 572	82 057	1 175 065
合计	31 220	3 227 314	245 800	3 504 334

资料来源:日本总务省统计局,《日本の统计》,2016年发行。

---

① 王玉珊.日本教育及其在经济中的作用研究[D].大连:东北财经大学,2012.

初中的课程是由各学科、道德、特别活动及综合学习四部分组成。与小学不同的是,其学科分为必修和选修两种,必修课包括语文、社会学科、数学、理科、音乐、美术、卫生体育、工艺、家政课,选修课包括外语、艺术及由地方教育部门设立的其他科目。另外,选修的修课规定与以往的纲要也有所不同,以往是在初中三年级才能够进行全学科的选修,而目前则是从一年级起就可以进行选修,目的是让学生能够得到多样性的发展。后期中等教育即高中实施普通教育和职业发展教育,不属于义务教育范围,招收初中毕业生或具有同等学力的学生。根据《教育基本法》的规定,高中阶段的教育目的是"在初中教育的基础上,以适应学生身心发展,实施高级普通教育及专业教育"。[①] 2014 年,日本高中生的人数已经达 350 万人左右。日本初升高的升学率高达 98.4%,高中毕业后继续升入大学的比例也达到了 53.8%,这表明日本的高中和大学教育已经相当普及。从日本初、高中升学率的变化情况看(见表 3-4),2004—2014 年,初中的升学率和高中的升学率逐年上升,其中女生的高中升学率一直高于男生。

表 3-4　2004—2014 年日本初高中毕业生就业率与升学率的推移　　　(%)

年份	初中毕业生		高中毕业生			就业率
	升学率	就业率	升学率			
			平均	男	女	
2004	97.5	0.7	45.3	43.6	47.1	16.9
2005	97.6	0.7	47.3	45.9	48.6	17.4
2006	97.7	0.7	49.3	48.1	50.6	18.0
2007	97.7	0.7	51.2	50.0	52.5	18.5
2008	97.8	0.7	52.8	51.4	54.3	19.0
2009	97.9	0.5	53.9	52.3	55.5	18.2
2010	98.0	0.4	54.3	52.7	55.9	15.8
2012	98.3	0.4	53.5	51.5	55.5	16.8
2013	98.4	0.4	53.2	50.9	55.5	17.0
2014	98.4	0.4	53.8	51.5	56.1	17.5

资料来源:日本总务省统计局,《日本の統計》,2016 年发行。

---

① 王玉珊.日本教育及其在经济中的作用研究[D].大连:东北财经大学,2012.

依据《教育基本法》规定的教育目的,高中分为普通学校、职业学校和综合学校三类。其中,普通学校以普通教育为主,主要是以升入大学为目标;职业学校以职业教育为主,学科繁多;综合学校以选修方式进行普通教育及专业教育,主要目的是为了适应学生的性格、能力、兴趣、特长等特点,为学生提供更多样化的选择。因此,综合高中所开设的科目比普通高中及职业高中更多,共有120种以上。除此之外,日本还有六年制以及单科高中等多种形式的高中。日本在高中阶段采取分流制度。2002年,经济合作与发展组织(OECD)及亚太经合组织(APEC)对39个国家教育分流状况的调查显示,日本初中毕业生选择职业高中的人数占28%,其余72%选择普通高中和综合高中。日本高中的授课方式分为全日制、通信制及定时制三种。其中,全日制是最主要的授课方式,即白天上课,年限为三年;通信制以通信的方式上课,年限为三年以上;定时制是在不同的时段上课,即半工半读,它同通信制一样,既可设立在全日制高中,也可单独开设,年限同样是三年以上。①

2013年,日本第二期教育振兴基本计划,培养中等教育阶段学生的社会生存能力,培养实现向未来飞跃的人才。

四、高等教育发展概况

日本高等教育机构依其办学形式,大致可分为高等专门学校、专修学校、短期大学、普通大学、研究生院五种,各类学校的数量如表3-1所示,人数如表3-5所示。从中可以看出,2014年高等专门学校共有57所,学生54 354人;专修学校共有3 206所,学生659 452人;短期大学共有352所,学生136 534人;普通大学共有781所,学生2 803 035人,其中大学生2 552 022人,研究生251 013人。从各学校的招生人数看,普通大学招生人数最多,高等专门学校招生人数最少;从与往年的比较看,专修学校人数趋于稳定,其他类型学校的招生人数均持续下降;从学生的性别看,在普通大学、研究生院和高等专门学校,男生的人数远远多于女生,而在专修学校和短期大学则是女生人数多于男生,其中短期大学女生的人数多达男生的近八倍。

---

① 王玉珊.日本教育及其在经济中的作用研究[D].大连:东北财经大学,2012.

表 3-5 2011—2014 年日本各类高等学校的学生人数　　　（人）

学校	2011 年	2012 年	2013 年	2014 年		
				合计	男生	女生
高等专门学校	55 521	55 243	54 864	54 354	44 970	9 384
专修学校	645 834	650 501	660 078	659 452	294 376	365 076
短期大学	150 007	141 970	138 260	136 534	15 812	120 722
普通大学	2 569 349	2 560 909	2 562 068	2 552 022	1 434 244	1 117 778
研究生院	272 566	263 289	255 386	251 013	173 368	77 645

资料来源：日本总务省统计局，《日本の統計》，2016 年发行。

下面主要介绍一下日本普通大学的情况。日本普通大学的教育方针以学术研究为中心，学制一般为四年，医科学院和牙科学院年限为六年，报考对象为高中毕业生或同等学力者，大学毕业后，可获得学士学位。高中毕业生或同等学力者要升入大学，必须通过日本各大学实施的入学考试。① 普通大学各专业学生人数如表 3-6 所示，从中可以看出，社会科学专业人数最多，其次为工学和人文学科专业。

表 3-6 2010—2014 年日本普通大学的专业设置及其学生人数　　　（人）

学校	2011 年	2012 年	2013 年	2014 年		
				合计	男生	女生
总数	2 893 489	2 876 134	2 868 872	2 855 529	1 635 438	1 220 091
大学(学部)	2 569 349	2 560 909	2 562 068	2 552 022	1 434 244	1 117 778
人文科学	385 268	379 288	377 182	371 201	127 715	243 486
社会科学	879 173	861 881	848 652	835 213	551 186	284 027
理学	80 960	80 990	80 490	80 684	59 375	21 309
工学	394 474	390 532	390 042	388 276	338 001	50 275
农学	75 770	75 741	75 724	75 593	42 108	33 485

① 李清晨子.大学生激励制度体系的优化研究：以浙江省某学院为例[D].江西师范大学,2014.

续表 3-6

学校	2011 年	2012 年	2013 年	2014 年		
				合计	男生	女生
保健	270 786	282 337	293 292	303 098	123 957	179 141
商船	—	—	—	119	104	15
家政	69 503	70 266	71 288	71 091	6 696	64 395
教育	172 971	178 421	183 783	187 549	77 097	110 452
艺术	72 073	70 929	70 137	69 163	19 922	49 241
其他	168 371	170 524	171 478	170 035	88 083	81 952

资料来源：日本总务省统计局，《日本の統計》，2016 年发行。

第二节　日本职业发展教育政策

一、日本职业发展教育的历史背景

日本的职业发展教育最早可追溯到 20 世纪 20 年代，其主要任务是为学生提供就业信息，帮助毕业生找到录用部门。第二次世界大战结束至 1955 年以前，日本的新生社会劳动力以初中毕业生为主，初中毕业生中升学与就业的比例相当。1955 年以后，日本新生劳动力的学历层次不断提高，从 1962 年开始高中毕业生成为社会劳动力的主要来源，1970 年以后则是高等学校毕业生就业的黄金时期。为帮助广大青年理性规划未来，1957 年 11 月，日本中央教育审议会在《科学技术教育振兴方案》中将"就业指导"更名为"进路指导"，在提供就业指导和升学指导的同时，为学生提供选择未来生活道路的咨询和指引。

1990 年以后，日本的就业环境和就业形势发生了变化。一方面，日本国民经济增长率持续走低，失业率居高不下，企业对求职者主观素质的要求日趋严格；另一方面，日本逐渐进入少子、高龄、富裕社会，年轻人的社会责任感下降，对劳动缺乏热情，出现了"啃老族"，有的年轻人即使求职成功，也很快因理想与现实的差距而离职。毕业生就不了业、不就业或短期就业后离职的现象，给日本的政治、经济乃至社会生活带来了严重冲击。日本政府认识到原有的"进路指导"已不能满足新时期社会发展的需要,以1984年文部省发布的《初高中学校进路指导手册》为转折点,日本的"进路指导"开始向职业发展教育转化。①

二、日本职业发展教育历程

日本曾经把"career"译成"进路",现在使用"职业发展"这一词汇。文部科学省将职业发展定义为"各个人一生中执行的一连串各种各样的立场、角色以及在其过程中自己与工作的关系或赋予其价值的积累"(文部科学省,2006)。为了明确现在日本通用的所谓职业发展教育(日语为"キャリア")的含义,参照日本文部科学省的定义,对职业发展的含义进行解析,它具有如下四个特点:首先,开头的"各个人"这一措辞是强调职业发展(career)离不开个人。只要把职业(occupation)与职业发展(career)做一比较,其语义便会明晰。职业是社会存在的一个方面,其存在是不以个人意志为转移的。反过来,由个人形成的职业发展(career)则不能离开个人而存在;其次,"一生中执行的各种各样的立场、角色"这一句强调职业发展(career)包含有偿和无偿的全部工作以及工作之外的子女和父母、区域居民的立场、角色;再次,"积累"这一词表明,职业发展(career)并非在某个时刻完成,而是要通过一生不断积累;最后,"自己与工作的关系或赋予其价值"这一句,说明与工作的关系、对工作赋予的价值会是各式各样的。

日本政府首次正式使用"职业发展教育"一词是在1999年文部科学省发表的《关于改善初等、中等教育与高等教育衔接》的报告中。该报告指出,有必要加强学校教育与职业生活的衔接,实施从小学阶段开始的职业发展教育,并将职业观和劳动观教育作为中小学职业发展教育的核心。②日本的职业发展教育正式实施于2004年,但作为其源流的职业指导早在大正年间(1912—1926年)就已经开始。

(一)日本职业指导的初创期

早在明治时期就有关于青少年职业选择的著述,进入大正时期后,开始引入欧美的职业指导。1915年,东京大学教授入泽宗寿著述《现今教育》一

---

①② 徐爱新,安月辉,于伟娜.解析日本的职业生涯教育[J].教育与职业,2011(18):81-83.

书,系统地介绍了欧美的职业指导运动,把美国的"vocation guidance"译成"职业指导",并正式使用该用语。1920年日本设立了第一个公立职业指导专门机关,即大阪市立少年职业商谈所。1921年,东京市中央职业介绍所设置了少年商谈部,1925年开设了东京府少年商谈所。

(二)学校教育引进职业指导

随着20世纪20年代职业指导的发展,学校教育也采用职业指导,尝试着对儿童进行职业指导。1922年,文部省开始举办职业指导讲习会,着手培养从事职业指导的人才。1927年,文部省发出《关于尊重儿童、学生的个性及职业指导文件》,决定将职业指导正式纳入学校教育中,以期促进学校职业指导。此举被视作日本学校职业(进路)指导的发端。职业指导既重视尊重儿童、学生的个性,又明确其在学校教育中的位置,学校教育开始实施以儿童、学生的个性为基础选择适当职业或学校的指导。

(三)战时体制下的职业指导

1938年,日本公布了《国家总动员法》,逐渐进入战时体制,同年10月由新设立的厚生省与文部省联合发出《关于小学校毕业者职业指导之件》的训令,以期进一步加强职业指导,使小学毕业生的职业与"国家的期望相适"。1939年日本推行职业指导强化运动,颁布国民征用令,国民按照其职业能力被征用,职业指导越发具有国家主义色彩。1941年起小学改称国民学校,《关于对国民学校的职业指导之件通牒》指出,"应高度国防国家体制,以培养职分奉公精神为国民陶冶的基础,振兴学校的职业指导,通过对升学与选职的指导,使职分奉公精神贯穿在皇国之道的修炼中"。职业指导以同国家要求相一致的形式被纳入国家体制之中,其对个性的尊重消失殆尽。

(四)战后新教育的职业指导

1946年11月日本公布了《日本国宪法》,翌年3月颁布了《教育基本法》与《学校教育法》。《学校教育法》制定了小学(第18条)、中学(第36条)和高中(第42条)的教育目标,[①]伴随着教育的民主化,开始强调适应个性发展,培养学生选择未来进路的能力。

战后日本职业指导的进程可分成如下四个阶段:

---

① 朴哲.日本职业生涯教育历史及其启示[J].延边大学学报(社会科学版),2012,45(01):35-38.

第一阶段:1946年—1950年。这一时期是确立民主主义和尊重个性的职业指导的开始阶段。战后的新学制刚启动不久,在教育课程上,一开始中学的职业指导被设置于"职业课"中,不久被安排在"职业·家庭课"之中。1947年和1949年,文部省分别颁布了《学习指导要领职业指导编》(试案)和《中学校(初中)·高等学校(高中)职业指导手册》。

第二阶段:1951年—1957年。这一时期,以"职业·家庭课"进路指导为中心,重视以导师为中心的课外活动、课程外的社会与心理辅导等。1957年,中央教育审议会《关于科学技术教育的振兴方案》(第14次答申报告)首次使用"进路指导"这一用语。

第三阶段:1958年—1968年。这一时期,中学以年级活动为中心,高中围绕"以导师为中心的课外活动"开展进路指导。1958年,日本修订了《中学学习指导要领》,职业指导更名为进路指导。1961年,文部省所编《初中·高中进路指导便览——年级主任编》,将进路指导定义为"通过学生的个人资料、进路情报、启发性经验以及商谈,让学生自己选择将来的进路,制订计划,决定就业或升学",并由教师组织进行的指导援助过程,至今仍作为学校进路指导的定义,成为进路指导定性的根本依据。

第四阶段:1969年—2003年。这一时期,进路指导强调其作为指导全部教育课程的角色,依托年级指导及以导师为中心的课外活动有计划地开展进路指导,这成为1969年《初中学习指导要领》(高中为翌年)的修订依据。1977年,学习指导要领中明确写出,要开展贯穿学校教育活动全部过程的进路指导,并一直沿用至今。20世纪60年代中期至80年代中期,在日本社会关心焦点"自我实现理论"(人被看作向自我实现不断成长的一种存在的诸理论)的强烈影响下,1983年初高中学校进路指导便览明确指出"职业的自我实现""社会的自我实现",同时关注以升学、就业指导为中心的进路指导。在此背景下,鉴于学生的成长和发展,为使毕业生在社会生活、职业生活中更进一步成长,进路指导将培养学生必要的能力、态度等作为中心任务。刚毕业学生的升学、就业对其未来的社会生活、职业生活起着重要作用,①因此在具体实行过程中容易把职业指导的着眼点放在入学、就业考试上,而忽视培

---

① 吕显然.日本职业生涯教育研究及启示[D].青岛大学,2014.

养学生作为主体开拓未来、参与策划社会的能力。事实上,由于没有充分考虑自己未来的发展及其相关问题,这导致学生出现接连不断的不适与挫败感。①

战后约60年间职业发展教育的变迁可概括为以下四点:第一,在定位方面,从原来课程中的职业指导转换成为贯穿学校所有教育活动的进路指导;第二,在内容方面,从对职业知识、理解的相关指导变成援助每个学生的职业发展;第三,在指导领域方面,从职业课程的领域转向特别活动或课程外的教育活动;第四,在指导教师方面,从职业课程教师变成定期指导年级学生的教师及进路指导主事。②

三、日本职业发展教育政策变革

20世纪70年代初,职业发展教育源自美国,不久传入日本,但当时并未引起政府当局的关注而得到重视和推广。直到1999年发布《关于改善初等、中等教育和高等教育的衔接》的咨询报告为推进职业发展教育,以1999年报告为基础,文部科学省2002年11月设置了"关于推进职业发展教育的调查研究协力者会议",并在2003年7月发表了中期报告。报告中指出,儿童的全部学习活动都会对职业发展意识产生影响,因此这种教育必须通过所有学校的教育活动来推动。在现行体制中,通过学习指导要领所规定的特别活动、道德、综合学习时间,展开与职业、出路发展相关的学习活动。不仅如此,还要通过各科学习,深入理解有关社会、产业的变化、劳动者的权利与义务,掌握选择升学专业、学科的能力以及选择职业的能力。③

为推进职业发展教育,日本政府相继推出了多个相互关联的法令或计划。2003年6月,由文部科学大臣、厚生劳动大臣、经济产业大臣、经济财政政策担当大臣参与制定了人才对策,即《年轻人自立挑战计划》,将推进发展教育作为实施该计划的重要支柱;2004年又推出了《培养每个学生的勤劳观、职业观——推进职业发展教育综合调查研究协会会议报告》,将职业体验活动作为推进发展教育的重要环节;从2005年开始,文部科学省在全国

---

① 朴哲.日本职业生涯教育历史及其启示[J].延边大学学报(社会科学版),2012,45(01):
② 吕显然.日本职业生涯教育研究及启示[D].青岛:青岛大学,2014.
③ 杨博艳.陕西地方本科高校大学生职业生涯规划教育问题与对策研究[D].西安:西安科技大学,2012.

138个地区开展"发展起步教育周",建立以初中生为主的五天职场体验制度及其支持体系,并编写了《初中职场体验指导书》,详细阐述了职场体验活动的目的和实施要领,并希望学校、单位、家庭相互支持形成体系;2006年日本又推出了"职业发展教育综合计划",实施以中小学生为对象的"新体验计划"、以大学生和研究生为对象的"高度职业发展计划"和以自由职业者为对象的"自由职业者再教育计划"。在一系列法令的推动和引导下,日本的职业发展教育超越了就业指导和进路指导的范畴,形成了一个伴随学生整个学习发展,以培养学生完整人格为目的的教育体系。①

目前,日本正在推进"职业发展教育综合计划"。这一计划由三部分组成,一是以小学至高中教育阶段的学生为对象的"新体验计划";二是主要以大学、研究生为对象,培养有高度专业能力人才的"高度职业发展计划";三是谋求自由职业者能力提高的"自由职业者再教育计划"。新体验计划是在小学至高中的全部学校中推进在职业和工作中学习初步经验的体验活动和实习,虽然次数有限,但开始接受小学生进行体验活动的机关团体在逐年增加。为促进高中阶段实习,2004年由经济团体、5678家长教师协会等设置了联络协议会。2004年决定依靠全国56所专门学校的信息技术、福利、生命科学等相关学科开发教育计划。制定企业实习与学校学习相结合的课程,形成培养职业人的结构体系。② 在这一计划的推动下,2003年日本高中学校开始实施"双轨制学习体系",要求学生在一定时期里,一周至少要有三天在企业实习,两天在学校里进行文化技能的学习。2005年4月,文部科学省又规定,初中生在一定时期里,要有五天以上的时间进行岗位体验活动,这项政策被称为"职业发展开始周"或"体验启动周"。学生们通过到各种劳动场所去体验了解劳动者的甘苦,学会与人交往的技能,树立劳动光荣的价值观。多种多样的体验活动收到了良好的效果。根据文部科学省的统计,2004学年实施就业体验的高中占学校总数的57%。到2010年,这一数字上升到77.2%,有职业体验经历的学生已达到学生总数的29%。"自由职业者再教育计划"是为自由职业者提供3至6个月的学习,为其开辟挑战正式职工的道路。

2008年,中央教育审议会职业发展教育·职业教育特别部会接受并审

---

① 徐爱新,安月辉,于伟娜.解析日本的职业生涯教育[J].教育与职业,2011(18):81-83.
② 李英,史景轩,宋晓平.日本职业生涯教育及其启示[J].成人教育,2007(12):93-94.

议了文部科学大臣"关于今后学校职业发展教育·职业教育的现状"的咨询,于2010年发表了题为《关于今后学校职业发展教育·职业教育的现状(第二次审议经过报告)》的报告。[1] 该报告提出,所谓学校的职业发展教育是指"为了每个人在社会上和职业上的自立,通过对必要的能力、态度的培育,促进发展的教育"。所谓职业教育则为"培养从事一定或特定职业所需知识、技能、能力及态度的教育"。从实践的角度来说,职业发展教育不分普通教育和专门教育而实施于各种教育活动中,这里也包含职业教育的实践。职业教育以具体的职业为对象进行基础性、通用性能力和态度的培养,它不仅作为职业发展教育的一环具有重要意义,而且在促成社会的、职业的自立方面也起到非常有效的作用。

日本职业发展教育的新理念主要有两点。一是培养学生积极的生活态度、正确的劳动观和职业观,高度重视每个人与生俱来的创造性,促进人的个性自主、有序的发展,实现个人与社会之间最有效的互动,使学生具有相应的职业知识和技能的同时,培养学生了解自己和主动选择人生道路的能力。二是逐步实现由就业教育到职业发展教育的转变。从指导目的来看,首先,职业发展教育是一种旨在培养学生完整人格的教育,从培养一个协调的社会人和职业人的角度出发,进行树人教育;其次,职业发展教育是一种有计划的教育,根据每个学生不同阶段的特点,指导学生通过个体或者团体性的活动,对自身的发展进行规划;最后,职业发展教育是一种有目的的教育,最大限度地拓展学生在今后生活中自我实现所必需的能力和态度,[2]要求从幼儿至成人的整个教育过程中,都要将传授知识与学生将来的工作和生存方式相结合,目的是通过职业发展教育促进人生价值实现,为社会提供适应时代要求的优质劳动者。

第三节 日本职业发展教育课程

1999年12月召开的中央教育审议会上提出,职业发展教育须贯穿于中小学发展阶段全过程,从小学阶段就开始实施,使职业发展教育与学生身心

---

[1] 蔡璐.日本中小学职业生涯教育研究[D].上海:上海师范大学,2017.
[2] 张玉改.生涯教育概念的多维透视[D].南京:南京师范大学,2018.

发展相融合,这就需要学校与社会之间的配合。2006年11月文部省制定了《小学、初中及高中职业发展教育推进指南》,又进一步印证在学校教育中推进职业发展教育势在必行,强调了职业发展教育与学生自身发展的必要性和重要性。小学阶段的职业发展教育主要注重培养学生学会表达自己的需求,尊重他人,与他人友好相处,这个阶段的学生不会考虑自身的性格、能力是否满足职业的需求,他们对职业世界的认识只是凭借自己的兴趣爱好,完全出于幻想之中;初中阶段的职业发展教育侧重于培养学生对自身特质进行全方位的了解,包括性格、能力、兴趣爱好和价值观等,并通过学校活动,对职业世界进行一番探索,建立良好的人际关系的能力,具备团队合作意识,懂得利用自己的个性优势。使其发挥到最优化;高中阶段的职业发展教育重在培养学生认知并接受职业选择信息的能力,灵活运用信息的能力,同时获得有关资料,了解个人兴趣和能力与工作机会的关系,认清与能力和兴趣相一致的工作领域,接受并参加学校举办的活动和训练,以培养技能,在自我认知、职业环境认知的基础上分析自己的优势和劣势,据此确定自己的职业发展方向,设计规划自己的未来,积极面对和解决未来决策过程中遇到的困难,心怀梦想,勇往直前。职业发展教育是全面发展的教育,注重培养学生终身学习的意识,注重培养学生的创新能力;职业发展教育是主体性和个体性的教育,在于发挥人的主观能动性,合理利用每个人得天独厚的创造性,提升个体的人文素质;职业发展教育加强了在个体价值观、心理、技能方面的指导,提升了个体的综合素质和能力,形成正确的职业观。推进职业发展教育基本有两个方向:首先是激发学生对工作的认同感,使他们对工作感兴趣,而不是负担;其次是帮助学生训练工作方面的技能,使他们将来能更自信地面对工作。学校必须根据学生的具体需求,及时给学生提供职业发展规划方面的指导。①

一、小学阶段的职业发展教育课程内容

在小学阶段,日本的职业发展教育将生涯教育与道德科等其他学科的教育教学相融合,并将职业发展教育的目标和内容关联到学生未来可能从

---

① 孙晋露.日本:系统化、分阶段的职业生涯教育[J].基础教育论文(文摘版),2015(3).

事的职业和生活中,①侧重于培养学生尊重和关心他人,同时也要学会爱护自己;学会表达自己的需求和兴趣爱好;树立学生积极向上、热爱劳动的生活态度;尝试吸引学生关注身边与职业环境有关的信息,培养认知职业信息的意识,了解工作的意义,发展学生对职业世界的正确态度;帮助学生树立目标和对未来生活的美好憧憬。② 小学阶段最重要的还是职业发展兴趣和意识的引导,基于对学生身心发展特点的考虑,这个时期他们对职业世界的认识全凭自己的兴趣爱好,不会考虑自身的性格、能力是否满足职业的需求,也不用选择去向问题。教育的起点和终点都是人,只有人得到全面的发展,其存在才有意义和内涵,传统的道德说教已经不能满足职业发展教育的发展,必须在学校的道德教育活动中以体验性的方式融入职业发展教育,活动可以涉及多个主体参与,比如:他人和家庭,既可以帮助学生在活动中学会与他人相处,尊重他人,又可以帮助学生掌握多种生活技能,同时还可以了解自己的多重角色和能力。因此,在小学阶段,学校必须重视职业发展教育与课程教学的结合,把学生个性的生涯与现实生活结合在一起,让学生感受到学有所用。

(一)基础科目学习

基础科目的学习旨在帮助学生学会表达需求,保持好奇心,不断探索新事物,开发个性生涯的创造性,尝试用各种不同的方式解决遇到的难题。在学习过程中,结果不是重点,最重要的是培养学生独立思考的能力,激发他们自身的创造性,帮助学生树立正确的人生观、价值观、学习观和成才观。③

(二)各类特别活动

在小学阶段,学生除了基础科目的学习,参加学校举办的各类活动也是必不可少的。书本上教的都是理论知识,学起来枯燥乏味,各类活动既能增加学生的学习兴趣,又能提高学生实际动手操作和临场应变的能力,还能培养学生之间的团队合作意识,形成良好的人际交往的能力,使学生的身心都得到很好的锻炼,养成积极健康的心态。

---

① 唐植君.日本小学职业生涯教育的本土化及启示[J].教学与管理,2015(2).
② 韩晓明.日本普遍高中学生职业生涯教育研究[D].沈阳:辽宁师范大学硕士论文,2009.
③ 谷峪.日本社会转型期的职业技术教育[D].长春:东北师范大学,2006.

(三)社会体验活动

学校举办的活动不能满足学生自身发展的需要,还需要参加一些体验性的活动,比如到实地去参观产品的制作过程和调查、参观当地的生产销售情况,引导学生活用书本上学到的知识进行调查分析等,或者运用资料进行调查分析,选择适当的学习课题开展学习活动。目的在于通过体验活动,让学生对职业世界有全新的认识,发展对工作的正确态度。

二、初中阶段的职业发展教育课程内容

小学阶段的职业发展教育注重培养学生的兴趣爱好,属于认知阶段。在初中阶段,日本职业发展教育的目标可以概括为:在学习知识的过程中,养成独立自主的性格,理解学习的意义;对自身特质进行全方位的了解,包括性格、能力和兴趣爱好,在自我认知的基础上分析自己的优势和劣势,设计自己未来的人生道路;树立正确的价值观和职业观。因此,初中阶段必须把职业发展教育与课程结合起来,合理调整课程结构,优化教学方法,把职业发展教育融入教学过程中。

(一)综合学习时间

在综合学习时间中,要求初中生参加参观和调查各类生产实践活动。日本初中阶段的课程结构更合理,教学内容符合学生自身生长发展。国语教学侧重启发学生对生活的态度,以及理解生活和社会的关系;理科教学能帮助学生锻炼逻辑思维能力,让学生了解和学习更多科学技术的工作原理,以及它与生活和社会之间的联系,从而更好地将所学的知识应用到生活和社会中。学校会以各种形式向学生展示学科学习以及它对未来职业的意义,比如每年新学期学校都会向学生及家长派发学习手册,学习手册主要是关于学科学习与生活和职业的关系,目的是让学生感受到学科学习对生活和未来职业的重要性。除此之外,学科理论知识的学习已不能满足学生自身发展的需要,因此,学校增设了各种实践课程,既能激发学生的学习兴趣和热情,又能锻炼学生的实际动手操作能力和人际交往能力。比如很多学校会安排学生进行职场体验活动。在此之前,教师会对学生的兴趣爱好以及以后向往的工作内容进行收集,然后学校会跟相应的体验单位取得联系,安排和协调好一切体验活动事宜。初中阶段的学生对自身的兴趣爱好已经

有一定的认知,活动之前学校会对学生进行培训,让学生了解职场体验的目的以及遇到问题应怎样处理。活动中根据自己的兴趣对未来职业展开思考,同时还能锻炼自己的人际交往能力,了解他人对职业的看法。体验活动结束之后,学生要写一份未来职业发展规划书,主要包括学生毕业后的职业去向和对未来职业的规划,学校会把学生每次的活动体验记录在案,方便学生和家长翻阅。职场体验活动既可以激发学生对学科学习的热情,还可以为学生未来的职业发展指引方向。①

(二)特别活动

特别活动主要包括:学校活动、年级活动、学生会活动。在学校活动中,学校会要求学生参加与职业去向和发展相关的体验活动和志愿者活动,帮助学生理解活动与生活和职业的意义;在年级活动中,会要求学校在年级内建立各种组织,便于解决学生和生活中出现的各种问题;在学生会活动中,学校为了丰富学生的校内生活,会组织各种志愿者服务活动,不仅提高了学生的劳动和服务意识,还可以培养他们的团队意识。通过开展特别活动,不仅解决了学生在学校生活中遇到的各种问题,还对学生进行了"做合格的社会成员"的教育。其中包括帮助学生确立人生的目标;在人际交往中,每个人都是独立的个体,学会理解和尊重他人,与他人和谐相处;学习中养成自律的精神,脚踏实地,勇往直前;树立正确的人生观、价值观、劳动观和职业观;以积极的心态面对未来的挑战。②

三、高中阶段的职业发展教育课程内容

学生在小学和初中阶段属于对自我人格的认知阶段,在高中阶段,学生自我认知基本已经形成,心理和生理也都逐渐成熟。交际范围也越来越广泛,此时,他们已经不仅仅是学生的角色,还会承担其他社会角色。他们不再只关注学习成绩,慢慢地会对自身进行全方位的定位,会对现实世界不断地尝试来修正自己的角色,同时思考人生的价值和生存的意义,发展对职业世界的正确态度。因此,高中阶段的职业发展教育侧重培养以下几点:学习状态从被动转变到主动;发挥主观能动性;培养学生独立自主的能力;学生

---

① 孙晋露.日本:系统化、分阶段的职业生涯教育[J].基础教育论文(文摘版),2015(3).
② 谷峪.日本社会转型期的职业技术教育[D].长春:东北师范大学,2006.

开始考虑自己的去向;对自我能力进行探索,形成正确的人生观、价值观和职业观,逐渐达到职业所需的基本素质和能力。

高中阶段的学生每到一个年级的心理和生理发育是不同的,接受各种职业信息的能力也不同,所以,高中阶段是把职业发展教育按年级的不同分阶段实施,在高中一年级,学生要对自身特质进行全方位的了解,包括性格、能力、兴趣爱好和价值观等,学校也会邀请各行各业的专家来校为学生演讲和做专业的指导,然后学生分析自身的优劣势,据此考虑个人的职业发展方向。在高中二年级,学校会组织学生去实地进行参观和调查,深入体验职场,分析职场中出现的各种问题。在高中三年级,学生除了面临紧张的升学压力,还要考虑升学问题。学生可以对梦想的大学进行实地考察,并与该校的大学生进行交流,了解该校专业的设置情况和专业的社会需求情况,等等。升学调查有两大好处,一是可以帮助学生对未来做出更加准确的选择;二是让学生意识到在校所学知识对生活和未来职业是有用的,以调动学生对所学知识的兴趣和热情。[1]

(一)综合学习时间

日本高中阶段的职业发展教育是与学科课程和教学融合在一起的,传统的课程体系设置和教学方法已不能满足学生自身的发展和社会市场的需求。新的课程设置融合了职业发展教育的内容,在教学方面,学科之间进行交叉贯通,能让所学知识融会贯通,比如,数学课可以和物理课结合起来,生物课也可以谈到家庭、环境和生活的关系。通过学科和教学间的交叉融合,学生能深刻地体会到知识对生活和社会的意义。为了适应时代的要求和社会经济的高速增长,部分高中对学科进行分类,分成普通学科、专门学科和综合学科。普通学科主要面对的是升学的学生,专门学科针对面向就业的学生,综合学科针对的是不定向的学生。在1999年3月,日本开始使用新的《高中学习指导要领》,对基础课程进行重新设置,基础课程数量不需要太多,主要是增加职业发展教育基础课程,同时教学方法和内容必须满足学习指导要求。为了适应科学的进步,增加了生命科学类学科;为了满足信息化技术的需要,减少了农业等传统职业课程的占比;为了适应老龄化社会需

---

[1] 谷峪,崔玉洁.日本高中阶段的职业生涯教育[J].外国教育研究,2010(12).

要,增设了福利专业。

高中新开设的课程中,最值得一提的是"产业社会和人"课程,这门课程是按照高中阶段的学习指导要求编制、设定的。学校根据这门课程把学生按照他们未来方向的意愿分成了不同的小组,希望他们能够认真学习这门课程,积极地投入职业体验活动中。学校组织学生对实地进行参观、调查和分析,并与社会上相关人员进行交流,进一步了解他们所从事的职业,为将来自己做职业选择的时候提供依据。学生参与这些活动,不仅可以感受到社会企业的实际运营情况,还可以帮助自己确定未来职业发展方向。部分高中自从开设这一科目,收效显著,学生和家长都做出了中肯的评价,表示一定会积极配合学校工作。调查显示,自从学生学习过这一科目,很多方面都有很大改变,比如学习积极性和自律性提高了,目标也明确了,学习热情更高涨了,学习态度也端正了许多。特别需要指出的是学生的出路意识较之以往得到了极大的提高。除此之外,学校还根据每个学生在专门学科的学习中,根据个人对未来预定职业选择的不同分成了不同小组。这些小组参与的活动不同于学校平时的活动,它充分利用了综合学习时间,探寻与出路相关的信息,实地调查和分析大学的专业设置情况,极大地提高了学生的学习热情。

(二)职业发展咨询活动

日本从小学开始,学校都组织有职业发展咨询活动(career counseling),是由学校专门的老师负责,老师会对你提出合适的建议。学生可以咨询与学习、生活和未来职业相关的问题,或者有些学生对自身定位不准确的,不清楚自己的兴趣爱好和能力,也可以让老师帮你发掘自己的潜力。此外,学校还为即将毕业的学生提供毕业去向指导。但是学校的职业发展教育不仅仅只是为了帮助学生指导他们职业方向选择的问题,更重要的是培养学生的价值观、劳动观和人生观,促进学生对社会的认识和自我的独立。

(三)实践活动

日本高校的职业发展教育实践活动集中体现在岗位体验和就职体验上,这两种体验活动激励学生走出校园,走进工厂、公司,亲自感受体会具体的职业环境,促进学生对社会工作的进一步了解,感受知识对生活和工作的意义,引导他们形成正确的人生观、价值观、劳动观和职业观。日本高中开展这两种实践活动,事先要与体验单位进行沟通联系,把准备工作做好。随着高中对职业发展教育越来越重视,高中进行这样的体验活动越来越多,导致体验单位数量不够。为了保证所有的学生都能参加这种体验活动,学校与当地的企业和主管机关进行协调,以获得他们的帮助,共同努力开拓新的体验场所。目前,为了保证这种体验活动能够顺利进行,日本上至国家、下至都道府县都在加紧收集体验单位的信息资料。作为国家行政机关,它们身先士卒,与当地的社会企业和组织共同安排前来体验活动的学生进行学习。

四、大学阶段的职业发展教育课程内容[①]

日本高校经过多年的实践,建立了完善的职业发展教育体系,此体系的三大支柱分别是:职业发展教育相关课程与讲座、体验式就业及课外支援活动。

(一)职业发展教育相关课程与讲座

日本高校实施的职业发展教育系统地建立了职业发展教育课程体系与效果测评系统。

1.课程设置

为了使学生掌握社会和职业中的基础知识、提高职业能力,各高校纷纷调整课程设置。各高校所设置的职业发展课程,大体包括四项内容:如何充实地度过大学生活、产业社会现状、职业发展规划及求职技巧。如大学生活动课程的教学目的是将学生生活与职业发展规划结合起来,引导那些还没有人生目标的学生开始规划自己的人生;鼓励学生在大学生活中勇于挑战和尝试;帮助学生在如今人情淡薄化的时代建立良好人际关系,并针对现今大学生基础知识匮乏、学习能力低下的问题,激发学生的学习能力、写文章的能力、自我表现力和沟通能力。产业社会现状课程的教学目标是帮助学生了解产业经济现状、动向和企业的组织结构,掌握商务礼仪。职业发展规划课程主要是通过审视自己的兴趣、能力、价值观,思考自己的职业观,进而建立人生规划。但学生的理想往往与自己的能力和现实的就业环境之间存

---

① 李晶.日本高校职业生涯教育及对中国的启示[J].当代教育科学,2012(17).

在差距,所以让学生学会如何处理好理想与现实的问题,建立良好的就业心态成为这门课程的重要内容。求职技巧课程主要是请企事业单位的领导、已经就业的毕业生等讲授自己的职场经验和求职技巧。

2.职业发展教育讲座

职业发展教育讲座可以分为两类。一是关于职业发展规划的讲座,二是关于资格取得的讲座。关于职业发展规划讲座最值得关注的是"工作与人生"系列讲座,该讲座面向全校学生开课,聘请了相关的专家,以系列讲座的形式,不仅讲授了顺利就业所需的知识与能力,还介绍了当今的就业环境及变化。该讲座的目的是为了加深学生对职业发展教育的认识和理解,同时对自己有更全方位的了解,据此确立个人的职业发展方向,并订立目标,从而使大学生活更有意义,而不是漫无目的。关于资格取得的讲座以立命馆大学为例进行介绍。立命馆大学设有专门负责组织各类讲座的机构称之为"讲座中心",举办诸如会计师考试讲座、公务员考试讲座、托福等英语讲座、系统维护等有关于信息处理的讲座等。并且学校举办讲座的数量和听讲座学生人数都在增加。这些讲座可以充分运用日常教学中学习到的知识,使学习内容多样化,教学效果突出,得到了学生和业内的高度认可。

3.效果测评系统

为了对职业发展教育的教学成果进行检验,各个高校都建立了效果测评系统,及时对职业发展教育进行评估、反馈和调整,促进职业发展教育向前发展。如武藏野大学开发了适应性测评系统,测试内容包括:性格倾向、社会适应程度、成长感、规划成熟度、事业观等,并对每个项目制定了详细的评价标准。对小学生每学期都会测评,根据测评的结果调整职业发展教育教学计划。四天王寺国际佛教大学为了更准确地对每门课程的教学效果做出评价,在开课前后对学生进行访谈和问卷调查,内容是教师为这门课设定的教学目标,即通过学习这门课程,学生的各方面能力有没有提高。通过问卷调查前后结果的比较,评价该课程的教学效果,并在以后的课程中不断加以改进。正因为有了客观全面的教学效果评价系统,日本高校的职业发展教育课程才得以在实践中不断完善。

(二)体验式就业

体验式就业是支撑高校职业发展教育体系的另一支柱。数据表明,到

2004年已有59%的高校把职业体验设置成专业课程,随着大学职业发展教育的深入,比例呈现一定程度的增长。特别是在日本与职业发展教育有关的院校,职业体验已经成为学生锻炼实践性技能的必要途径,很多企业已经专门在线上建立网站,发布职业体验活动需求的信息,或者利用媒体向大家宣传,比如报纸和电视,然后学校与体验单位联系,组织学生统一进行体验活动,或者个人通过网上报名直接到实地参观和调查。武藏野大学将实习纳入必修课,开设于三年级暑假,2学分,目的在于使学生通过就业体验更好地规划未来。文京学院则将其称作体验式学习,开设在三年级上学期,长达15周。并有两类供学生选择,一类是在日本国内企业中的体验式学习,另一类则是去国外有合作关系的大学进行"跨文化交流体验式学习"。

学生实习环节得以顺利实施,需要"产学官"通力合作作为保障。所谓"产学官"合作是指产业界、高等教育界和政府的联合协作。2003年6月,为解决年轻人就业问题,日本政府发表了"年轻人自立、挑战计划"。在各省厅的联合协作下,自2004年起的三年中实施了若干解决年轻人就业问题的措施。其中包括与产业界合作,通过派遣职员到学校教授就业经验及让学生到企业进行就业体验等手段,帮助学生更好规划自己的职业发展等。2003年日本经济团体联合会和日本工商会议所联合发表了《关于促进以年轻人为中心的就业问题及人才培养的共同宣言》,具体措施包括官民合作推进企业实习、试雇佣的进行;官民合作提供就业信息;大力开展学校内的职业发展教育;为更好地创业提供职业发展教育等。学生实习对职业发展教育来说是必要的环节,同时也作为"产学官"合作的一项重要内容受到政府、企业、高校以及全社会的高度关注。

(三)课外支援活动

日本高校职业发展教育不仅贯穿于课程、讲座之中,而且提供了针对每位学生的个性化服务和丰富多彩的课外活动。

1.咨询指导服务

法政大学开设咨询指导室,学生可以通过预约得到专业指导人员一对一的咨询指导。咨询师对低年级学生在如何度过大学生活方面的困惑给予辅导和帮助,并在指导他们了解自身性格的基础上建立起早期的职业规划;对高年级学生在求职面试、职业选择中遇到的问题给予建议和指导,并帮助

他们调整就业心态。此项服务对职业指导人员配备数量及专业知识和经验提出了很高要求。高校根据学生的规模配备相应数量的具有专业知识背景的职业发展教育指导人员,他们既要掌握教育学、心理学知识,熟练掌握心理量表、职业适应性量表以及各种计算机辅助软件等现代化的职业发展指导工具,又要熟悉当前就业形势和就业政策,同时具有学生工作、教务工作乃至国际交流工作等相关经验。

2.由学生组织参与的职业发展支援活动

如日本法政大学针对新生,由高年级志愿者负责组织和开展的拓展活动。内容包括:在学或已工作学长的经验演讲、新生自我介绍和采访、大学生活规划讲演、交流会等。这样的活动一方面给予新生相互交流、向学长学习及自我审视的机会,另一方面也给高年级学生提供参与策划、组织的实践机会,取得了良好效果。

可见,日本高校的职业发展教育从大一到大四是相互贯穿融合的,针对不同年级学生对自身发展的需求不同,制订相应合理的教学计划。一年级,学生对自身定位还不清楚,还处在迷茫期,这时应该帮助学生提高自我认知,明确自身发展方向。通过如何度过大学生活相关课程,使学生从低年级就开始思考人生规划,并加强写作、沟通等基础能力的培养。二年级,主要是加强学生对自身特质进行全方位的了解,开设职业发展规划相关课程,帮助学生形成早期的职业发展设计方案。三年级的侧重点是培养学生的各项技能,开设产业社会现状相关课程,帮助学生了解社会,开设各类专业资格证书的讲座。引导学生多参加职业体验活动,让学生较早接触到职业环境,通过身心体验社会,树立良好的职业观。到了四年级,主要是帮助学生解决就业问题,同时开展求职类的讲座,通过招聘会和企业宣讲会,让学生能及时了解市场对人才的需求信息,尽可能地就业,同时也可以帮助学生确定发展方向,选择最合适自己发展的事业。而咨询师的一对一咨询指导和学生自发组织的各类活动则贯穿大学四年,从各个方面为学生提供无微不至的帮助。文京学院大学就制定了一套完整的职业发展教育计划,称作"Bunkyo-Career Design Program"。

综上所述,大学职业发展教育不仅有完整的课程和教学体系,而且内容丰富,手段先进,能够帮助学生更好地融入社会,引导学生确定自己的职业发展方向,并制定出相应的计划和目标。职业发展教育使高校对学生的教育落实到实处,而不是只局限于理论知识的学习,更多的是让学生切身体验到生活的意义,激发学生学习的热情,使他们更加坚定自己的人生目标,憧憬未来,形成正确的人生观、价值观、劳动观和职业观。

第四节　日本职业发展教育特色

一、职业发展教育政策支持

日本的职业发展教育是以政府为中心主导推行的,其相关部门负责引导和协作。日本文部省以 1999 年报告为基础,为推进职业发展教育,于 2002 年 11 月设置了"关于推进职业发展教育的调查研究协力者会议",并在 2003 年 7 月发表了中期报告。报告表明,与学生学习有关的活动都会对职业发展意识的形成产生作用,因此学校必须增加职业发展教育方面的内容。另外,为了帮助学校、政府和企业等更好地推行实施职业发展教育,政府制定了与之相关的政策法规。从 2005 年开始,政府加大企业对人才培养的力度,并采取一些激励政策,如免除一定比例的企业教育培训费用,以此鼓励企业积极进行人才培养。2010 年 5 月,日本职业发展教育发布针对义务教育和高中教育的报告《未来职业发展学校》,强调各学校应充分认识职业发展教育的重要性和必要性,提出了学校对未来职业发展教育的应对策略。通过日本政府对职业发展的高度重视和全力支持,使得职业发展教育在日本已经形成系统的中小学学习全过程的教育。

二、全程化的职业发展教育

2004 年,文部省为了大力推进职业发展教育,邀请相关方面专家针对职业发展教育的研究召开会议。会议提出了对未来职业发展教育的应对策略,特别强调职业发展教育必须以学生为核心,并把发展教育融入中小学学习全过程。日本形成了完整的中小学职业发展教育教学大纲体系,并明确规定了各个阶段的教学内容和任务。小学阶段主要强调对小学生生活方式的引导,养成良好的生活态度和生活习惯,有着健康安全的生活意识,对生

活充满憧憬,通过学校开展的教育活动对小学生各个方面进行指导,形成正确的生活观、劳动观和职业观;初中阶段强调提高学生的认知能力和选择判断的能力,提高学生适应集体生活的能力,帮助学生克服青少年时期的烦恼,同时了解工作的意义、发展对工作的正确态度。理解和尊重自己与他人,建立良好的人际关系,理解学习对于自身的意义,积极规划将来;高中阶段学生被要求从被动学习状态转变到主动,发挥主观能动性。着重培养学生独立自主的能力,学生可以自我选择、自我监督地学习,对自我能力进行探索,形成正确的人生观、价值观和职业观,逐渐达到职业所需的基本素质和能力。职业发展教育已经被日本融入中小学各个阶段的教育之中,各个阶段的知识是连贯的、依次衔接的,与学生职业发展相关的内容也非常丰富,包括养成良好的人生观、价值观和劳动观,养成良好的社交能力,了解个人兴趣和能力及其与职业机会的关系,探索并获得积极的自我认知,认知并接受职业选择信息。因此,日本中小学职业发展教育已经形成了完整的分阶段有序衔接的体系。

三、学科专业重组

随着教育改革的兴起,职业发展教育越来越受到高校的重视,并在各个高校全面实施,高校认识到传统的学科专业设置已不符合时代要求,必须提供满足社会需求的经济实用的教育,职业发展教育恰好填补了这一空缺,使得高校的专业设置更加丰富和合理。学生就业一直是社会高度重视的问题,影响就业的原因有很多,比如高校设置的专业与社会需求脱钩,满足不了市场需求;学生理论知识丰富,但实用技能差;学生缺乏正确的就业观、择业观等。要想解决就业这一难题,必须不断地更新高校专业,并及时修订高校专业教学大纲,设置合理的专业结构,满足劳动力市场和行业岗位对人才的需求,增加学生的就业机会,同时也能推动社会的经济增长和发展。因此,为了适应时代要求,各个高校间互相交流学习,校内积极开展了院系间合作,院内开展学科交叉,专业重组,形成了一套新的经营管理方法和运营体系。各高校学科专业重组后,不仅激发了学生学习的兴趣,拓宽了知识眼界,而且丰富了专业体系内容,使得各学科专业领域的知识相互渗透融合。学科专业的重组,推动了国立大学所有教育学部的解体,成立了国际协力研究科、综合研究科等交叉学科。另外,还有许多高校正在大力发展职业发展教育研究生院的建设,积极打造一支专业的职业发展教育人才。

四、灵活运用体验式就业

20世纪90年代后期,主要以学生的职业劳动观为核心,为了培养学生对职业信息的认知,开始引入一些职业体验式的活动。1998年开始,高中教育阶段推进职业体验式活动,并做出相应的计划;1999年高中阶段的学校把职业体验列入高中教学计划当中。进入新世纪以来,日本制定了与职业发展教育相关的计划,主要是以中小学生为对象,实行"职业体验计划"。"职业体验计划"是一种在职业和工作中学习初步经验的体验活动和实习,包括职业现场体验、实习等,已在小学至高中的全部学校中推进,虽然体验的次数有限制,进行体验活动的组织单位数量也不多,但设置接受中小学生进行职业体验活动的组织和团体在逐步增加。职业体验活动的效果初期非常明显,调查显示,大部分学生在职业体验活动中受益匪浅,包括:有助于认知并接受职业选择信息,同时获得有关资料;有助于了解个人兴趣和能力及其与工作机会的关系;有助于认清与能力和兴趣相一致的工作领域;有助于形成良好的职业观;提高自己的社交能力;增强自身意志和责任感。职业体验活动是一项有价值的活动,但期望这样珍贵的体验不要只是例行公事和做面子活,而要落到实处,坚持下去,做好体验前后的指导工作。

五、强调毕业大学生体验资料存档管理

高校鼓励并引导学生建立个人职业生涯规划资料档案存档,帮助学生对自身特质、职业环境进行全方位的了解,在自我认知、职业环境认知的基础上分析自己的优势和劣势,据此确定个人的职业发展方向,并制订出行动计划,随着生涯发展对规划及时进行评估、反馈和调整,使规划始终具有可指导性。高校指导学生职业生涯规划的形式有很多,包括就业讲座、就业咨询、就业体验等。非常值得学习的是,几乎全部的高校都建立了就业指导中心,专门为学生就业服务,提供各种信息资料,其中包括往届毕业生的就业体验活动经历、就业资料,这些资料能够帮助大学生通过理论分析和实践指导,认清自身优势劣势,不断修正自己,使大学生职业生涯规划的探索体验

更加完善,补齐自身在职业生涯规划能力方面的不足,少走弯路,科学确定职业发展方向。

六、注重"产学合作"

职业发展教育在日本高校得到进一步发展,在其发展进程中"产学合作"逐步受到重视。21世纪以来,日本为了应对出现的社会经济问题和国际的挑战,尤其是日趋严峻的大学生就业问题以及实施教育改革过程中的问题,加快了"产学合作"的进程。日本文部科学省于2005年4月发布的《第三期科学计划的基本政策》中,指出要构建可持续发展的"产学合作"模式,日本经济进入高速增长期,需要大批实用性和高质量人才,这就需要学校和企业加强合作交流,在具备基础理论知识的同时,与社会外部环境相接触与企业接轨。① 日本政府鼓励各高校改变以往传统的培训模式,促使学校和企业间加大合作力度。大学可以为企业提供人才,同时企业帮助大学研究开发新项目和培养人才,比如通过建立大学科技产业园,一方面学生可以在产业园得到技能锻炼,为企业培养实用性人才,加强学生的创新创业意识;另一方面可以吸引社会各界专业人士进行创业投资。为了加强"产学合作",日本创建了大批的研究基地,其中最为著名的是"筑波科学城",这是一个集教学、科研、生产于一体的综合基地。除此之外,各高校还邀请各行各业专家及有经验的人士来高校做演讲,向学生讲授他们职业发展的亲身经验,希望能够帮助学生更好地迎接未来的人生。

产学合作这种把学校教育与企业培训结合起来的教育模式促进了日本经济的高速增长,缓解了大学生就业问题,成为企业培养各类优秀人才的最佳途径。高等院校走产学研相结合的道路是当今社会新的发展趋势,高校与企业合作的范围比较广泛,形式也多种多样,高校根据企业对人才的需要,开设相应的课程,包括理论课程和实用课程,同时加强学生的职业发展意识;企业为了适应社会的发展,会派职工到高校进修学习,也会委托学校搞一些科研项目,企业提供一定的经费;高校会派学生到企业锻炼学习,亲身体验职场的运营,同时也邀请或聘任企业的技术专家为客座教授,为学生

---

① 杨思帆.国外学生人生规划教育的若干特点与启示[J].教育与考试,2010(02):87-89+92.

讲授经验。"产学合作"使高校和企业的联系变得更加紧密，既满足了企业的发展需要，又开阔了高校的办学空间，提高了高校学生的毕业就业率，推动了日本经济的发展。

七、立足学生的终身发展，注重对学生人格教养的教育

为了应对新的就业形势、满足社会对人才的需求和迎接经济全球化的挑战，全面发展的职业发展教育理念渐渐取代了传统的就业理念。社会需要的是全面发展的人和终身发展的人，社会对人才的需求标准也发生了变化，学历不再是找工作唯一的敲门砖，企业更看重的是个人的能力和能为企业创造多大的价值。当然这并不意味着企业不再重视学历，只是在重视学历的同时，对人才的质量要求更高，主要表现在企业对求职者的职业价值观、社交能力、管理能力、性格等方面的要求也越来越严格。企业常常被问到这样一个问题："你招募员工时最看重求职者哪方面？"企业基本上很一致地认为人品最重要，我们在日常生活中也经常说"这个人人品很好"，而企业所追求的"人品"指的是虽然有些时候技能没有完全体现出来，业绩不是最好的，但是个人的品德、热情、态度、进取精神、敬业奉献精神、正直诚信有责任感等会在将来的工作中发挥出来的能力。学校一定要以学生的终身发展和人格素养的发展为出发点，在完成对学生基础知识和基本技能的基础上，融合专业教育、职业素养教育和人格素养教育，注重培养学生的专业进取精神、与人合作的团队精神、敬业奉献精神、正直诚信精神、有责任感、热情、礼貌等。这些品格是企业无法计量评价的，是伴随人终身的可持续发展的能力，更是一种财富，也是"人品"的重要组成部分。职业发展教育正好填补了这一空白，不仅仅关注对学生知识的传授，更加关注对学生的人格素养教育的培养。

东京经济大学为了学生在毕业后能更好地适应社会，特别注重培养学生的冒险挑战精神、自信、勇气、尊重意识、礼仪意识、职业规划能力、交际能力等。传统保守的人格特征已经适应不了社会的发展，现在的社会需要的是具有挑战精神和冒险精神，敢于尝试别人不敢做的自信和勇气的人。职场中，每个人都是一种独立的人格，即使自己与别人的价值观不同，我们也要学会尊重别人；个体不能独立存在于宇宙中，在待人接物上我们要拥有一

定的礼仪规范;职业规划能力是指个体依据相关的理论指导,在了解自己、了解环境的基础上,确定适合自己的生涯目标并制定相应的实施计划的过程的能力。职业规划不是简单的找工作,而是把个人的追求、专长和创造力紧密联系在一起,为规划者带来适宜的就业机遇和良好的职业发展前景;所有的行业都是建立在人与人之间的交流沟通上的,因此,要在理解他人的基础上,充分表达自己的能力。东京经济大学培养的是综合型人才,它要求个体对自身特质和职业环境有全方位的了解,养成他们积极主动地选择和决定自己未来发展的态度和能力,积极培养学生适应社会变化的可持续发展的能力。

八、立足经济社会发展,变革职业发展教育体系

社会不断向前发展,日本的劳动力市场随着社会经济的发展也发生了一些改变,使得雇佣方式变得具有灵活性;雇佣标准更多元,传统的雇佣标准几乎都是以学历标准作为参考,现在不仅看重学历,更看重的是能力;雇佣重心已开始转向第三产业。同时,与经济社会发展密切相关的职业发展教育也发生改变,包括职业发展教育的理念观、教学观、发展观。由单一形式向灵活、多元的办学格局转变;由传统教学向注重以学生为本的教学方式转变;由终结教育向可持续发展的现代职业发展教育转变。素质要求不断提高,人本意识不断增强,多元格局逐渐形成。

思考题:

1. 日本职业发展教育课程在不同教育阶段的表现有哪些?
2. 日本职业发展教育的新理念包括哪两点?对我国发展职业发展教育有什么启示?
3. 日本高等教育机构分为几类?
4. 日本职业发展教育的特色是什么?

推荐书目:

[1]朱文富,李文英.日本近代职业发展教育研究[M].石家庄:河北教育出版社,2016.

[2]谷峪,姚树伟.职业教育·生涯教育·终身教育:转型期日本职业教育[M].北京:高等教育出版社,2010.

[3]罗海鸥,陈俊英.日本职业教育:比较与就业过程视角下的职业教育学[M].北京:人民教育出版社,2014.

国外论文导读与阅读(一):

导读:日本的"终身雇佣制度"及其对职业指导的影响

作者:瓦茨(A.G. Watts)

论文围绕日本"终身就业制度"的讨论展开,全文包括三个部分。

第一部分介绍了日本"终身雇佣制度"的概念、特点和效果。"终身雇佣制度"并未进入日本法律,主要是基于劳动者和管理者之间的默契。对于终身雇佣有文化解释和功能主义解释两种解释视角,文化主义解释认为它源于日本社会中强烈的封建压力,如尊重家庭和权威人士,强调合作对共同利益的重要性;功能主义解释认为终身雇佣制度不是源于封建关系,而是源于雇主在现代工业增长初期应对技术工人短缺和高劳动力流动的合理经济计算,终身雇佣是雇主维持培训投资成果的最有效的方法。终身雇佣制度曾给日本经济社会发展带来了明显成效,但对其能否继续维持也存在一些质疑。

第二部分分析了终身雇佣制度对日本教育系统的影响。在终身雇佣制度的影响下,教育的最高成就被认为是确保进入好的公司或组织,大学或学院的选择与就业之间的联系比较紧密,初始教育水平对于决定个人进入哪个组织方面至关重要,但对于他们在进入这个组织后的职业前景和进步水平方面的作用要有所减弱,因为晋升更多的是基于入职后的成绩与表现。日本企业对教育系统的主要期望是它能为学生提供高标准的通识教育并培养学生的工作纪律和职业道德,很少关注课程是否拥有足够的职业性质。

第三部分探讨了终身雇佣制度对日本就业指导的影响。1953年日本通过法律规定每所中学至少有一名职业指导教师组织实施学校的职业指导计划,他们与企业和公共就业指导服务部门保持联系,收集就业信息并进行分类,然后通过班主任给予学生具体的职业帮助。此外大多数学校还有一个或多个指导人际关系等问题的一般教师。日本公共就业保障办公室专门负

责为日本初中、高中和大学生以及成人提供就业服务,并通过印刷品、定期召开职业指导教师会议等形式向学校传播职业信息,同时还提供就业咨询和进行心理测试。日本几乎所有的大学都设有就业办公室,为学生提供关于商业等领域的职位空缺并处理学生的就业申请,安排学生到公司进行访问以熟悉公司情况,还会举行一些职业考试和预选面试等。

文章来源:

A.G.Watts.The Japanese'Lifetime Employment System'and Its Implications for Careers Guidance. International Journal for the Advancement of Counselling, 1985(8):91-114.

国外论文导读与阅读(二):

导读:唐纳德·舒伯对日本职业指导和职业咨询的贡献

作者:艾格尼丝·渡边·村冈(Agnes M. Watanabe-Muraoka),托马斯-阿奎那·武舍仙崎(Thomas-Aquinas Takeshe Senzaki),埃德温·赫尔(Edwin L. Herr)

论文主要介绍了唐纳德·舒伯对日本职业指导和职业咨询的两大重要贡献。

一是为建立中学职业指导体系的理论参考框架做出了贡献。20世纪50年代,日本中学的职业指导和咨询作为国家政策的工具,主要使用的模型是工作匹配模型,重点是如何在从学校到工作的过渡时期选择一个最适合的工作或职业。唐纳德博士提出的中学职业指导理论框架即将职业指导的重点从工作匹配模式转向职业发展模式。这一理论对日本职业指导带来的影响充分体现在日本教育部1947—1962年编写的《职业指导教师手册》中。例如:1947年日本职业指导教师手册,学校职业指导被定义为帮助学生选择职业,做好准备并找到适当的工作的过程。1949年修订的"手册"将学校职业指导重新定义为通过提供适当的职业培训帮助学生发现和利用自己的潜能,并帮助他们获得有益的生活经验。1961年版本的"手册"还建议日本中学实施系统和纵向的职业指导计划,旨在帮助每个学生培养自我理解、决策、生活规划和采取行动的能力,以便能够调整他们的职业选择。尽管此后到1990年"教师手册"修订了四次,但这项建议仍未改变。然而遗憾的是由于没有提供实践计划,大多数教师无法将职业指导从人/工作匹配模式转向职业发展模式。

二是他的工作对日本20世纪90年代经济动荡和劳资关系变化所迫切需要的职业咨询的理论框架和实践框架的影响。20世纪90年代伴随着日本经济社会和就业环境急剧变化,传统的终身就业制度和年资工资制度也在发生变化,从而导致了工人职业模式和职业道路的变化,工作匹配模式对此反应有限,职业咨询的价值得到重视。有研究者发现唐纳德博士的"一生生涯的彩虹图:生活广度、生活空间方法"对重返社会的妇女、职业生涯中期的求职者和老年工人是最适用和最有回报的方法;其关于职业生涯中期职业成熟要素的假设也适用于满足条件的日本成年男性。

论文最后,作者预测唐纳德的"发展—个体—现象—社会"方法的重要性将会增加,并成为帮助每一代日本人在这个不可预测的社会中积极生活的主要参考框架。

文章来源:

Agnes M. Watanabe-Muraoka, Thomas-Aquinas Takeshe Senzaki, Edwin L. Herr. Donald Super's Contribution to Career Guidance and Counselling in Japan [J]. International Journal for Educational and Vocational Guidance, 2001(1): 99-106.

(节选的英文原文见附录4)

第四章 英国职业发展教育

本章要点：
1. 英国职业指导的框架体系；
2. 英国职业发展教育的课程；
3. 英国职业发展教育的特色。

英国的职业发展教育始于19世纪末，至今已有一百多年的历史，政策法规完备，教育体系成熟，课程模式多样，对我国开展职业发展教育具有重要的借鉴意义和价值。本章在介绍当代英国教育概况的基础上，对英国职业发展教育的政策、课程以及特色进行阐述和解读。

第一节 当代英国教育概况

英国教育在世界教育史上占有重要地位，教育发展体系完备，无论基础教育还是高等教育都为英国的经济发展和人才培养做出了重要贡献。

一、基础教育概况

从历史的角度看，英国的基础教育有两种传统：一是为培养领导人才而设的公学和文法学校的传统；二是为训练底层劳动者而设的小学的传统。当时，这种小学的毕业生是不能升入公学或文法学校就读的，只有专为公学和文法中学而设的预备学校的学生才有此机会，直到20世纪初这种阶级或等级的界限仍然很明显。20世纪20年代和30年代，使劳动人民的子女有机会接受中等教育的社会诉求越来越强，在这种情况下，1945年英国教育部正式确立了中等教育"三轨制"原则,即有三类中等学校:一是公学和文法中学;二是技术中学;三是现代中学。学生入读不同中学的根据是"11岁考试"。但是,随着社会的发展,人们认为11岁考试"定终身"是不合理的,考试成绩的差别在相当程度上受家庭背景影响,对广大社会下层家庭子女很不利;同时,大量的社会学调查表明,人为的选拔和后来的分流带有阶级的偏见,与教育民主化和教育机会均等原则相矛盾,许多人特别是工党内部的一些人认为,改革中等教育机构,是消除社会不平等,进行社会改良的重要途径和手段。从20世纪60年代起,英国中等教育进行了综合化改革,出现了多边中学、综合中学等学校类型,其中综合中学七年一贯制(11~18岁)形式得到政府的提倡而发展迅速,缘于它主要吸收除残疾儿童以外的所有适龄儿童入学,而不问能力如何,可以说是真正属于普通性质的学校。80年代以后,综合中学成为英国中学各种类型中最多的一种。据统计,1985年,综合中学在英格兰占中学总数的84.5%,在威尔士占98.4%,在苏格兰占96.4%。从另一种统计数字中,也可以看出自70年代以来几种主要类型的中学发展变化情况。1971年,在整个英国由地方管理的中学中,文法学校占18%,现代中学占38%,技术中学占7%,综合中学占34%,而到1986年,文法中学已下降到3%,现代中学下降到4%,技术中学下降到只占1%,综合中学则达到了86%。① 中等教育综合化改革后,11岁考试普遍被废除,学生初等学校毕业后进入统一的综合中学。许多技术中学和现代中学重组或合并为综合中学。综合中学既有学术性的文化科学知识课程,又有实用性和职业性课程,适应了普及中学教育的需要。

二、高等教育概况

英国最古老、最著名的两所大学是创立于12世纪和13世纪的牛津大学和剑桥大学。15世纪,英国又先后建立了圣安德鲁、格拉斯哥、阿伯丁等三所苏格兰大学。爱丁堡大学成立于16世纪。19世纪30年代,新大学在伦敦及其他主要城市纷纷建立。这些大学都是独立的自治机构,学校在学位授予、入学、课程设置等方面拥有高度自治权。这种学术自治的传统一直延

---

① 江山野.关于英国中学课程设置的考察报告[J].课程.教材.教法,1989(10).

续至今,令人称道。与此同时,许多规模较小、专门从事教师培训的院校也在英国各地兴办。20世纪初,英国的高等教育仍然是纯学术的精英教育,适龄青年入学率较低。1919年英国成立大学拨款委员会,负责管理政府对大学的拨款。20世纪50—60年代,几乎每年都有一所新大学成立。同时,各地纷纷创办工学院。1963—1979年,适龄青年入学率发生了较大的变化,从原来的5%上升到12%。1992年,政府通过立法,结束了大学与工学院的"双轨"制,所有工学院都获得了大学的地位,拥有学位授予权,大学的数量由此增加了一倍。20世纪90年代初,英国18~21岁青年的入学率上升至33%,2000年达到40%。[1] 在2008年欧债危机爆发后,英国经济陷入困境。布朗政府重新认识知识和技术对未来经济发展的战略地位,分别于2009年和2010年提出了《崇高志向:知识经济中的大学未来》和《确保高等教育可持续发展的未来》两份报告。这两份报告认为下一阶段应该在公平入学机会,拓展高等教育的资金来源,促进研究、技术和创新的相互转化,培养世界级高水平的劳动力等方面做出积极努力,建立起支撑世界一流水平的教育体系。2016年,政府《高等教育:知识经济的成功之源》提出英国高等教育在提升教学水平、促进社会流动、丰富学生选择等方面是未来工作的重点。[2] 在上述进程中,英国逐渐构建了政府主导、多元合作、市场导向、学生为主,以培养世界一流大学和优势学科专业为目标的现代高等教育体系。

第二节 英国职业发展教育政策

英国职业发展教育从19世纪末开始萌芽,第二次世界大战后快速发展。英国最早的"职业指导服务中心"叫作"任命委员会"(Appointment Committee),成立于1892年的牛津大学,1970年开始称为CAS(Career Advisor Service)。英国大学生职业指导和服务真正获得重大发展是在20世纪90年代,大学生职业发展教育和指导工作引起政府和社会的普遍关注,成立了全英职业指导服务协会——"英国高校学生(研究生)就业协会"。政府还陆续发布《面向21世纪的教育与培训》教育白皮书以及"国家教育和培训目标"

---

[1] 彭伟强译.21世纪的英国高等教育[J].世界教育信息,2001(9).
[2] 周凌.英国现代高等教育发展对我国"双一流"建设的启示[J].中国高教研究,2017(11).

等法规,将职业发展教育与培训指导置于优先战略地位,为振兴英国经济做出了巨大贡献。

一、职业发展教育的法案法规

英国的职业发展教育政策表现在一系列的法案法规之中。

1.政策之一:《雇佣和训练法》

1948年,英国政府通过《雇佣和训练法》,明确规定各中学对所有在校学生实施职业指导。中学的职业指导由中央青年雇用委员会全面负责。此委员会由劳动部、教育和科学部以及苏格兰教育部选拔人员联合组成。地方中学职业指导由地方劳动局或教育当局负责。20世纪80年代以后,英国政府又颁布了一系列文件,强调职业指导应成为学校课程的一部分,并规定最迟在中学二年级阶段设置该方面课程的固定教学时刻表。普通中学的职业发展教育和职业发展指导要由学校的指导教师和校外的职业官员协作负责。指导教师的任务主要是实施职业发展教育讨论,帮助职业发展教育官员安排学生咨询,并提供最新的职业信息等。校外的职业官员的主要职责是为学生进行个别和集体咨询,帮助制定职业发展教育训练计划,协助使用计算机辅助职业指导系统,参加家长会议,举办咨询日、职业参观,组织职业演讲等活动。

2.政策之二:《新课程中的生涯发展教育》

2000年,英国教育与就业部颁布《新课程中的生涯发展教育》(Career Education in the New Curriculum),该文件对生涯教育的具体目标做了明确规定:第一,自我发展。自我发展主要指学会正确认识个人的兴趣、能力、态度、价值观和培养个人的责任感。第二,生涯探索。主要指探索职业与工作领域的关系,了解工作领域中不同的职业类型和获得该职业应具备的知识与技能。第三,生涯管理。是指在认知自我后,学会运用所学知识确定自身的个人目标,选择符合自己特长的职业类型,做出现实的生涯决策,实现自身价值。

3.政策之三:《为了发展的技能:国家技能战略》

2009年11月,英国国会发布《为了发展的技能:国家技能战略》(Skills

for Growth:The National Skills Strategy),从促进经济复苏和实现可持续经济增长的角度提出,技能开发是英国经济复苏计划的关键部分及面临的紧迫挑战。全球化知识经济中的现代工作非常需要技能型人才,技能型公民具有更强的生产力和创造性,只有通过受过良好教育、有事业心及具有良好技能的公民的努力工作才能提高企业的生产水平,实现国家的美好未来。该战略对英国现有的技能开发体系做出重要改革,具体包括:通过更加先进的学徒制培养一流的现代技术工人,对有利于未来经济发展和创造就业所需要的技能进行投资,通过技能审计及提供更好的信息和课程服务为人们提供更多的培训选择机会,为培训机构引进监督机制,等等。

为支持《国家技能战略》的实施,英国政府同时发布《技能投资战略2010—2011》,提出2010年至2011年,英国政府对继续教育和技能开发的投资将达到44亿英镑。其中,对培训位置的投资预计将超过35亿英镑,比2009—2010年度增长约3%。经历与行业广泛的咨询过程,这一战略还提出,为对经济增长的关键行业培养高技能工人,将对培训资源进行更有效的整合。目前,这些目标都已经实现。

4.政策之四:《学徒制、技能、儿童与学习法案》

2009年12月9日,《学徒制、技能、儿童与学习法案》(Apprenticeships,Skills,Children and Learning Act)获得通过。法案为技能体系改革奠定了必要的法律基础,具体包括:取消学习和技能理事会,把其对14～18岁教育与培训进行拨款的责任转移到地方权威机构;设立新的技能拨款主管职位,领导技能拨款署,负责对19岁以后的教育与培训进行拨款;设立一个新的机构——青年人学习局,对相应的地方权威机构进行支持。法案涉及的范围非常广泛,并提出要加强学徒制的发展,包括发布新的资格框架和证书体系,为公民赋予一种新的权利,使其可以申请时间参加培训,等等。

5.政策之五:"盖茨比基准"

2014年,英国STEM学习中心的创立者约翰·霍曼爵士受盖茨比基金会委托,通过对全球职业生涯指导深入的调查、走访与案例分析后,列出了可供学校用于提升职业生涯指导体系的八项指导基准:[①]

[①] 谢银迪.英国:发布中学职业生涯教育指南[N].中国教师报,2018-5-2(3).

（1）制订一个职业生涯教育指导计划。每所学校都要有一个高级管理团队支持的职业生涯规划组织，有1名经过培训的负责人，并有一份学生、家长、教师、校长和公司雇主认可的职业生涯教育指导计划。职业生涯教育指导计划应在学校网站上发布，以便于学生、家长、教师和企业雇主访问，网站要接受学生、家长、教师和企业雇主的定期评估反馈，成为评估过程的一部分。

（2）学习如何获得职业信息。学生和父母都能获取有关未来学习选择和人力市场情况的高质量信息，并得到一名咨询顾问的帮助，以充分利用这些信息。到14岁时，所有学生都可以访问并使用职业发展路径和人力市场信息，获悉学习选择的决定。鼓励家长搜集并使用有关人力市场和未来学习选择的信息，为子女提供支持。

（3）满足学生需求。学生在不同阶段有不同的职业指导需求。学校要从平等和多样化角度出发，根据每个学生的需求量身定制指导计划，具体包括：学校的职业生涯指导计划要打破思维定式，寻求突破和创新；学校要把对每个学生的职业选择建议和决定进行系统性记录；所有学生都有权查阅记录以支持职业发展；学校应该为每个学生的教育、培训和实习收集并保存准确的数据。

（4）STEM（science，technology，engineering，mathematics）的意义和影响。到14岁时，每个学生都有机会了解不同的STEM课程如何帮助自己进入职场并成为优秀的工作者。

（5）接触公司雇主和员工。学生有多种机会向雇主学习有关工作、就业的技能。这些可以通过访问、指导和企业策划等一系列活动实现。从11岁开始，学生每年至少参加一次与雇主有意义的接触。这种"有意义的接触"是指学生有机会了解工作是什么样的，或如何在职场取得成功。

（6）到工作场所实习。学生通过工作访问的方式到工作场所体验生活、实践学习，扩大社交范围。到16岁时，每个学生至少有一次工作经验(除兼职外)；到18岁时，每个学生都要有一次更为深刻的工作经历（除兼职外）。

（7）接触继续教育和高等教育。所有学生都应该了解自己可以获得的全部学习机会，包括学术和职业路线以及学校、学院、大学和工作场所的学习。到16岁时，每个学生都会与全部学习机会进行有意义的接触，包括第六级学院、学院、大学和学徒提供者(包括员工和学生见面机会);到18岁时,所有考虑申请大学的学生都至少有2次到大学访问和接触学生与教师的机会。

(8)接受个性化指导。无论何时进行学习或职业选择,学生都有机会与职业生涯顾问面谈。只要经过培训达到合格水平,顾问可以来自校内,也可以来自校外。当学生需要进行重大的学习或职业抉择时,能够得到生涯顾问的指导和帮助。学生在16岁以前至少有一次与职业生涯顾问咨询的机会,并且18岁前还有一次接受更深入咨询的机会。

6.政策之六:《职业生涯战略:充分发挥每个人的技能和才华》

2016年,英国首相特蕾莎·梅提出建设更公平的英国,促进社会流动,为每个人创造机会的执政蓝图。为此,英国政府于2017年12月4日发布了《职业生涯战略:充分发挥每个人的技能和才华》,将职业生涯体系的相关部门联合在一起,政府、教育部门、雇主、职业协会或其他组织需要建立强有力的伙伴关系,通过高质量的信息、教育、建议和指导,主要从五个方面为青少年提供帮助:第一,了解自己的选择和不同的达成路径,规划自己的职业路线和步骤;第二,对自己还不了解(可能还不存在)的新机会或者还不能实现的想法保持好奇心和兴趣;第三,充分了解自己具备的知识和技能,并知道如何将其运用到工作中;第四,在工作中有获得感、有坚持、有进步,不管年龄、能力和背景如何;第五,在整个职业生涯中增加劳动所得,通过做自己擅长和喜欢的工作获得满足感。

7.政策之七:《学生职业生涯教育指南》[①]

为了构建职业生涯体系,帮助年轻人发现个人价值和潜能,选择适合自己的职业,从而建设一个更加强大公平的社会,2018年1月,英国教育部发布了《学生职业生涯教育指南》,该指南发布对象为学校董事会、校领导和教职工,旨在为中学实施职业生涯教育提供路线方向。该指南是政府2017年《职业生涯战略:充分发挥每个人的技能和才华》的重要组成部分。

根据时间顺序,《职业生涯教育指南》对学校提出了关键行动计划(见表4-1)。

---

① 谢银迪.英国:发布中学职业生涯教育指南[N].中国教师报,2018-5-2(3).

表 4-1 《职业生涯教育指南》对学校提出的关键行动计划

时间节点	主要行动
持续工作（2012 年 9 月开始生效）	每所学校必须确保为 8~13 年级的全部学生提供单独的职业指导
2018 年 1 月开始（2018 年 1 月 2 日生效）	1.每所学校必须确保 8~13 年级的全部学生有参加一系列教育和培训机构活动的机会,以使他们了解技术教育资格认证或学徒制度 2.每所学校必须出一份政策声明,列出提供职业指导的具体安排并保证落实
2018 年 1 月~2020 年年底	1.每所学校都应该使用"盖茨比基准"改进现在的职业指南,并在 2020 年年底前完成 2.每所学校都应该为每个学生提供 7 次与雇主接触的机会(7~13 年级至少每年一次),到 2020 年年底全部满足(其中一些应该是与科学、工程、技术、数学等方面雇主的接触)
2018 年 9 月开始	每所学校都应该任命 1 名有才能的人担任职业领导者的角色来引领职业指导计划 每所学校都要向学生和家长公布具体的职业生涯规划细节

与此同时,为帮助每所学校顺利完成转型,政府也为学校提供相应的支持（见表 4-2）。

表 4-2 政府为学校提供的支持行动计划

时间节点	主要行动
2018 年 9 月开始	为职业领导者开发的工作规范和标准投入使用 作为经费支持方,职业与企业公司将在所有的"盖茨比基准"中发挥更广泛的作用
2018 年—2019 年	职业与企业公司将为学校提供达到"盖茨比基准"的相应工具 资助 500 所学校和学院的职业领导者进行培训
2020 年底	所有学校都能找到至少 1 名企业顾问

作为职业生涯指导的主要实施者,学校需要肩负起提供指导和教育的责任。所有8~13年级的学生都有权要求学校提供以下机会:第一,作为职业生涯指导的一部分,了解技术教育资格认证和学徒制度,并获取各种培训信息;第二,通过可选活动、集会、小组讨论和品酒会等,获悉一系列当地公司雇主提供的机会(包括技术教育资格认证和学徒制度);第三,了解如何申请全部学术和技术课程。同时,学校也将许多活动整合到职业生涯指导中,提供雇主进入校内与学生、家长交流的机会,根据学校自身情况将大厅、教室或私人会议室提供给学生使用,同时提供其他专业设备支持活动,具体时间将根据活动安排进行讨论和商定(见表4-3)。

表4-3 学校需要提供的支持活动

	春季学期	秋季学期	夏季学期
8年级	大学和技术学院入校活动	生活技能:会议和导师交谈机会	生活技能:会议和导师交谈机会
9年级	大学和技术学院入校活动	第四学段(14~16岁)选修活动	
10年级	生活技能:准备实习的交流会		生活技能:会议和导师交谈机会
11年级	生活技能:16岁通过会议的接触机会;大学和技术学院入校活动	16岁后晚会 16岁后品酒会	
12年级	高等教育展览会;18岁后交流会;学徒申请	小组会议:未来教育、培训和就业选择	小组会议:未来教育、培训和就业选择
13年级	研讨会:高等教育和更高级的学徒申请		

除以上政策法规外,2003年,英国教育与技能部还制定了《全国11~19岁生涯教育与指导框架》(Careers Education and Guidance in England: A National Framework 11~19),该政策文件对生涯教育目标、具体的生涯教育内容、活动方式都做了说明与规定,并附有生涯实施实例,为英国学校的生

涯教育实施提供了标准和参照。2005年,教育与技能部发表了纲领性官方指导文件《14~19岁教育与技能白皮书》,该文件再次重申加强中学阶段生涯辅导,并要求通过行业技能委员会,使雇主广泛地参与现行的教育改革中。2009年,英国政府推出了一项职业指导计划,该计划强调职业生涯教育是学校教育的重要组成部分,规定职业生涯教育最迟要在中学二年级开始实施,综合中学、公学、文法中学、现代中学、技术中学等都有法定责任为学段三(7~9年级)和学段四(10~11年级)的学生提供最新的生涯信息和生涯指导。2012年,英国生涯教育与指导协会还制定《生涯教育与工作相关教育框架》(A Frame-work for Careers and Work-related Education),规定了生涯教育的理论依据和实施内容。

二、英国职业发展教育的指导机构

英国职业发展教育的指导机构类型多样,下面对这些机构做简要介绍。

1. 青年就业处(Careers Servers)

许多年来,英国首要的职业指导代理机构是"青年就业处"。它为各种年龄的人提供就业指导,主要的服务对象是在学校就读的高年级学生。1993年英国政府立法规定"青年就业处"的职能在于:为所有超过13岁的全日制学生服务;为半工半读的学生提供服务;为21岁以下的离开全日制教育系统两年的学生服务。

2001年4月,英国政府发布新的政策,决定用"联合就业服务处"(Connexions Services)取代"青年就业处",为所有13~19岁的人提供服务。"联合就业服务处"的服务范围比就业指导更广泛,除了职业指导外,它还提供为少年妈妈的服务,财政建议,住房和毒品问题咨询服务。在职业指导工作的各个方面,"联合就业服务处"都发挥了重要作用。

2. 国家信息咨询与指导委员会(NIAGB)

"国家信息咨询与指导委员会"隶属于教育与科学部,协调教育与科学部和劳工与福利部为成年人和青年人提供职业指导。促进教育和就业之间的平衡。除了一些私人和非营利组织外,它可以调整大部分职业服务机构。

3. 指导理事会(The Guidance Council)

"指导理事会"是1993年注册的慈善团体,有自己的秘书处。主要活动是代表职业指导领域进行政策规划和宣传,促进指导质量,进行政策研究。

4.国家就业训练组织(EMPNTO)

国家就业训练组织是一个全国性的组织,负责制定训练标准,协助指导咨询的机构和仲裁行业。其标准是在国家职业委员会质量标准的国家资格上发展起来的,负责管理职业指导机构的质量标准模型。

5.大学毕业生就业指导联合会(AGCAS)

代表高等教育机构的职业服务机构,发展了一套实践编码,是职业指导领域的重要质量保证组织。

6.职业指导专业协会联盟(FPAG)

近年形成的保护团体,代表各个部门的职业指导从业人员的利益。如全国职业指导教师联盟,全国成人教育指导联盟。其分支组织在全国大约有1万个。

7.职业指导协会(ICG)

职业指导协会代表职业指导的从业者,起着游说议员、倡导政策的作用。同时它还代替职业指导证书机构颁发职业指导合格证,起着一定程度上的质量保证作用。2013年,职业指导协会与其他几家机构合并成立了新的职业发展研究协会(Career Development Institute,CDI),旨在创建一种支持青年从学校到工作转换的完整服务。

三、英国职业指导的框架体系

英国的职业指导框架体系主要由学校和公共服务机构提供的职业指导服务构成。

(一)基于学校的职业指导服务

基于学校的职业指导服务强调学校和外部机构的合作,强调专家之间的合作与共享。英国学校的职业指导内容包括四个方面:发展自我意识、增进职业机会意识、发展决策技能、学会从学校到职业世界的转变。

英国还专门立法保证青年人接受职业指导的权利,例如英国《1997年教育法》规定:所有的学校都应当保证提供最低标准的职业发展教育,保证所有13岁以上的年轻人接受平等的职业指导的权利。所有学校都建立了学生可以利用的"职业库"。"职业库"包含有最新的就业机会信息,以及大学或训练机构等继续学习机会的信息。

英国高等教育领域里的职业指导机构较多,一方面是由于法律对大学职业指导服务义务的空白规定造成的,另一方面是由于英国大学的传统自治色彩浓厚所致。大多数大学都有完备的独立的职业指导服务机构,一些学校通过各个院系提供,一些则由综合学生就业处提供。英国大学的职业指导服务形式多种多样,如文本信息和网上信息、个人咨询与指导、个人自助、就业博览会、雇主会谈、毕业生职位空缺发布、面试技巧训练、职业经营技巧训练、课程本位的职业发展教育。这些服务机构经验丰富,有悠久的历史,与其他国家相比,很有特色。

(二)公共服务机构提供的职业指导

2002年4月,英国就业服务与福利部、管理失业基金和福利基金的机构合二为一。接受劳动与退休部的管理,劳动与退休部的下属机构"附属工作中心"承担就业和福利服务的角色。

"附属工作中心"是英国提供职业指导服务的重要机构。英国还专门为此颁布了一项"新协定计划",这项计划使得"附属工作中心"起了重要的作用。"新协定计划"将失业人员的问题专门列入就业指导机构的合同之中。随着"附属工作中心"的建立,英国建立起了许多更现代的、更具吸引力的服务中心,其中包括很方便利用的视频触摸终端,它可以用来发布职位空缺信息。

(三)服务于成人的职业指导

英国还有专门服务于成人的职业指导,主要包括以下内容:

1.信息咨询与指导伙伴(IAG)

英国教育与就业部在1998年的《学习化时代》白皮书中建议"扩大和加深成人职业指导"。1999年英国建立了地方"信息咨询与指导伙伴"机构。其运行和资金筹措依靠学习和技能委员会。"信息咨询与指导伙伴"机构立足于地方,接受政府资助,通常由公共的、私人的、志愿者和社区团体组成。

伙伴机构与公共就业组织进行有效的合作,为就业者的信息共享提供了有效帮助。"信息咨询与指导伙伴"机构被视为英国政府的重要助手,在发挥政府解决社会边缘人问题的政策战略上发挥了重要的作用。

2.学习引领(learn direct)

"学习引领"是英国成人职业指导服务的新方式。它与传统的个人会谈指导方式截然不同。"学习引领"发端于1998年,以电话技术为基础,向成人提供职业指导服务。目前,英国全国范围内有两个"学习引领"中心,位于曼彻斯特和莱斯特两大城市。"学习引领"由英国产业大学提供经费资助,以免费的方式帮助成人获得继续教育和训练的机会。"学习引领"中心向所有的成人开放。"学习引领"中心的电话帮助热线一年365天开放,每天从8:00到22:00,方便了那些出狱者、外国学生、居无定所的人以及流离失所的人。自开放以来,有50多万人拨打学习引领中心的热线电话求助。

3.工会学习代表(IULR)

"工会学习代表"是由工会组织和政府联合发起的一种新的职业指导形式,"工会学习代表"是较有特色的组织,其宗旨在于为低技能和低资格的就业提供信息建议,鼓励他们接受教育和训练。这是一种更好的为特定人群服务的方式:如老人、异教徒、少数民族、兼职者,他们获得的职业训练往往少于其他人。英国《劳动就业法》还专门赋予"工会学习代表"法定的权利来完成他们的职责。

第三节 英国职业发展教育课程

英国进行职业发展教育的历史较早,既重视中学的职业发展教育也重视高校的职业发展教育。中学的职业发展教育课程主要代表是14~16岁专业学院课程,而高校的职业发展教育课程代表是职业发展教育管理技能(CMS)课程。

一、14~16岁专业学院课程

为了弥补大学毕业生对职业市场需求反应迟缓的弊端,英国特别重视初中阶段学生的职业生涯教育。具体做法就是很多州立大学设置14~16岁专业学院,设立这样的学院也是各州立大学为了响应英国教育标准局对大学教育改革的号召。英国9年级的儿童都可自愿申请就读14~16岁学院,2017年为了招收更多的学生,有的学院招生简章特别强调录取公平、一视同仁的原则。

剑桥地区学院 14~16 岁专业学院将课程类型分为职业型课程、核心中等教育课程、选修课程。在设计开发课程体系前期，学院会做充分调研和论证，如师资条件、实验条件等，其间会邀请用人单位和行业相关专业人员以及家长群体等社会力量共同参与课程体系设计，以保证这一设计的科学合理性。课程体系是否符合学校的培养目标和地区要求仍要当地审批部门审核，并受英国教育标准局监管。学生要选择职业方向，接受普通中等教育证书(general certificate of secondary education, GCSE)[①]课程以及全日制的职业课程或学徒制课程，将职业技术性课程与 GCSE 的核心课程相融合。剑桥地区学院 14~16 岁专业学院规定的 GCSE 核心课程包括：英语语言、英语文学、数学和科学四门，GCSE 选修课为一门历史或地理，同时也会根据学生需求设置不同课程。学生将接受每周 16 小时的 GCSE 课程，课程开设两年，与此同时，他们还将学习信息技术、艺术或媒体课程。该学院为准备就业的学生设置了职业性课程，具体包括酒店服务、建筑、机械、美容美发、健康护理、社会工作和汽修等。学生选择一种职业型课程进行学习，学院会根据专业情况采取一对一学徒教学或小班化组织教学的方式，提供实训基地并使合作企业确保学生在实践中获得发展。

14~16 岁专业学院重视学生职业发展的学习与指导，学生可以获得相应职业技能证书，为未来就业打下基础。比如，圣海伦 14~16 岁专业学院第一年的职业课程内容多为职业生涯规划课程和兴趣课程，第二年逐步加深到专业指导课程并参加集训实践。通过集训实践，学生在学习的过程中有机会考取获得英国职业资格二级证书以及相应行业内的二级从业证书。获得英国职业资格二级证书的学生有机会进入学院合作的校企进行半工半读式的学习，也可留在校企工作。对于毕业后想继续留在继续教育学院的学生，据个人情况，学院采用资格证书衔接和教学单元衔接。16~18 岁可申请深层次学徒制或职业技能培训教育（相当于大专水平），19 岁后仍然可以接受成人教育甚至申请与职业相关专业的本科文凭，完成 14~16 岁初中教育与继续职业教育的衔接。[②]

---

① GCSE 考试是英国 14~16 岁的学生完成第一阶段中等教育后参加的主要会考，相当于中国的初中毕业文凭考试，是评价基础教育质量的重要依据，也是决定英国中等教育阶段学生升入高中阶段乃至大学的重要评价指标。

② 邵小雪. 14~16 岁专业学院：英国初中与职业教育衔接的典型模式评价[J].中华少年,2017(32).

二、职业生涯管理技能课程[①]

早在20世纪90年代初,职业生涯管理技能短缺严重影响和制约着英国大学生就业。英国高校试图以大学生"职业生涯管理技能(career management skills,简称CMS)"培训项目的研究、探索和实施来促进大学生就业。英国政府实施的"教学研究中心"(Center of Excellence in Teaching and Learning)项目,用5年时间投入390万英镑支持雷丁大学(又译"里丁大学")开展大学生职业生涯管理技能培训项目的探讨、实施和推广工作。在英国高校就业指导体系中,职业生涯管理技能课程为各大学普遍采用。

(一)职业生涯管理技能课程目标

职业生涯管理技能课程目标主要体现在以下三个方面:

1.重在唤醒,由"DOTS"向"SODT"模式的转化

英国高校认为,职业发展管理技能是指通过一系列行之有效的外在方法不断提高大学生的自我认知、自我发展、自我表达和自我管理的技能、知识、经验、素质与品质。掌握这些技能有利于促进学生以理性、实际和积极的人生态度进行职业决策,并帮助学生管理好自己职业发展的方向和路径。其着眼点是唤醒学生的内在潜力,使学生顺利度过择业阶段并在其职业发展中不断学习,掌握职业选择的主动权。雷丁大学的课程目标就是让学生进一步明确自己的就业优势和毕业后可供选择的职业,从而理性地做出决定,进一步学习获得理想职位所需的各项技能。具体而言,就是实现"DOTS"模式向"SODT"模式的转变。

"DOTS"模式是雷丁大学职业生涯管理技能课程中学生进行自我诊断性分析的一系列测试。该模式包含四个层次:第一个层次为"做出决定"(D:decision-making),即毕业生能够做出决定,使自己可以获得最好的机遇;第二个层次为"就业的机遇意识"(O:awareness of opportunities),即毕业生能够增强就业机遇意识,熟悉各个职业和雇主的喜好;第三个层次为"过渡的能力"(T:skills for making the transition),即毕业生能迅速转换自己的思维,

---

[①] 王占仁,常飒飒.英国高校职业生涯管理技能课程研究——以英国里丁大学为个案[J].中国高教研究,2012(10).

掌握制作简历的技能以及面试的技巧;第四个层次为"了解自己"(S:awareness about your self),即毕业生能够了解自己的优势和特长。学生通过上述四个层次诊断性的自我剖析,会对自己的职业倾向以及今后职业生涯的发展有一个理性的认识。雷丁大学的职业生涯管理技能课程便是以此为根据,进行四个层次的重组,通过"DOTS"模式向"SODT"模式(S:awareness about your self;O:awareness of opportunities;D:decision-making;T:skills for making the transition)的转变,达到增强学生职业生涯管理技能的目标。

在实际授课中,雷丁大学将毕业生了解自己的优势设定为职业生涯管理技能的第一个层次;将毕业生能够增强就业机遇意识,熟悉各个职业和雇主的喜好作为职业生涯管理技能课程需要达到的第二个层次。通过上述两个层次的授课,最终使得学生可以达到职业管理技能的第三个层次——"做出决定",即毕业生能够做出决定,实现自我与职业发展倾向的良好对接。最后,职业管理技能课程所需要做的,便是帮助学生获得"过渡的能力",即帮助毕业生迅速转换自己的思维,掌握制作简历的技能以及面试的技巧。

通过四个层次的顺序调整,可以看出雷丁大学职业生涯管理技能课程是把唤醒学生的内在潜能,使学生能够充分了解自己,能够获得辨认适合的工作机会的能力作为首要目标。

2. 分群类教,深入人心的"客户观"

英国高校的职业生涯管理技能课程以满足学生的需求为根本,把学生当作"客户"。这与英国大学生就业市场化历史悠久,就业服务体系已经进入到比较成熟的阶段有关。为更好地提升学生的就业能力,英国高校的职业管理技能课程非常注重"客户"——学生的意见和反馈,根据学生的需求确定具体授课的内容和形式,并将学生需求调查作为一项常规工作制度。以雷丁大学为例,该校的每个学生都有一个账户,学生可登录职业管理技能课程的网站,提交自己想要获得的课程形式和内容,学校会统计选择不同课程形式和内容的学生数量,并根据统计数据设置课程。除此之外,在课程结束时,学校会向学生发放评估表,一是了解学生对课程的掌握程度、反馈意见;二是根据评估完善就业服务管理层的工作。把学生当作客户,还表现在实施个性化教育和培养。学校针对不同专业、不同阶段、不同类型的学生群

体进行"分群类教"。雷丁大学职业生涯管理技能课程既有针对本科生的内容,也有针对硕士和博士生的学习主题(topics)。在针对本科生的内容中,涵盖了学生大二到大四这三年中会遇到的各种问题。根据专业与课程内容间的联系程度不同,授课的方式、人员也会相应不同。

3."授之以渔",注重传授支持学生长远发展的技能

英国高校的职业生涯管理技能课程以促进学生长远发展为目标,既高度关注现实又面向未来,使每一个学生既能够得到直接指向"寻找工作"的指导和服务,也能够得到面向一生职业发展的知识和技能。雷丁大学职业生涯管理技能课程教授给学生的职业生涯管理技能既可以帮助学生更好地定位自己,学会研究和判断,最终保证他们能够在就业市场中拥有一席之地;同时,也能够帮助学生在离校后抓住机遇,最终获得持续的成功。所以,他们既开展提高学生自我认知的各种活动,在职业选择过程中使学生明确自己的性格、价值观、技能、发展动力以及优势和不足,也帮助学生掌握专业范围内各种类型工作和学习机会的信息,了解劳动市场结构,学会在就业市场中增加自己就业机会的各种知识;既让学生拥有关于职业生涯的信息资源并知道如何利用这些信息来争取机会,也帮助学生了解用人单位的招聘流程及选聘方法,懂得自我推荐并展示自己的技能和能力;既帮助学生获得学位要求的一般技能、专业技能和通用技能,也帮助学生认识到个人因素会影响其职业选择,了解实现职业生涯决策的具体策略方法,反思、调整职业发展规划能力。

(二)职业生涯管理技能课程的实施

职业生涯管理技能课程自2002年应用于本科教学以来,取得了很好的效果。在此期间经过不断探索,课程的实施对象范围不断扩大,运行模式不断更新。根据各个学校的不同情况,职业生涯管理技能课程的开设方式和实施过程也略有不同。下面将雷丁大学的职业生涯管理技能课程的实施周期及对象、运行模式、授课方式和实施教师逐一介绍。

1.实施周期及对象

职业生涯管理技能课程旨在全面跟踪指导学生在校期间的发展,在不同的阶段会相应地调整课程设置和教学方式。雷丁大学自2002年起,所有

本科生教育都融入了职业生涯管理技能课程。学生在大学一年级时，就开始在学校的职业生涯管理技能课程网站上进行接触性学习；进入大学二年级，学生开始正式参加该课程学习，形式以一对一辅导为主；三年级后，学校提倡学生继续关注职业生涯网站，从网站丰富的资源库中寻找资料，进行独立学习，以此来帮助学生做好毕业后工作或继续学习的准备。

2006年雷丁大学针对课程的实施对象进行过一项调研。统计数据显示，在参加课程学习的学生中，20%非常想参加此类课程学习，40%~60%对于课程有些疑问，20%不想参加。学校把不想参加课程学习的这类学生称作"很难接触的学生"（untouched students）。课程开发人员的目标是希望所有学生最终都能够参与到课程学习中来，显然这里产生了矛盾。雷丁大学经过调查发现，通过课程运行模式及开设方式的多样化可以解决这一矛盾。为此，该课程实施对象除本科生以外，还延伸到了部分硕士和博士研究生，主要是结合他们的学科特点有针对性地开设。

2.运行模式

由于职业生涯管理技能课程与学生所学专业课程的联系程度不同，该课程的运行模式主要分为三种：离散模式（discrete）、分摊模式（distributed）和全面渗透模式（pervasive）。在三种模式中，讲授课程的教师、授课的方式、适合的学科有所差异。

离散模式适用于与学生所学专业相联系的情况，课程由多个模块组成。职业生涯指导课程被融入这些模块中，成为其中的一部分。这种运行模式的教师一般由本专业的教师担任。分摊模式适用于职业管理技能课程与学生本专业课程没有联系的情况。职业生涯管理技能课程自成一体、单独讲述，属于通识教育范畴，由就业指导中心开设，并由从事就业指导的专职教师讲授，这是雷丁大学本科生的必修科目。全面渗透模式是一种全程贯穿和整体融入性的教学模式，学生主要通过职业规划课程来学习工作技能，学习内容由学生所学专业课程的特点决定。这种模式主要适合于技能性较强的专业，如汽修专业等。

3.授课方式

职业生涯管理技能课程的讲授面向所有专业和学位的学生，一般分为

两部分:讲授课程和网络课程。雷丁大学的职业生涯管理技能课程和学生的学分挂钩,每个学生需要修满5学分,每个学分相当于10个小时的学习时间,因此要求学生学习满50个小时。此外,根据该校实际情况,雷丁大学的职业生涯管理课程采取了"混合学习"(mixed learning)模式,包括三个部分:一是共三次每次两个小时的授课;二是在线练习;三是学生提交完成的作业。

讲授课程(taught session)。这是整个课程实施的起点,主要通过三次授课进行,每次授课两个小时并需要学生完成相应的在线学习和作业。课程的内容以互动的形式为主,主要包括闪问游戏(flash question)、性格类型测试(MBTI)和同伴评估。

在线学习(on-line work)。这个部分是学生学习和反馈的过程。学生需要做在线练习,网站有约200页的资料,既有互动性的练习,也有信息提供平台。这部分的主要资源包括PPT资料、作业、讨论区、视频、其他资源等。通过网站,课程能适合不同风格学生的学习。网站上的视频涉及雇主、教学人员、就业指导人员、学生等各类人群。

完成作业(assignment)。其目的是让学生对所学内容有一个整体的理解和感知,并对学习结果进行评估。评估分学生自我评估和由教研人员的"形成性评价"(formative evaluation)。学生作业的内容,一是回答问题,问题内容根据学生与雇主和校友会面中所涉及内容及教师授课内容设定;二是简历制作、申请书撰写;三是完成教师在授课后布置的问题和作业。

4.实施教师

由于课程运行模式不同,实施教师的队伍结构也有所变化。一种是就业指导中心(careers advisory service)的专职职员,另一种是专业教师,还有一种是两者的结合。在雷丁大学每个院系都有一名讲授职业生涯管理技能的教师。

雷丁大学的职业生涯管理技能课程与学位课程相协调和适应。教师可以自由选择授课内容,学生也可以选择所学内容。每个学生都可以在网站上提交他乐于接受的学习内容,课程的开发者也可以根据大多数学生的需求进行调整。该校的职业生涯管理技能课程也用于提升和完善其他就业指导服务。

对于授课教师的专业,英国高校没有严格限制。以雷丁大学为例,他们更希望就业指导人员的背景越宽泛越好,但要有就业指导资格,需要参加一年培训拿到证书,授课教师的学历要求起点至少是硕士。

(三)职业生涯管理技能课程举例——"毕业生去向课程"

雷丁大学的职业生涯管理技能课程中最为著名的是"毕业生去向课程"(destinations)。该课程是专门为高校本科生开设的在线职业发展教育管理技能课程,部分内容也适用于研究生。其开发机构是雷丁大学职业发展教育管理技能中心。该课程具有五个方面的特点。

1.灵活的设计理念使课程充分满足学生的个性化需求

毕业生去向课程的设计致力于保障每一个使用者(学生)都能够自由地使用,项目施教者(教师)可以灵活操作。使用者在使用毕业生去向课程的网站时没有固定"路线",清晰的导航确保使用者可以独立地锁定特定的主题或者进行自由探索体验;职业生涯管理技能课程的开发者和教授者可以通过虚拟学习环境(VLE)呈现他们所选择的内容。这就使得课程设计可以充分实现个性化学习。

2.系统、全面的主题使课程涵盖职业发展教育管理的方方面面

毕业生去向课程网站包括多个主题,主要包括:工作申请表的制作、职业生涯的规划、雇佣单位的分析、兴趣的培养和发展、面试的方法和技巧、职业生涯的管理、继续深造的相关事宜,等等。

3.丰富多样的视频资源使课程生动易学

毕业生去向课程以收录超过200个专业的视频为特色,并且每个视频都有文字记录。所有视频可以分为两类,一类是嵌入网页中的视频,另一类是作为视频资源图书馆的视频。嵌入式视频在毕业生去向课程中经常被使用,这些视频是纸质材料的有效补充,许多视频为使用者提供了恰当的建议。视频资源图书馆是一种以闪存为基础的资源,囊括了超过200个专业录制的视频。使用者可以根据自身需要对视频资源进行关键词搜索、分类浏览以及添加个人视频。

4.互动式练习使课程学习者与教授者能及时沟通

毕业生去向课程是互动式的,这使得它特别有吸引力,很受学生欢迎。课程包含超过500个关于信息、建议和互动性练习的自主式网页。另外,该课程也提供许多多媒体资料,非常适合用户进行在线学习。

5.面向全球市场的设计使课程特别容易满足客户需求

毕业生去向课程是使用层叠样式表(cascading style sheets)设计的,这意味着可以通过编辑一个文件来改变它的设计和风格。因此,该课程特别容易满足客户需求,不同的客户可以根据自身需求将新的内容和视频编辑进去。

第四节 英国职业发展教育特色

英国职业发展教育的特色鲜明,主要包括以下几个方面:

一、重视内外部相互协调,学校与社会机构共同配合

当今时代,学校教育改革必须与社区、家长保持互动,注重教育内外部的相互协调,注意发挥各方的合力,确保教育目的的实现。英国教育部门在教育改革的实践中也比较关注社会与教育的相互作用,并注意利用各方力量。英国在一些法令中规定,相关社会部门要为学生熟悉各种职业提供便利条件。大学校园、企业、事业单位、工场要和学校建立广泛的合作关系,给学生们提供参观和就地实习的机会,以熟悉各专业、职业和工种,利于学生做出正确的选择。英国的每个社区都设有青少年实习培训中心,政府和企业为其提供实习岗位,学生在技能培训之后,可根据自己的能力和兴趣申请实习岗位。在大学申请和工作简历中,这些职业实习经验都是被认可的。在英国的部分职业启蒙试点小学,学生还有机会进入企业和大学校园参观,切身感受未来的专业学习和相关的职业环境,更好地促进学生的职业意识和观念的正确塑造。同时,学校也比较注意赢得学生家长的支持。如定期举办家长培训,请他们注意从小对自己的孩子进行职业意识的灌输,锻炼他们的独立能力,这些都保证了学校教育改革得以有序地进行。

二、注重改进学校职业服务质量

为了提高学校职业发展教育质量,英国政府在2002年就职业发展教育与指导的发展方向与未来的规划问题进行了广泛咨询和调查。《1997年教育法》规定,职业发展教育是9~11岁学生的课程之一。目前,英国政府准备进一步将学生职业指导的年限进一步扩展。

同时,英国政府改进学校职业指导的措施之一在于强调发挥初等、中等学校和大学的积极性,让学校自主安排职业发展指导方案,包括整合课程和时间安排。这种改革政策的优势在于给予学校和各类职业发展教育组织以充分自由。鉴于这种改革可能造成学校职业指导质量的差异,英国政府正在努力发展一种质量保证体系和应用标准,使国家的资格证授予制度和自我评估形式相结合。英国政府正集中精力解决这些问题,开始提高学校举办基准,提供最好的服务,加大职业发展教育视察力度。例如,在政府创办"联合就业处"时,就运用了法律的手段,主张不能降低已有的为青年人服务的职业指导质量和数量。

英国政府还采用一定措施来保证学校职业发展教育的质量和均衡性,例如,采取国家指令性职业发展教育课程、指令性教师任职资格和更加具体详细的学生权利规范。英国政府认为,为了保证学校职业指导的质量,联合就业处以及学校职业指导教师的技能、资格和能力至关重要。为了保证职业指导的技能和资格标准,联合就业处必须面对职业发展教育从业人员的两种资格需求,即职业指导角色和个人顾问角色的均衡发展。

三、强调提升职业指导从业人员的资格标准

英国职业指导证书的特色在于其广度和深度。许多机构的指导者都有正式的从业资格,专门的技能和知识,而且职业指导资格的获得形式多样,层级有别,方便不同层次的指导者取得资格。

2002年改革后,职业指导从业人员的证书类型主要有三种:第一种是职业指导资格证书。即需要在大学提供的研究性课程里专职学习一年或者兼职两年,然后被职业指导协会认可或授予证书。第二种是国家咨询与指导行业的四级证书。即通过以工作为本的途径获得。这种证书在英国的证

书体系中比较普遍,通常要经过 12~18 个月的从业时间去获得。第三种是国家咨询与指导行业的三级证书,即授予给那些兼职业指导者。

联合就业处的指导者要求取得个人顾问毕业证书和职业指导资格证书。毕业证书注重为青年人服务的一般能力,如与被推荐人和各种代理机构沟通的能力。联合就业处指导者一般要求拥有国家咨询与指导四级证书,其他职业指导者有两种证书中的一种则可。从事全国职业发展教育的指导者还拥有其他类别的证书。据英国教育研究基金会关于学校职业发展教育的调查表明,许多职业指导者拥有各种基本证书甚至硕士水平证书。"学习引领"的工作人员要求视工作性质而定,必须获得国家二级或者三级证书。

四、重构成人职业指导新思维

成人职业指导是英国的创新,是向着终身职业指导体制迈进的具体举措,是英国终身学习体制的组成部分。这一点很值得其他国家学习。

英国最近的成人职业指导改革最为引人注目的是重构成人指导新思维,相对于英国过去的成人教育形式是重构,相对于欧洲国家更是如此。例如,"学习引领中心"将现代市场和大众传媒、电话、网络技术相结合,社区里巡回服务,为顾客提供在线职业指导服务。

在英国,私人成人职业发展教育服务市场往往不太成功。原因是大量的人不愿意购买学习引领中心的自我评估工具,尽管价钱很低。同时网上也有许多相似的评估工具免费提供。在别的 OECD 国家里,成人指导的私人市场有一定的发展,如企业为被解雇后的人员提供的职业再介绍服务市场。英国目前的成人指导则是政府提供和私人提供之间的平衡。英国政府认识到这样的事实,即成人指导是政府投资的事业,也是私人市场和个人负责的事情。这种政策主张进一步拓宽了职业指导的广泛性。

五、深化职业指导的理论基础

相对于欧洲国家而言,英国的职业指导服务有着丰厚的理论研究基础。英国具有专门的职业指导政策研究与分析中心——全国职业教育与咨询协会和德比大学的职业指导研究中心。除此之外,英国各大学以及社会各界有许多对职业指导感兴趣的专家和研究人员。

英国职业指导的知识基础雄厚的一个关键原因在于：英国对职业指导从业者有较高的资格要求,大学能提供这种资格训练甚至具有研究生水平的课程方案。因此,英国大学里有专门的学术研究人员,职业指导实践领域有专门的技术人员。英国政府愿意委托相关机构进行职业指导政策研究,职业指导的政策制定和实施以研究为基础。因此,英国关于职业指导的理论十分丰富,甚至成为其他欧洲国家重要的参考资料。

英国曾经专门召开指导研究中心和指导委员会共同组织的会议:全国职业指导研究论坛。目前,英国职业指导研究的主要论题有:发展与政策和实践相关的一致性职业指导课题研究;促进对重大科研选题的认同机制,找到研究差异;寻求职业指导的研究同盟军,支援职业指导投资;广纳相关利益主体参与全国职业指导研究议程,影响职业指导政策和实践。

思考题:

1.英国职业指导的框架体系是怎样的?

2.英国职业发展教育的特色是什么?

3.以雷丁大学为例,论述职业发展教育管理技能课程的目标及实施。

推荐书目:

1.王占仁,常飒飒.英国高校职业生涯管理技能课程研究——以英国里丁大学为个案[J].中国高教研究,2012(10).

2.刘晓倩.英国中学生涯教育述评[J].外国中小学教育,2014(6).

3.李蕾,陈鹏.发达国家职业启蒙教育的经验与启示[J].职教论坛,2017(21).

4.谢银迪.英国:发布中学职业生涯教育指南[N].中国教师报,2018-5-2(3).

国外论文导读与阅读:

导读:青年职业发展教育:英国和其他欧洲国家的基本理念和规定

作者:瓦茨(A. G. WATTS)

论文比较了英国与其他欧洲国家在青年职业发展教育方面的差异,包括三个部分:

一是职业发展教育理念不断发展。在新技术和市场全球化的影响下,企业雇主与求职者的契约时长缩短,个体工作的不稳定性加剧,职业发展教育的理念发生改变。一方面,职业概念由强调个体组织内部层级晋升,发展为更加注重生涯特性;另一方面,职业发展教育由仅仅停留在就业前的职业指导阶段,发展为日益可持续化和多元化,即构建起从学校环境到工作场景连贯一体化的职业发展教育机制,关注个体自我认知和职业管理能力的提升,以及注重专家指导、网络技术运用和家庭参与等因素。

二是介绍以英国为代表的欧洲国家对职业发展教育的规定。以英国为例:根据1997年教育法,英国规定学校有法定责任为9~11年级的学生提供职业发展教育方案。职业发展教育目标包括四个部分——自我意识、机会意识、决策学习、过渡学习;开展形式有跨课程主题模式、课程渗透、个人及社会教育计划、职业教育日、教牧/辅导模式、学校课外活动、个人、社会和健康教育(PSHE)项目和工作体验或实习等;职业发展教育时长随年级而增强。除基础教育外,英国的职业发展教育还包括高等教育,继续教育和社会成人教育等方面。目前,英格兰和威尔士职业发展教育较为复杂。其他欧洲国家:丹麦、德国、希腊、荷兰、葡萄牙等都推出了职业发展教育方案,为基础教育阶段的中学生提供一系列职业发展教育课程;比利时和法国规定由专家顾问来主持学校的职业小组会议;工作经验方案在各国普遍实施,使学生获得社会工作体验。

三是分析时间、内容、方法、交付模式、进展和评估这六个方面存在的问题。时间上:职业发展教育仍然局限于职业过渡点,职业发展教育计划应从小学尽早开展;内容上:职业发展教育各课程培养目标的差异性,使学生难以形成明确的职业偏好;方法上:职业发展教育课程中教师传授、小组体验式学习以及实践工作体验等教育方法的效果难以平衡;交付模式上:四种交付模式(具体封闭模式、扩展封闭模型、整合模式、课外模式)都存在缺陷。例如,整合模式很有吸引力,但是在教师培训和课堂教学等层面很难实施;封闭模式导致学生学习的功利性和教师培训的困难性;课外模式虽然摆脱了课程的限制和约束,但容易被边缘化,与学校和学习过程的主流脱节;进展上:劳(Law)提出职业发展学习具有周期性和螺旋形,可分为感知阶段、筛选阶段、聚焦阶段和理解阶段;这些过程与自我意识、机会意识、决策学习和转型学习四个目标相对应;评估上:学生过分注重外在知识技能的自我表现,忽视自我意识与学习能力的发展;应注重评估方式与职业发展教育目标的一致性,建立多元化的评估模型。

文献来源:

Watts A G. Career Education for Young People: Rationale and Provision in the UK and Other European Countries[J]. International Journal for Educational and Vocational Guidance, 2001, 1(3):209-222.

(节选的英文原文见附录5)

第五章　德国职业发展教育

本章要点：
1.德国职业发展教育的政策；
2.德国职业发展教育课程的特点；
3.德国职业发展教育的特色。

德国特别重视职业发展教育，其职业教育特色鲜明，发展成就有目共睹。德国的职业发展教育和它的职业教育紧密结合，相互渗透。本章在介绍当代德国教育概况的基础上，对德国职业发展教育的政策、课程以及特色进行阐述和解读。

第一节　当代德国教育概况

德国教育在世界教育发展史上占有重要地位，无论义务教育还是高等教育都具有鲜明的特征，下面对德国教育做一概括介绍。

一、德国的初等教育

德国的初等教育是强制性的，也就是我国小学阶段的教育，学制是统一的四年制(个别州如柏林为六年)。孩子年满六岁入学。一年级和二年级通常只有一位教师进行教育教学工作，三年级教师数量增多，分别担任不同科目的教学。教学内容和形式要根据学生的身心发展状况、个性特点来制定，进行个别教育。教育的目的之一是培养学生终身学习和接受教育的素质和能力。因此，在教学内容的设置上，有读、写、数学、文化、语言、音乐、乡土实物课程、艺术、体育和宗教课等。从三年级起开设外语课。在评定学生成绩方面,一、二年级不采用计分制,采用评语制,即由任课教师对学生的学习情况做出评价,三、四年级才采用计分制,为的是保护这个年龄阶段孩子活泼好动的个性,避免计分制压制学生的学习兴趣。从二年级开始,任课教师将根据孩子的学习情况来决定其是否能继续升到高年级。

二、德国的中学教育

中学教育又分为初阶(sekundarstufe I)和高阶(sekundarstufe II)两个阶段,下述四种中学分别包含了初阶和高阶两个阶段。大体上相当于我国的初中和高中阶段,但在内容和结构上又有相当大的不同,比较复杂,有些甚至连德国人也搞不清楚。以下分别予以说明。学生在完成小学阶段四年基础教育后开始中学阶段的学习。根据成绩将学生分流至四类中学,由此开始初阶的学习。这四类中学分别是:五年制普通中学(hauptschule),六年制实科中学(reals-chule),六年制综合中学(gesamtschule)和九年制文理中学(gymnasium)。中学的学习年限根据各州的具体情况有所不同。大多数州的学校将五至六年级作为定向观察期,为七年级的分流做准备。在这个阶段,学校和家长会根据学生的学习情况及个人禀赋来决定让孩子进哪一类中学。这样做可以防止将学生过早分流,保留了充足的时间考察学生究竟适合进哪一类中学。

(一)普通中学

普通中学成立于19世纪60年代,前身是原国民中学(volksschule)高年级阶段。如果学生不能或不愿进入其他的三类中学,则必须升入普通中学继续学业,从而最低限度地落实《基本法》所规定的义务教育政策。普通中学的学制为五~九年级,少数州要上到十年级(如下萨克森州),但学生可以自己决定是否继续升级。中学的所有课程都具备实用性和实操性。此外,还教授学生如何择业。这一阶段基本可理解为职业发展教育的准备期,其主要目的是让学生掌握进一步接受正式职业发展教育所必备的基本知识,具备今后工作所需的基本职业素质。学生按规定完成上述五~九年级初阶的全部课程并通过考试后,取得普通中学毕业文凭,这相当于实科中学学历,从而获得进入高阶学校的资格,或者转学。但普通中学的毕业生基本没

有资格进入高等专科学校和大学,且毕业后从事的职业大多是掌握专业技能的技术工人和手工业劳动者,因此很多家长不想让孩子读普通中学,近年来德国教育界一直对此存有争议。

(二)实科中学

实科中学的教育教学方向介于普通中学和文理中学之间,在教育内容上,它比普通中学具有更进一步的普及性,也分为初阶和高阶两个阶段。相对于普通中学,实科中学的学生毕业后具有更加灵活的个人发展方向,这种办学形式在当代德国中学是比较成功的。在教学内容上,以北威州为例,实科中学的普及教育阶段(初阶)课程有德语、社会学、地理学、数学、自然科学(生物、化学、物理、信息技术)、艺术、音乐、手工编织(女生)、宗教和体育。除以上科目外,学生还必须学一门外语(一般是英语),从六年级开始还要学第二外语,一般为法语、荷兰语或西班牙语等,二外课是普通中学所不具备的。另外,作为必修课的补充,七年级开始增设选修课,学生自主选课,可充分考虑自身兴趣和知识侧重点。

(三)文理中学

文理中学相当于大学预科,因为只有从文理中学毕业,才有直接升入大学的资格。而从其他三类中学毕业的学生,均没有资格直接升入大学。但是,近年来文理中学的毕业生人数增长很快,因此,并不是每个毕业生都能直接上大学。大学的入学条件中要求学生应具备小学四年基础教育的良好成绩,此外,家长还需要征求小学任课教师的意见,由教师根据学生个人的学习情况帮助其选择适合自己的那类学校。如果学生想进实科中学和文理中学,一些州如巴伐利亚、巴登-符腾堡、北威等的教育部则特别规定学生应提供教师出具的建议信。而其他州如黑森州、汉堡等,教师的建议则只是给学生家长提供参考。在教学内容上,文理中学虽也属于普通中学教育范畴,但其教学深度要超过其他三类中学。因为大多数文理中学的学生今后要进入大学接受高等教育,所以它比其他三类中学有更高的入学条件要求。

(四)综合中学

20世纪60年代中后期,联邦德国出现了一种称为综合中学的中等教育机构。综合中学产生的原因是某些党派认为三分制的中学体系阻碍了中下层阶级子女同样享受同等教育的机会。因此,他们呼吁将过去三种中学合并到这种新型中学中来。综合中学于1969年正式被联邦政府认可,随后各州都开始了综合中学的实验。但是,总的来说,综合中学发展较为缓慢。①目前,只有为数不多的几个联邦州有综合中学。学生在小学四年级毕业后,不是分别进入不同的学校,而是进入同一所学校,即所谓的综合中学。综合中学把普通中学、实科中学和文理中学三种学校的教学方向相融合。课程分为两种:一种是基本课程,即安排不同程度的同年级的学生共同上课;另一种是能力课程,即根据学生程度分别教学。综合中学的学习年限分为两个阶段:一是义务教育阶段,由五到十年级或七到十年级(如果小学是到六年级的话);二是自愿教育阶段,最高可到十三年级。十三年级毕业生的学历等同于文理中学的毕业生。

三、德国的高等教育

德国的高等教育产生于中世纪晚期,其产生方式不同于欧洲早期的大学,虽然采取了巴黎大学自治团体的模式,但它不是作为学者联合体自发产生的,而是由代表封建邦国的诸侯建立的。因此,从一开始德国的大学就既有着学术自治的传统,又有着受政府控制的特点。经过多次教育的改革,当今双重身份的角色依然存在,并成为德国大学有别于其他国家大学的显著特征。从管理的角度看,双重身份意味着对大学进行管理的权限也一分为二:作为国家机构的高等学校要服从国家的管理,而作为社团法人的高等学校又享有一定的自我管理的权利(主要在教学、学术研究活动领域)。这种权限的分割及国家政权联邦制的特点,就使得以教授为中心的基层教学科研组织和分散行使国家权力的州政府成为整个高等教育管理结构中的两个关键层次。

德国高等教育在历史上曾经有过很高的声誉,即使现在也是大家争相研究的国家之一,有着自己的特点。这些特点是德国教育界一直引以为自豪的,但也在发生着悄悄的变革。

(一)高等学校的分类与特色

与美国不同,德国大学之间的水平差异不很显著,高等学校的分类特点

---

① 杨明,赵凌.德国教育战略研究[M].杭州:浙江教育出版社,2015:980.

主要体现在大学与高等专业学院的分工。大学与高等专业学院有着不同的使命和定位,均可颁发文凭(diplom)和学位(magister)。大学与我们常识性的理解相一致,为学术性高等学校(颁发博士学位),注重基础研究,功利性不强,通常都设置有广泛的学科,几乎包括所有的专业领域,因此规模都很大(但很多综合大学通常不含工程技术专业)。高等专业学院为职业应用性高等学校,注重培养实际应用型人才,为职业实践做准备。高等专业学院与企业界有着更紧密的联系,其师资除学术资格外一般还需要至少5年的非学校实际工作经验。根据《高等学校总纲法》的规定,大学的基本学制为10个学期(医科专业为12个学期),高等专业学院为8个学期。

(二)高等教育的学位特点及学校质量认证

德国的学位制度是比较特殊的,例如它原本没有学士(bachelor)学位,而有 diplom、magister、国家考试(staatsexamen)和博士(doctorate)四种形式。德国人认为 diplom 和 magister 均高于学士学位。大学毕业时获得什么文凭主要依赖于所学学科。例如,diplom 主要颁发给理、工及大多数社会科学和经济学的学生,magister 主要授予艺术、人文科学及部分社会科学的学生,magister 考核还必须包括两个主修学科或一个主修学科和两个辅修学科;staatsexamen 由州或联邦规定,那些想要从事公共服务工作(如教师、法官)和国家监管职业(如医生、律师、药剂师)的学生需通过国家考试获得入门资格;doctorate 也就是我们所说的博士学位,只能由大学颁发。有专门的机构评估和认证各州高等学校的教学质量,确保高等学校的相互承认。认证的程序有自评、外部评估和改进,外部评估由专门机构进行,包括请国外的专家。目前,德国各州基本上都具备这样的机构。评估的基本内容包括:第一,学习的内容是否符合未来科学的发展;第二,学生是否符合劳动力市场的需要;第三,学生是否有对外交流和研究的能力;第四,学校教学科研设施和场所。

自1997年以来,德国许多大学设立了国际学位课程。学习3年,考试合格可以获得学士学位。在此基础修读3到4个学期可以获得硕士学位。如果成绩优异、经教授同意,可以继续攻读博士学位。

(三)学额分配机制

在德国,文理中学的毕业生具备进入大学学习的当然资格,因此出现了热门专业的学额分配问题。德国有一个分配学额的机构,叫作学习岗位分配中心,其遵循三种分配程序。

第一,普通分配程序。为一般性专业,主要根据学生个人志愿选择,都能保证入学。当第一志愿申请人数过多时,可向第二或第三志愿学校调整。学额分配不但要考虑学生想上什么学校,而且还要考虑学生的家庭住址及是否有需要照顾的因素(如残疾人)。

第二,挑选程序。为比较热门专业,现有学习岗位容纳不了,分配中心按学习成绩和等待时间对申请学生进行排队,55%按成绩,25%按等待时间,剩下的20%由学校自主决定。

第三,特别挑选程序。为最热门专业,申请者需再参加一个测试,测试结果与中学毕业考试成绩同等重要。

第二节　德国职业发展教育政策

德国职业发展教育的政策包括义务教育阶段的政策、职业法规方面的政策以及政府部门的就业公共服务政策。

一、职业义务教育政策

德国的职业义务教育始于19世纪60年代。1869年颁布的北德意志联邦工商条例规定,不足18岁的伙计、帮工和学徒,有进入补习学校接受职业补习教育的义务。1872年,帝国政府颁布了《普通学校法》,规定6至14岁的8年初等教育为强迫义务教育阶段,并要求18岁以下已经就业的青年,尽可能地继续接受职业补习教育。1873年萨克森州对不足15周岁的男孩实行三年职业义务教育,成为德国第一个实行三年职业义务教育的州。1900年以前,普鲁士多数大城市实行职业义务教育。

由于义务教育的推行,整个德意志民族的文化素养得到了极大提高。1919年魏玛共和国成立。《魏玛宪法》规定儿童6岁入学,接受8年普通义务教育,职业义务教育到18岁停止。1938年颁布的《帝国义务教育法》明确规定,属德国国籍、在国内有住址或长期居住的所有儿童和青少年,都必须接受8年学校义务教育。这种义务教育必须由德国的学校来实施。职业

义务教育为2至3年,即农业职业义务教育为2年,其他为3年。至此,德国的义务教育基本定形。

为了统一联邦各州的教育,1964年各州文化部长在汉堡举行会议。会议协议规定,义务教育从6岁开始,年限为12年。德国的义务教育有其独特之处,即接受完9年全日制义务教育的青少年,便开始接受3年部分实践制职业学校的义务教育。这种义务教育,也是对所有青少年的普遍要求。接受这种义务教育的人不仅包括离开主要学校接受学徒培训或就业的青少年,而且包括待业在家或操持家务或在父母的企业中工作的青少年。进入实科学校学习的青少年,可免除职业义务教育。

德国的实科中学是一种具有普通教育性质兼具职业教育性质的学校,定位于培养全面发展的实用型人才。早在1984年,职业指导就已经作为实科中学的及教学计划内容被实施且纳入社会学的入门课程。实科中学的职业指导是一种职业预备教育,学校通过对学生职业潜力、兴趣、能力的分析评定,结合社会、职业劳动市场的需求,引导、促使学生自主合理地为升学或就业做好准备,既实现了学生个性化的职业定向支持,又保障了学生未来进入高级职业学校的竞争力。以德国巴登-符腾堡州为例,其实科中学职业指导的实施主要通过主修课程、潜力分析、合作机构指导、主题项目完善以及特色实践保障等方式进行。实科中学除了包含普通中学的基础课程外还设有职业导向的实践性课程。为了使学生更好地规划职业生涯,学校会设置三大主修课程组供学生选择,内容涵盖数学、自然科学、技术、经济、语言、艺术等。潜力分析的方式主要为专业教师通过合作项目或实践活动等观察学生的各项能力,与学生进行谈话,结合社区、家庭等因素,对学生的职业潜能进行分析。实科中学与公司或企业合作,形成了以学校为中心、合作机构共同协作的职业指导体系。企业定期举办"车间工作日"学生由经验丰富的培训师傅引导,进行定期的企业参访登记,明确自身在各职业领域中的强项并得到有关职业定向的初步介绍。①

---

① 关世卿,刘辉.德国实科中学:为学生提供个性化职业预备教育[J].中小学管理,2017(07):53-55.

二、职业培训与就业促进法规政策

德国通过完善法律保障体系,将大学生就业纳入法制化轨道。1969年,德国颁布《联邦劳动促进法》,这是德国劳动部门实施职业培训促进的法律依据。后来,政府先后颁布了《职业教育法》《就业促进法》《训练促进法》《大学生法》《非全日工作法》等,《大学生法》规定在校大学生要保证一定时间的实习。在德国,与包括大学毕业生在内的求职者直接相关的法律还有失业保险法、劳动中介法、社会保险法等。

《联邦劳动促进法》第1条明确规定,联邦劳工部负责职业培训;第2条和第3条要求联邦劳工部根据联邦政府的社会福利政策和经济发展需要,进行下列具体工作:

(1)消除已有的失业,保证向国民经济各部门提供充足的劳动力和限制一切低于法定价值标准的职业活动;

(2)消除因技术进步和经济结构变化所引起的影响从业者正常就业的一切不利因素,努力增强从业者的职业流动性和职业应变能力;

(3)向有各种程度身心障碍者提供必要的财政支持,为其谋取职业创造有利条件;

(4)为那些由于结婚或家务繁重而离职、若干年后又想重返工作岗位却难以胜任该项工作的妇女和那些就业竞争能力差、难以在正常劳务市场条件下谋取职业的年老者以及其他成年人,创造各种必要条件,努力安排其就业;

(5)根据经济区域和经济部门的特点,调整职业结构。

职业教育领域的生涯教育同样受到重视。1969年,联邦德国议会颁布《职业培训法》,指出"在联邦德国,职业培训是'双元'体制的,由行业及相关公共服务机构、专业机构、家庭等同职业院校及其他(职业)教育机构合作培养技术技能型人才;在该体制中,行业负责职业培训的实践部分,职业院校则提供必要的理论知识教育;受训者具有双重身份,既是学生又是学徒"。[①] 1981年,德国又颁布与《职业培训法》配套的《联邦职业教育促进

---

① Walter E. Theurkauf, Andreas Weiner. The German Dual System of Vocational Education and Implications for Human Resource Development in America[A]. Paper presented at the American Vocational Association Convention(Nashville, TN, December 6, 1993). ERIC.3-4.

法》,规定了涉及职业教育规划、统计和研究内容的条款,并确立了联邦职业教育研究所在职业教育领域的法律地位。2005年,德国合并1969年《职业培训法》和1981年《联邦职业教育促进法》,在此基础上,修订颁布了《联邦职业教育促进法》。这对受教育者的职业生涯发展极为重要。

除了国家层面的法律规范外,德国还通过各州《教育法》、德国各州文教部长联席会议与联邦政府签署的各项框架协议、德国联邦主管行业部门同联邦教育与研究部协商后颁布制定的与各培训职业相对应、全国统一的《职业培训条例》等法律及职业教育规范来约束"双元制"的实施。[1] 具体看来,职业院校要在国家《联邦职业教育法》、各州《教育法》、《职业培训条例》及《职业教育框架教学计划》的规范下,开展教学活动。企业则必须遵守《联邦职业教育法》并按照《职业培训条例》的相关标准开展"基于工作"的人才培养活动,培养学生的综合能力和职业发展能力。

职业培训是人的职业成长发展的重要环节。《职业培训条例》是德国职业教育的重要规范性文件之一,其制定或修订遵循"共识"原则,由来自联邦政府、州政府、雇主、行业协会、职业教育领域等的诸多利益主体共同协作完成。《职业培训条例》的开发周期一般为两年(24个月),大致分为基准确定、条例制定和条例颁布三个阶段。[2] 基准的确定由相关联邦部门、联邦教育与研究部、社会合作者、各州及联邦政府相关人员在协商一致的原则下确定。在制定阶段,各州还要根据联邦政府起草的《职业培训条例》制定《框架教学计划》作为职业院校开展教学的框架指南。

三、学生就业公共服务机构与政策

为保障大学生顺利就业,德国政府成立了专门机构并制定了相应的政策措施。

(一)学生就业公共服务机构

1.联邦劳工部

德国联邦劳工部建于1952年,为联邦级的社会自治机构,其人员由三方

---

[1] 德国职业教育双元制中国本土化创新研究编写组.德国职业教育双元制中国本土化创新研究[M].北京:人民出版社,2017:3.
[2] 同[1],17.

组成,雇员代表、雇主代表和公共部门代表各占三分之一。联邦劳工部由负责行政事务的理事会和制定政策的董事会共同管理。董事会成员包括雇主协会和雇员协会以及州和地方政府人员。从组织上讲,联邦劳工部在纽伦堡设有一个中央办公室,11个地区办公室和184个地方劳工办公室,共有近700个分支机构。德国联邦及各州劳工部是政府主管全社会就业的机构,亦是主管大学生就业的机构。它主要负责四个领域:工作咨询和安置,职业咨询服务,失业保险金和研究。联邦劳工部的主要任务之一是制定联邦的就业政策,促进就业,减少失业,并就这些问题与各州、各地方相关部门以及议会劳动与社会委员会协商。各州劳工部则负责制定本州范围内的就业与社会政策。从服务对象上讲,不仅包括在校青年,也包括离校青年,后者占使用该服务青年人数的一半左右。近年来,服务的重点转向在寻找培训场所和进入劳动力市场方面遇到困难的青年。这类青年可以参加各种职前课程以及其他方面课程。还为特定群体(例如对非传统职业感兴趣的女孩和年轻妇女)和特定职业领域举行特别活动。联邦劳工部提供针对所有年龄段的职业指导服务,但是它为青年和成年提供的服务是分开的。对于青年,指导和安置都由职业咨询师负责。对于成年,指导和安置的职能由工作顾问和安置人员划分。残疾人和残障人士则由专业的康复咨询师提供服务。在服务方式上,青年可以通过电话与服务部门联系。此外,职业咨询师可以进行短期会面,现在越来越多的会面需要经过提前筛选。联邦劳工部发布职业信息,运营职业信息中心(BIZ),在学校和劳工办公室提供职业指导,为公民提供职业培训,并促进职业培训和国际合作。职业信息中心与雇主协会,手工艺品和商业组织、商会、手工艺品工会以及政府在建立针对学生的培训场所方面有着密切的联系并合作。联邦劳工部的研究所调查基本的劳动力市场,职业和教育统计数据,然后将其分发至职业指导部门。由职业指导人员和联邦劳工部其他专家组成的工作组将这些统计数据转换为职业和教育信息。联邦劳工部为员工、学生、离校生、雇主和一般公众免费提供各种出版物。例如,所有普通中学和实科中学的学生都会获得一本介绍双元制可以提供的职业和培训机会的出版物。文理中学的学生则会收到介绍教育计划和教育机会的出版物。这两种出版物都是每年更新一次。

2.各地区劳工局

劳工局为个人、企业和机构提供有关培训和就业服务。具体而言包括介绍培训和就业职位；提供就职咨询；为雇主提供咨询；资助职业培训；资助残疾人就业；促进创造和保存就业岗位以及对就业市场和职业发展进行数据统计和跟踪研究等。同时，劳工局与政府、企业、私人就业服务机构和高校密切合作。劳工局执行政府的就业政策，为企业提供信息和咨询，与私人职业中介机构合作实现信息共享，设立专门的高校服务组为大学生提供就业信息和就业指导。劳工局高校服务组是高校学生获得就业信息和就业指导的一个主要渠道。它的核心任务是为高校在校生和毕业生（毕业后一年以内）提供就业市场和劳工局服务信息，指导专业学习重点规划、专业转换、职业选择、职业素质培养、从学业到职业的转换和进修，提供职业申请指导和培训等。高校服务组多设在大学附近，便于为学生就近服务，每学期都开展形式多样、内容丰富的活动。以柏林地区为例，劳工局共设有柏林北部区、市中心区和南部区三个高校服务组，分别服务于三地附近的19所高校学生。每年的夏季学期，柏林三个劳工局高校服务组都会举办针对某个专业的就业市场发展、大学生在中小企业的就业机会等几十场报告会，组织企业自我介绍或参观活动。此外，还举办有"优势—劣势分析""跨文化合作的关键能力"以及其他关于学业、实习的讲座，开设"职业申请材料准备""面试技巧"等培训课程。

(二)学生就业公共服务政策

政府部门为学生制定的就业公共服务的政策包括：第一，规定职业学校、高等学校毕业生最低待遇标准。第二，降低劳动成本和税率，减轻企业负担，鼓励企业开辟新劳动岗位。第三，鼓励毕业生自主创业，为此制定专门政策，并为毕业生自主创业提供银行贷款。第四，减少加班时间，设立志愿者岗位，每年可安排近百万人就业。在经济不景气的情况下，德国政府还会采取以下措施促进就业：向企业提供补贴，鼓励它们雇佣高校毕业生；为毕业一年尚未就业的高校毕业生提供失业保险金，使之尽快找到合适的工作等。对大学生毕业后因知识、技能欠缺在一定时间没有找到工作的，政府为其进行3个月的培训、补课，费用由国家劳工部支付。员工失业后，在1到

2年之内,劳工部还将按该员工平均月工资60%的标准补助失业者。此外,劳工部还搭建了一个网络平台,用于向社会提供各种信息,企业可以在这个平台上发布信息,个人也可以在这个平台上找工作。这些措施为高校毕业生整个就业机制的正常运行都产生了重要而积极的影响。

第三节　德国职业发展教育课程

德国的职业发展教育课程旨在为学生树立正确的职业意识和观念,使学生获得寻找工作的技能与方法,最终帮其找到理想的职业,并在以后的职业生活中继续受益。

一、德国职业发展教育课程内容

(一)基础教育阶段的职业发展教育课程

德国基础教育阶段的职业发展教育课程有两种形式,由普通学校实施的职业教育和由职业学校实施的职业教育。① 由职业学校实施的职业发展教育通常是为期一年的课程,因此也称为"职业预备教育年",由普通学校实施的职业发展教育包括两方面内容:一是通过劳动学课程进行技术、经济、社会生活的初步教育,二是职业定向教育。

劳动学课程旨在帮助学生了解相关职业信息并初步确定自己的职业道路。② 劳动学课程是综合了劳动、职业、技术、经济、社会、政治等各个领域的入门教育,其内容包含关于经济和劳动世界的一般定向;劳动行为的教育;职业选择的入门教育等方面。劳动学课程主要以接受义务教育后走上谋生道路的青少年为对象,特别以普通学校七至九年级的学生为对象。在课程实施方面也有别于一般基础课程,授业者包括专职劳技教师、职业咨询员、社会工作者、工厂师傅等,在组织形式上,不局限于课堂教学,而是结合访问职业信息中心,参观工厂、进企业实习等。劳动学课程本身不是职业训练,而是为以后的职业训练打好基础。劳动学课程的主要任务是通过学校教学

---

① 李扬.联邦德国学校的职业指导[J].比较教育研究,1994(1).
② 傅小芳.德国基础教育阶段的职业指导课程[J].教育理论与实践,1999(19).

和企业中的直观劳动,使学生了解现代社会技术化的劳动程序,熟悉现代生产和服务行业中的劳动,从而为选择职业做好准备。

普通学校职业发展教育的第二个方面即职业定向教育。职业定向教育通常贯穿于义务教育的第八年和第九年,直到选定了某一教育途径或某门训练职业或职业领域为止。职业定向教育由联邦劳工部及其下属机构与普通教育学校和职业教育学校共同承担。工作主要包含以下几个方面:提供职业信息、提供职业咨询、学校与教学中的职业定向。职业信息的提供是多部门合作的结果,联邦统计局从不同的角度编制职业分类,联邦劳工部和联邦职业教育研究所从不同角度提供有关职业的描述。职业咨询信息的提供则是联邦劳工部的主要任务之一,1998年以前职业指导和安置由联邦劳工部垄断,开放后私营部门发展了各种服务。学校和教学中的职业定向主要以三种形式开展:职业选择课、企业考察和企业实践。职业选择可一般在普通学校学生毕业离校的前两年开设,内容主要以职业选择和职业定向为主。企业考察是为学生初步接触和观察劳动世界或企业现实而特别安排的一种教学活动。企业实践则给学生亲身体验企业内各种活动的机会,让学生获得对劳动世界的初步经验。

(二)高等教育阶段的职业发展教育课程

德国高等教育阶段的职业发展教育显著特点是大学、企业界、劳动局的全方位合作。德国高校学生的职业发展教育由联邦劳工部和各州联邦政府的劳工局全面负责,大学生职业指导处下特设一个信息中心。信息中心建立了网络平台,全国有职业指导需求的人员可以共享资源。大学里设立了就业市场学院,专门负责学生专业能力以外其他能力的培训,如独立工作能力和社交能力。企业界常年为大学生提供实习基地,负责其培训与考核。《高等教育框架法》要求高等教育机构向学生和申请人告知学习的机会和条件,学习课程的内容,结构和要求,并在整个学期间向学生提供学业指导。在提供此类指导时,它还要求机构与负责职业指导的部门合作。遵循《高等教育框架法》以及各州的相关法令,大多数大学和一些职业学校都建立了学生咨询服务中心。他们一半以上的工作是针对未来的学生(包括开放日和学校参观日),其余针对在校学生。大部分工作是对信息和建议的简短答复(有些是通过电话和电子邮件),但大多数工作还为那些不确定自己的选择、想要改变方向、在学业和生活方面遇到困难的学生提供更深入的咨询。他们的指导人员来自各种学术背景,有些人在指导和咨询方面具有特定的资格。高等教育机构与联邦劳工部的高等教育团队之间的合作关系是根据劳工部与校长常务委员会之间的一份全国性协议展开的。该服务机构的高等教育团队分布在每个拥有超过 10 000 名学生的高等教育机构。他们通常在高等教育机构提供服务,靠近该机构的学生咨询服务中心。原则上,他们专注于提供职业指导和安置服务,而学生咨询服务中心的服务则专注于教育指导。在实践中,两者之间存在一些重叠,特别是在学生改变学科或辍学的情况下,他们通常会合作组织诸如招聘会和研讨会之类的活动。但是,学生咨询服务中心与雇主之间的联系很少。传统上,德国的高等教育机构对离开大学后将学生推向职业生涯几乎没有责任。但是,随着机构之间竞争的加剧以及与劳动力市场的联系变得越来越复杂,这种情况开始改变。近年来,相当多的大学建立了自己的职业服务机构,有时将它们与联邦劳工部的高等教育团队或学生咨询服务中心及其他学生服务中心安排在一块。

二、德国职业发展教育课程特色

总体来说,德国的职业发展教育课程具有以下特点:

(一)呈现明显的职业化倾向

德国高校课程设置呈现出了明显的职业化倾向,并且在职业化过程中具备自己的独特之处。德国大学课程致力于培养学生广泛的职业适应力,避免给学生传授狭窄的职业知识。其大学教育的目的不是培养学生的职业技能或对某些特殊职业的能力,而是培养学生掌握和运用科学知识和方法,在某一领域进行创造性工作的能力。同时,德国高校课程发展趋势的突出特点是将职业化和基础化相结合。

德国的教学计划把教学内容分为理论课、实验课、实训课、企业实习等几部分,先在教室里讲理论,再在实验室里进行实验,然后到实训课中练习,最后才把学生放到企业中实习。根据专业不同,德国大学对实习分为义务和自愿两种。实习的期限大致 2 个月至半年,有的专业甚至要求一年。实习时间可以累计。义务实习要求在写毕业论文之前完成,学校在《学习准则》中都会对实习的内容甚至岗位做明确规定。实习结束,相关单位要对学生

在实习中的表现进行鉴定。学生把实习报告和鉴定书交给学校专门负责实习管理的部门进行认定,实习管理部门会根据鉴定书和实习报告,认定哪些岗位的哪些时间段的实习符合《学习准则》的要求,并出具一个实习时间确认书,学生据此获得实习的学分。①

(二)注重"关键能力"的培养

"关键能力"是一种普遍的、可迁移的,在个人的职业生涯、个性发展和社会活动等各个方面起关键作用的能力,是指与专业不直接相关的知识和技能,包括在不同场合和职责情况下做出判断、选择的能力和处理人生生涯中不可预计各种变化的能力。"关键能力"包括专门能力、语言能力、方法能力、自我能力和社会能力、跨文化交际能力等。德国高校强调"关键能力"不仅是学生将来在职业生涯中应对各种变化所必需的能力,而且是成功完成大学学业所应该具备的能力。德国高校主要有两种培养学生"关键能力"的课程形式:一种是一体化课程,一般由专业院系开设,课程内容与专业知识有关,教师在传授专业知识的过程中,注重培养学生的"关键能力",如相关专业学习和工作技巧、项目管理、科学工作等。另一种是补充式课程,一般由学校设立专门机构,开设跨专业或者一般性"关键能力"培养课程,如外语、领导能力和跨文化能力课程等,与专业知识的关系不大。

(三)重视创业课程体系建设

德国政府和金融研究机构联合在中学、大学开设创业课程,让学生尝试自己开公司,接触和熟悉企业管理及经营知识。许多德国高校已经建设了一套比较完善的创业教育课程体系。包括企业家精神训练、创业法律法规、企业创业管理、商业计划书、市场调研、新产品开发、财务管理、市场营销战略等几十门课程,课程涵盖了创业精神、创业意识、创业能力、创业知识、创业实践操作等领域。慕尼黑技术大学的创业教育设计的课程就包括企业财政、风险投资、商业发展计划等,这些课是面向全校的通选课。主要为创业者服务的有生物技术与医药产业的筹资与评估、创新企业家等课程。为促进创业教育目标的实现,慕尼黑技术大学还通过大量分析典型案例、为学生提供实践机会等方式增长学生的创业实践经验,从而全面提升学生的创业

---

① 张颂. 德国大学生的就业指导和实习管理[J]. 河北师范大学学报(教育科学版),2009(12).

能力。据德国经济与劳工部统计,德国50%以上的劳动力通过自主创业实现就业。

(四)帮助学生合理选择职业道路

开设职业发展教育课程的目的就是帮助学生合理选择职业道路。德国学校、劳动部门和信息中心加强合作,通过《现今的职业》《阶梯》等书籍和分门别类的职业资料、影片,向学生详细介绍各种职业的性质、要求、工作范围、发展前景,以及本地区劳动力市场的形势等,让学生对社会可以提供的职业有一个广泛、深入的了解。在帮助学生了解职业世界的同时,指导学生客观评估学习成绩,参加各类心理、生理自测,使学生学会理性地进行自我分析,有的放矢地进行职业选择。在职业咨询员、教师、家长等的帮助下,学生有效地协调能力与兴趣、爱好、客观条件与主观愿望、供与需等各种矛盾,重新选择职业,从而使职业选择的过程科学、合理、系统。教师指导学生书写求职信的格式、内容、技巧等,增加获得面试的可能性;帮助学生调整心理状态,修饰外表形象,练习自我介绍,把握谈话过程,过好面试关;对某些要求笔试的行业,教师还会精选一些试卷,有的放矢地训练学生的计算能力、逻辑推理能力和形象思维能力,以便在笔试中获得良好成绩。

第四节 德国职业发展教育特色

德国职业发展教育的特色多样,主要体现在以下几个方面:

一、以高校为主体进行专业化指导

德国高校具有自主办学的传统,强调教学和科研的独立性,学生就业直接进入市场,学校不需承担任何责任,但这并不意味着高校不关注毕业生的就业,相反,大学深知其中的利害。因为毕业生就业情况的好坏与招生生源和社会捐助息息相关,影响学校的经济效益和社会效益。因此,各高校主动参与就业指导,都设置了形式不同的专门机构,保证必要的经费投入和人员编制,主要针对教学的缺陷和学生的不适应性,通过开设相关的职业指导课程,培养学生正确的职业观、职业操守和职业规范,以提高学生的基本素质和生存能力为目标,帮助大学生进行职业生涯规划和人生设计,重视学生就业前实用职业技能的培训。

职业服务中心是德国高校为大学生提供就业指导的专职机构,其职责范围并不局限于对大学生提供直接的就业咨询和指导服务,还包括举办招聘会、举办和就业有关的讲座和报告会、进行各种招聘的模拟实验以及心理测评等。以德国亚琛工业技术大学为例,该校的就业指导与服务中心隶属于学校人力资源部。它的服务对象既包括在校学生,也包括在校的教职员工,为他们提供相关就业辅导以及职业选择支持与服务。该部门还负责对接企业来校招聘的广告受理,按照一个广告100欧元的标准收取费用,也向用人单位提供在校内宣传和推销的机会,按照一次400欧元的标准收取费用。该部门开展的针对毕业生的日常活动主要有简历指导、联系企业、模拟面试、咨询服务、发布奖学金项目信息等,其中有些项目也要向学生收取10~20欧元不等的费用。20世纪90年代,德国在亚琛工业技术大学还创建了一个规模较大的大学生协会,协会有英文网站,目标是创造一个为大学生提供就业服务的免费平台,工作人员都是大学生。目前,该组织在德国的诸多大学都设有分部。[①] 柏林技术大学对那些毕业后有创业打算的学生还提供体贴入微的培训和服务,学校设有专门的咨询机构,分专业由专人对学生创业的创意、项目的形成、项目风险的预测方法、公司建立所需要的程序等提供细致的咨询和培训。培训与咨询人员全部来自提供创业服务的企业和成功创业的公司。[②]

在德国各高校,从事大学生就业指导工作的人员专业化水平都很高,能够满足大学生对职业指导的需求。专业化的就业指导就是指把大学生分成不同类别,区别加以对待,分类予以指导。除了按常规的专业和学科分类外,更多的是按大学生的就业期望、性格特点、自身条件和要求等进行分类,并针对不同类型的学生进行不同方式、不同内容、不同程度的指导。对职业声望要求高的学生,帮助他们分析职业行情,分析职业发展的动态、前景和趋势,引导大学生正确认识和估价自我,合理"定位",明确职业选择的目标;对重视工资待遇的学生,则帮助他们分析各行各业的薪酬情况,引导大学生

---

① 教育部高校毕业生就业指导考察团. 欧洲高校毕业生就业制度与服务体系建设[J]. 世界教育信息,2012(09).
② 张颂. 德国大学生的就业指导和实习管理[J]. 河北师范大学学报(教育科学版),2009(12).

合理"报价",并向他们传授面谈待遇的技巧等;而对有自卑感的学生,则鼓励他们增强自信心,学会心理调适,化解心理危机。在职业指导中,通过开展一对一面谈、性向测评等方式,了解大学生的兴趣、特长、能力、气质、价值观等个性特点,引导他们正确认识和评价自我,纠正认知偏差,调整心理误区,扬长避短,充分展示个性,实现人——职的最佳匹配。

除了对在校大学生进行就业指导外,德国的高校还非常注重为高中毕业生提供入大学前的咨询服务。高校每年都举办面向高中毕业生的入学咨询服务活动,其内容主要是为高中毕业生提供包括学校专业设置情况介绍、学生如何选读相应专业、各专业就业前景以及如何设计职业生涯等咨询服务,为学生实现成功就业打下良好基础。

二、充分利用社会资源

德国就业指导的一个明显特点,就是充分利用各种社会资源,形成一个规范有序、高效合理和多元参与的社会化就业服务体系。

1.企业积极配合

德国企业积极配合大学生就业工作,具有较强的社会责任意识。在德国的社会教育观念里,企业对高校的教育、教学和就业承担着一定的社会义务。企业密切同德国高校合作进行各种科研活动,为高校提供大量的科研经费,甚至直接在相关高校设立实验室,充分利用高校的人才和科技储备为企业服务。企业主动为大学生提供顶岗带薪的实习岗位,选派有经验的专家指导学生,以提高其职业适应能力为目标,重视培养大学生的动手能力、创造能力和设计分析能力。企业之所以愿意接收大学生实习,主要原因有两个:第一,德国政府对提供实习位置的企业都有不同的税收减免的鼓励;第二,接受实习生也是企业节约人力成本的措施。另外,一些用人单位通过实习发现了人才,为了留住这些人才,还资助他们完成学业。

德国企业还乐意接受大学生在企业里做毕业论文。在德国,学生的毕业论文可以在学校按照老师给的题目写,也可以在学校批准的情况下在企业里完成。在企业里做论文实际上是互利的事情。企业根据自身急需解决的问题列出论文选题,学生就可以从中选择自己的论文题目,这样既锻炼了

自己的实际问题解决能力,也使得被企业录用的概率大增。部分大学生毕业前就确定了劳动雇佣关系。

2.基金会等社会组织提供经费支持

德国社会组织范围广、规模大、类型多、历史悠久。早在1995年,德国社会组织(不包括宗教团体)的经济规模就达到944亿美元,占国家GDP的3.9%。在众多的社会组织中,基金会的地位举足轻重。2010年,德国有合法登记的基金会达1.5万多个,其中95%是公益性的,5%是非公益性的私人家族基金会。没有合法形式的基金会多达2.5万多个。所谓合法登记的基金会是按民法规定以私人名义成立,发起人注入基金,有权决定组织机构、理事会成员、运作方式和活动范围,但基金与发起人财产脱钩,为社会所有,政府派员参加监事会,并要求基金会提供年度报告,监督其是否按照宗旨、章程规定运作。没有合法形式的基金会,主要包括以信托方式成立的基金会,以有限责任公司名义成立的基金会以及以社团名义成立的基金会等。① 这些基金会为德国高校就业指导提供了大量经费支持。

3.私人介绍所是重要补充

1998年以前,联邦劳工部是唯一合法的提供就业指导和安置服务的部门,垄断结束后,私人介绍所得到快速发展。德国于1994年出现私人介绍所,它的运营需要经劳工部的批准注册,多数属于营利性机构,但是只面向企业一方收费,是求职者与用人单位之间联系的桥梁。私人介绍所具有较强的竞争力,它的优势主要体现在服务的范围广、灵活性强。有效补充了政府、企业以及学校服务的不足之处。私人介绍所可以为毕业生开展各种职业测评服务,并解释测评结果,为毕业生设计职业发展目标,帮助毕业生提高求职技巧并进行有效的就业决策等。私人介绍所发挥作用的另一个领域是发布职业信息,其中一些是由联邦就业服务局签约的,此外,书籍,杂志,CD-ROM和其他媒体的商业市场也在增长。私人介绍所提供的这些服务与政府和高校为学生提供的就业政策措施形成合力,是职业发展教育的重要补充。

---

① 张凤有.德国大学生就业工作考察报告[J].中国大学生就业,2010(S1).

三、重视实用技能的培训

培训是德国大学生就业指导的一大"亮点",有利于大学生更快地适应新的工作岗位。在德国,无论政府、学校还是企业,都非常重视对毕业生进行实用技能方面的培训。政府就业指导部门通过开设培训班和设立市场学院等形式,聘请企业的高层主管、工程师、设计师等担任培训师资,根据社会各行各业的需求,对学生进行各种实用能力的培训。这些实用课程的学分,占学生毕业所需学分18%左右,增加了毕业生工作的"附加值",也缩短了毕业生就业后的适应期,使毕业生在市场上很受欢迎。德国下萨克森州政府为大学生提供各种职业的入职培训,比如生物工程和材料等专业,培训教师经常是各个行业联合会的成员,有利于学生把自己的专业和未来的职业更好地结合起来。高校也通过设置不同形式的课程来提供培训,同时在互联网上提供下载课程或专业书籍以帮助就业。德国下萨克森州的汉诺威科学技术大学等一些学校每年定期举办校企手牵手活动,一方面便于学生找工作,更重要的是企业能为学生提供免费的实习机会,以提高学生的动手实践能力。柏林技术大学为学生定期开办讲座和实训,内容既包括如何制作简历、如何应对面试、如何和企业就工资和待遇进行谈判等具体问题,也有相关专业的发展趋势等。主持讲座和实训的人员全部来自校外的企业和管理部门,如劳工局大学生就业管理部门、银行和保险公司的人事管理部门和毕业生工作介绍公司等,内容针对性强,非常实用。

四、强调发展性

强调发展性是指重视人与职业的和谐发展,力求人在职场中有广阔的个人发展空间,个人能力、创造性和主动性能得以充分发挥等。在具体的就业指导工作中,则注重引导学生将个人的发展前途、发展空间和企业的发展前景、企业的潜力和培训体系等因素作为择业的重要条件,重视企业文化和管理理念对个人成长发展的作用,并把就业指导贯穿于学生职业生涯规划和人生规划当中。从进入大学起,就业指导人员就主动对学生进行性向测评,了解其特长、兴趣、爱好、能力等,建立学生个人的特性档案,帮助他们做好学业的发展计划和职业发展的规划,并结合学生的性格特征和职业意向,

为其设计科学合理的课程结构,重视培养其终身学习能力、适应能力、创造能力、管理沟通能力、团队协作精神以及各种职业技能等。① 面对经济社会发展带来的职业领域的变革及对技术技能型人才的能力个素质要求的转变,德国职业发展教育注重学生的职业能力培养,包括对专业能力、社会能力、方法能力、学习能力等的综合培养,以使学习者能够更好地适应经济社会发展变化。

五、具有全纳性

德国的职业教育作为社会融合的重要推力,具有"全纳性"的特点。"全纳教育"作为一种教育理念,指的是实施一种无排斥、无歧视、无分类的教育以促进社会融合。德国不仅要向"被社会忽视的人群"(即那些学习能力较差的弱者、残疾人、移民、女性等)提供更多接受职业教育的机会,而且还要向那些实践动手能力强的年轻人(即技能的"天才""精英"等)提供"职业英才计划"以及优秀毕业生嘉奖等项目,出台多种激励措施并培养其成为高素质技术技能型人才,进而推动社会融合。例如,针对大学辍学者,德国联邦教育与研究部门实施了"工作启动着+培训市场结构"项目,其中一个关注点就是吸引大学辍学学生到中小型企业参加职业培训。这一方面帮助辍学大学生得到职业教育与培训机会,另一方面缓解了中小型企业培训场地闲置带来的困难,满足企业的用人需求。针对年轻父母,则提供兼职职业培训。根据《联邦职业教育法》第八款的规定,向民众提供参加兼职职业培训的机会,尤其是青年父母。兼职职业培训帮助青年父母将职业培训同家庭责任相联系,具有灵活性。针对残疾群体,《联邦职业教育法》和《手工艺法》规定必须考虑残疾人担任特殊需求,在特定的培训职业领域对残疾人进行培训。2011年6月,德国实施《联合国残疾人权利公约》全国行动计划,进一步促进残疾人融入社会。在该行动计划下,通过"全纳倡议"等项目的实施,增加了残疾人在基于企业的培训和企业有关的培训中的参与。在推动残疾人与社会的融合方面,《德国社会规范》规定残疾青年人应得到更多的支持,除了国家实施的一系列职业导向和咨询服务外,还与特殊学校的第三方提供者合

---

① 王保义.中德大学生就业指导比较研究[J].高等工程教育研究,2004(04).

作制定职业导向措施,如果由于残疾程度和类型导师企业不适合开展针对性职业培训,则可以根据个人需求在非企业住宅性培训或基地与继续培训组织中获得职业资格证书。①

德国联邦劳工部提供的职业指导服务向所有人开放,服务对象不仅包括在校学生、未就业成年人还包括就业人员,除此之外,还有针对特殊群体、残障人士的服务。2001年,德国联邦政府、企业协会和工会成立了工作、培训和竞争力联盟,建立职业教育背景下的终身学习框架,重点关注以往被忽视的已就业人员的指导服务。此外,面对出生率的下降和预期寿命的延长,德国开始关注老年工人的就业指导服务,旨在鼓励老年工人参与职业指导服务和应对退休延迟。

六、与信息技术深度融合

在数字化社会和工业4.0的大背景下,德国职业发展教育与信息技术深度融合,不仅体现在其职业指导服务的提供方式上,也体现在其职业人才的培养方面。德国的就业指导服务受到一系列信息技术和其他自助服务的支持。例如就业研究中心基于数据调查得出中长期劳动力市场需求预测,建立关于培训机会、学徒和培训职位空缺的数据库,利于计算机进行职业选择和其他自我探索。就业办公室下设有职业信息中心,无论是青年客户还是成年客户都在职业信息中心进行独立的职业探索。普通中学和实科中学的学生在14至15岁以班级为单位到职业信息中心进行职业探索。文理中学的学生通常根据自己的时间安排前往职业信息中心进行职业探索。无论是单独还是成组参加,他们首先都会先了解职业信息中心以及如何使用其资源。每个职业指导官负责五到六所学校。他们的演讲主题涉及职业信息中心服务到职业决策技能等方面。指导人员还给普通中学及实科中学的学生讲授"劳动经济学与技术"课程。职业信息中心有一个称为STEP-PLUS的计算机化的职业指导工具,专为初中和高中学生设计,将自我评估的兴趣与大约250个职业的需求进行比较,帮助学生与职业指导人员的对话做好

---

① 德国职业教育双元制中国本土化创新研究编写组.德国职业教育双元制中国本土化创新研究[M].北京:人民出版社,2017:59.

准备。

人才培养方面,德国进行教育改革推进职业教育4.0,迎接职业教育数字化转型发展。职业教育4.0是德国在推进工业4.0过程中形成的概念,它突出人才的数字技术能力,同时强调人才的社会能力和个人能力。职业教育4.0聚焦于数字化劳动对职业资格与能力的要求,以及在此基础上的职业教育标准与规范、教学内容与资源及教育方式方法的转变。[①] 2016年,德国联邦教研部在《面向数字化知识社会的教育行动》框架内启动实施了《"职业教育4.0"框架倡议》,旨在研究数字化发展对相关职业资格要求的变化,推动职业教育适应经济发展日益数字化、网络化的要求。在教学方面,开发适应需求的应用于职业教育与培训的学习与教学方案,包括移动学习、贴近劳动岗位的学习以及基于互联网的相关技术支持下的教学,为职业教育实践提供新的数字化的学习和教学方案。

思考题:

1.德国职业发展教育的政策是怎样的?
2.德国职业发展教育课程的特点有哪些?
3.德国职业发展教育的特色是什么?

推荐书目:

1.王保义.中德大学生就业指导比较研究[J].高等工程教育研究,2004(04).

3.傅小芳.德国基础教育阶段的职业指导课程[J].教育理论与实践,2005(8).

4.张凤有.德国大学生就业工作考察报告[J].中国大学生就业,2010(S1).

5.教育部高校毕业生就业指导考察团.欧洲高校毕业生就业制度与服务体系建设[J].世界教育信息,2012(09).

---

① 殷文,刘红,刘立新.工业4.0背景下德国职业教育发展战略[M].北京:教育科学出版社,2019:4.

国外论文导读与阅读(一):

导读:德国一项针对视力障碍青年的生涯教育项目

作者:拉斯·瓦尔德特劳特(Rath Waldtraut),阿佩尔汉斯·彼得(Appelhans Peter)

论文从三个部分展开。

一是项目背景。在德国,每个残疾人都有接受职业培训的权利。在长期高失业率和劳动力市场不断调整的背景下,尽管德国政府为视障青年提供了针对过渡点时期的扶持项目,但视障人群难以进行职业融合。主要是由于全国性视障中心较少,导致大部分视障青年选择在家附近参加学徒培训或职业培训课程,不利于他们得到视障教师的专业援助。由于学校无法保障大多数视障学生的特殊职业需求,1983年,德国北部的石勒苏益格—荷尔斯泰因州成立了石勒苏益格州视障服务中心,来促使视障青年融入职业培训和工作环境。

二是项目介绍。1986年,该中心指导下的学校启动了为期5年的视障青年职业教育项目,目的在于改善视障青年的学习和生活状况,并确保他们长期的职业融合和就业。该示范项目为学生提供了多元化的咨询服务,例如对个人视力障碍的认知,社会生活技能的学习,职业培训教育等。

三是实施结果与影响。从实施数据来看,该项目提高了视障人士的就业比例;为视障人士成功提供了专家援助和资源支持,尤其是视障领域专业咨询师所提供的个人咨询,还构建了特殊专家关系网。从此以后,视障青年能够在本地实现专业职业训练,而不必前往州外的特殊机构,为视障人士从学校过渡到工作期间需要的咨询和支持奠定了坚实基础。

文献来源:

Rath W, Appelhans P. A Career Education Project in Germany for Youth with Visual Impairments[J]. Re View, 1994(26):29-34.

国外论文导读与阅读(二):

导读:父母行为与青少年职业探索

作者:巴贝尔·克拉克(Bärbel Kracke)

这项研究探讨了父母的教育和行为对青少年职业探索的影响。参与者

是德国中级轨道学校的236名9年级学生。研究结果表明,父母的权威性、对青少年问题的开放性以及父母对职业探索的关注度与子女的职业探索密切相关,而父母的教育背景和青少年性别与青少年的职业探索无关。

导论部分提出了四个研究问题:第一,父母行为以及青少年的探索行为是否随父母的教育背景而变化?第二,父母行为在多大程度上有助于青少年的探索?第三,父母行为和青少年职业探索之间的关系是否随父母的教育背景而变化?第四,父母的哪些行为对青少年的职业发展具有重大影响?

方法部分介绍了研究对象和数据收集方法。研究对象为德国中级轨道学校的236名9年级学生,参加者中,有94名是女生,而142名是男生。平均年龄为15.2岁,只有198名青少年报告了父母的学校教育。职业探索是通过包含自我探索、环境探索以及探索的广度等6个项目的量表来测量的。父母行为的测量包含4个项目,父母对青少年问题的开放度包含5个项目,父母对职业准备的支持度包含6个项目。

结果和讨论部分阐释了问卷调查和统计分析的结果。本研究调查了不同父母教育背景的家庭中各种父母行为与青少年职业探索之间的关系。结果表明,父母教育程度对父母行为没有影响,如对青少年问题的开放态度,父母与青少年之间的对等关系以及父母对职业发展的刺激。与父母教育唯一的关系是权威型父母的养育反映出温暖,支持和自主的行为。以儿童为中心,具有支持性以及父母与青少年具有对等关系的家庭,孩子表现出更积极的探索行为。这种关系独立于父母的教育程度和青少年的性别。

文献来源:

Bärbel Kracke. Parental Behaviors and Adolescents' Career Exploration [J]. The Career Development Quarterly, 1997(45):341-350.

国外论文导读与阅读(三):

导读:低素质的成年人如何规划职业生涯——来自德国叙事研究的发现

作者:彼得·韦伯(Peter C. Webera),亚历山大·科钦布(Alexander J. Kochemb),西尔维·韦伯·豪塞克(and Sylvie Weber-Hauserc)

职业道路,职业发展和成人教育在很大程度上取决于早期生活中的学习和进入劳动力市场的经验。但是在教育和职业背景相对较弱的人群中,人们在如何看待自己的处境以及如何描述、计划和实现自己的职业方面存在差异。基于对低素质成年人的叙事性访谈,本研究描述了个体情况和终身学习与职业发展的方法。本文基于既定的职业概念,说明如何将职业和学习观念的差异理解为情境化的行为。调查显示,内部资源和外部约束对这一群体的教育和职业发展有潜在影响。讨论的重点是职业咨询和指导的后果。

文章分为五部分,分别为引言和理论背景、目标和分析方法、叙事分析结果、研究问题讨论和结论。

引言和理论背景介绍了当前的职业研究通常集中在代际差异上,以找到关于假设的经验证据。少有研究深入探讨人们如何实践其职业生涯或人们如何体验这些过程。作者将职业发展过程理解为主观建构及内外环境制约共同作用的结果。认为在后现代社会中,职业顾问(和其他专业人员)需要有关人们如何体验其教育,工作和职业以及他们如何实现自己的生活和职业的具体知识。从这个意义上讲,职业规划不仅仅是建立一个身份,还可能与我们多元化社会中的各类人的咨询有关。越来越多的人没有高技能的工作和职业机会所要求的技能,那些生活在危险和不稳定状况下的人需要特别注意,因此作者将目光投向低技能人群,了解他们对教育和工作的看法。

第二部分指出进行研究的目的是根据叙事性尝试初步发现低资历背景人士的学习和职业发展过程的动态发展。作者提出四个研究问题,第一,目标人群主观上认为什么对他们的职业问题产生了影响?哪些因素影响了个人职业选择和生活?第二,有关低素质人士及其教育程度或职业成就的发现相当结构化、社会化或个性化,并且大多基于汇总数据。但是,可以根据主观职业兴趣以及人们如何塑造和实施职业来识别差异吗?第三,一方面职业是个人的建构过程。另一方面,我们假设机构机会和制约是相关因素。在个人的职业过程中,个人经验、资源和体制因素有多大程度的联系?第四,假设个人职业生涯的设计是一个能动的过程,需要主观的意义和反思,那么是否可以从这个群体的叙述中识别出行动方案和反思过程?这种"传记行动计划"是什么样的?文章采用内容分析和叙事研究相结合的方法,样本量是对15个人,5个男性和10个年龄在25~42岁的女性,一共进行了23次叙述性访谈。

第三部分为叙事分析的结果。在与给定的演绎代码系统一起进行编码的过程中,产生的数据证实了关于影响低学历群体职业发展的经验知识。教育问题和劳动力市场融入障碍得到了支持。例如,在这种情况下,环境和家庭背景(即社会和文化资本)对于教育和劳动力市场的进入也具有重要意义。教育道路上的早期负面经历影响了整个人生的教育成就。开放编码的第二步和对案例内在动力的解释使我们能够探索案例之间的模式和差异,并发展出关于这一群体的个人如何开展职业的初步类型学。

第四部分是研究问题的讨论。第一个研究问题询问与个人职业行为过程有关的方面。已定职业生涯是个人行动的基础。研究表明,制定职业生涯是一个长期的过程,有时会进行许多尝试以达到更稳定的职业或教育水平,有时会获得一些成功和某种程度的稳定性。所有案例表明,该目标人群的职业不仅与工作和教育相关,而且与家庭、休闲、文化、宗教等其他问题相关,并且人们试图与这些不同领域的人建立联系。人们会采取行动来理解其身份建构中的平行方面,他们正在努力取得连贯性,并尝试在不同的层次(例如工作,教育,家庭)实现自己。对于第二个问题,我们在此提出了可以确定的主观职业兴趣之间的差异,以及人们如何塑造和实施自己的职业。这似乎很重要,因为有时会对群体(如所谓的低素质群体)进行标记和集体对待。例如,根据人们展示自己制定职业生涯的实际方法,我们已经确定了差异。从人们对教育和工作的谈论方式上,这些叙事也反映了这些差异,在某些情况下是指一种更积极的方法,有时带有消极和痛苦的观念。对于某些人来说,寻找替代工作和职业机会的选择似乎非常重要。关于第三个研究问题,我们承认,一方面,个人职业是(心理—社会)建设性的过程;另一方面,我们认为与机构机会和制约因素是相关的。叙述表明个人可以理解为自己职业的演员,但资源却截然不同。除了内部和传记资源之外,制度方面似乎对个人职业生涯的制定有很大影响。但是,今天的个人教育经历,自我概念或生活动机已经面临结构性限制,有时还存在着机会,这些机会对于个人如何(或不能)从事自己的职业至关重要。对于第四项研究问题,我们尝试将叙述性研究与理论研究联系起来。我们认为,个人以两种方式将其职业互动与环境联系起来。一方面,他们根据自己的内在经验和资源将他们计划和做的事情情境化。另一方面,他们根据自己对环境的主观看法,将他们计划和做的事情与背景联系起来。反映并规划自己的资格和职业道路的能力似乎对于完成这项任务至关重要。

第五部分是结论。本研究是基于叙述性研究的探索,提出了一些与咨询实践和理论讨论进一步发展有关的问题。同时,它提供了一个有适应职业和生活特殊问题的群体,发现这些人实现自己职业和生活的实际方式似乎很有趣且重要。当生活和身份的多元化是主要模式,并且集体支持结构受到侵蚀或改变时,可以洞察生活和职业的主观观念的研究和实践可能会非常有意义。

文献来源:

Peter C. Webera, Alexander J. Kochemb and Sylvie Weber-Hauserc. How low-qualified adults enact their career – findings from a narrative study in Germany[J]. British Journal of Guidance & Counselling, 2016(44): 158-170.

(节选的英文原文见附录6)

第六章 国外其他国家职业发展教育

本章要点：
1. 澳大利亚职业发展教育的主要特点；
2. 澳大利亚职业发展教育的蝴蝶模型；
3. 加拿大职业发展教育的课程特色；
4. 新西兰职业发展教育的标准框架。

职业发展教育起源于西方国家，虽然美国、英国、日本、德国对职业发展教育的探索和研究比较成熟，在机构设置和实施策略上都具有高度的系统性和规范性，但是一些正处于职业发展摸索期的国家也能提供一些独特的借鉴价值，如澳大利亚职业发展的蝴蝶模型能激发学生自主性以思考未来职业发展，为其成功规划职业发展起到良好的铺垫作用；加拿大的"现实的系列游戏"让学生预知了未来，对学生未来职业选择有非常大的影响；等等。所以每个国家的职业发展教育都各具特色，都具有适合本国发展特点的教育模式，应从不同角度来探究这些国家职业发展教育的科学性。

第一节 澳大利亚职业发展教育

一、澳大利亚职业发展教育的历史背景

澳大利亚的义务教育具有一定的政治性，是为国家服务的工具。教育所培养的人要达到国家的要求，满足企业的需求。学校教育的对象将是社会的公民，教育在培养方式上注重与企业的需要挂钩。培养学生具有公民

意识,培养学生具备企业所需求的技能,这正是早期生涯教育的萌芽。澳大利亚教育体制建立于19世纪70年代,该体制的构想借鉴了世界其他国家特别是英国的教育体制。1872年,国会指出教育要强调权威、整齐、服从和命令,因此学校毕业生毫无疑问要服从企业的需要,同时也要对企业和国家忠诚。学校、公民和工作之间的联系一直存在于澳大利亚,正因如此,某些形式的职业发展教育已经成为中学课程的一部分。

早在20世纪初,教育既提供学术教育,也提供贸易和家庭艺术方面的教育,这种分流教育满足了当时社会的需求,当时的社会认为那些在行业或贸易领域充当赚钱养家者角色的人,与在家承担家庭工作的人是有区别的,这种分流教育持续到20世纪70年代,随后逐渐衰退。在那时,学校已经引入了职业发展教育,并把培养职业道德与提供工作、职业信息相联系。一些测试已经展开,主要目的是探索年轻人的资质、兴趣与大量的工作之间是否能恰当地相匹配。

20世纪70年代的经济萧条始于制造业部分劳动力市场的衰落,后来扩展到所有的工作领域,这些工作可以通过使用技术而被更有效、更低成本地完成。青年雇佣方式的变化,导致了全职工作机会的减少。伴随经济领域的变化,年轻人的工作理念、工作类型和工作场所的性质也发生了变化。随之,教育更加强调课程与劳动市场的联系,以及现代社会对于个人在社会中角色的关注,因此职业发展教育的模式开始出现。基于发展心理学的研究成果,这种模式承认个人与其所处社会的内在联系对其做出职业决定起到了显著作用。教师要为学生获得知识提供便利,支持年轻人去探索和了解他们各自的需要和期望。

二、澳大利亚职业发展教育的开展[①]

1997年,麦克恩和麦考齐向澳大利亚中小学和大学生涯教育工作人员发布了生涯教育向导,它阐述了1992年澳大利亚教育委员会职业发展教育工作组的成果。将深化对学校体制中职业发展教育的理解作为重点,提出了学校教育应该发展的四个关键要素:一般雇佣性能力、企业教育、职业发

---

① 陶倍帆.澳大利亚职业生涯教育研究[D].上海:华东师范大学,2014:12-14.

展教育、基于社区与工作的学习。职业发展教育开始被学校视为关键的发展领域之一,受到学校的关注。①

2001年,《通往未来的足迹》(Footprints to the Future)建议应该向所有年轻人提供机会去参与专业的职业发展教育。它指出职业发展教育对于年轻人益处颇多,它给予年轻人一些设计巧妙的、可利用的信息,并提供了一些指导服务和后续服务,这些信息和服务把劳动力市场、教育和社会咨询融合起来,可以帮助年轻人做出恰当的选择。报告同时指出,如果学校想要提供高质量的职业发展教育服务,那么就应该由那些具有合适资格和技能的人们来提供,并且把职业发展服务融入课程中。报告认识到向年轻人提供职业发展教育的重要性,认为应向所有年轻人提供职业发展教育的指导和服务。

2003年,《技能融合》(Bridging the Skills Divide)报告指出所有的中学生都应该获得经过专业培训、具有良好知识结构的生涯顾问的辅导,不管这些职业发展顾问是在学校内,还是通过其他渠道(企业合作关系或外部资源配置)工作。同时,报告指出生涯发展单元应该成为教师教育课程的一部分。该报告强调所有中学生都应当获得来自于专业工作人员的职业发展教育辅导,因此教师也应加强职业发展教育课程的学习。

2003年,经济合作组织报告澳大利亚在评价其职业发展教育服务和项目时,建议所有州和领地的所有学校都应该招募一名具有职业发展教育与指导专业背景的工作人员,因此,学校应扩展向职业发展教育实践者所提供的教育。

《学会工作》(Learning to Work)报告也体现了澳大利亚政府对提高生涯教育工作的支持。所有的州和领地都支持政府的决定,有些州和领地也在发展地方性的课程。2004年《学会工作》报告提出越来越多的人已达成共识,认为学生能够成功地完成离校转变的一个最为重要的因素是有效的生涯教育服务。职业发展教育应该成为学校核心课程中强制性的一部分,并由专业的职业指导教师教授。委员会建议所有中学都至少有一位全职的、

---

① 刘欢. 英、美、澳初中物理教材中职业生涯教育内容比较研究及启示[D].武汉:华中师范大学,2018.

专业的职业发展顾问,这个专业顾问具有相关专业的背景,将在学校里提供一个详细的职业发展教育服务,并与学校里职业发展教育和培训的协调者合作。

2004年,《生涯转变和服务框架报告》(Career and Transition Services Framework)认为年轻人想要完成从学校到继续教育、培训和雇佣的转变,以及做出有关工作、课程、职业路径的重要决定,需要从专业的顾问处获取信息和支持。满足年轻人需要的生涯教育必须由经过专业培训,并且能从社区、学校获得支持,由尽职尽责的工作人员来实施。这些工作人员不仅仅作为职业指导教师,还需要在学校里担任其他重要的角色,以此使他们职业指导教师的角色发挥更大的影响作用。职业发展教育不仅是必需的,而且应当在学校教育中占据重要地位,并发挥更大的作用。

为了职业发展教育得到更好的实施,澳大利亚联邦政府也出台了一系列有关举措。一是制定了生涯教育的国家标准,形成了对生涯教育实践者的评定过程;二是联邦政府对于澳大利亚生涯发展蓝图进行了一些创造和试验,这个蓝图是以引领世界生涯教育的加拿大生涯教育研究成果为基础;三是联邦政府建立了旨在向职业发展实践者以及年轻人提供建议的职业发展研究机构;四是联邦政府提供奖学金来保证提供职业发展教育的教师能够获得深造及短期在企业实习的机会。

由此可见,在澳大利亚国内,人们不断提升对职业发展教育重要性的认识,国家和学校也逐渐提高职业发展教育的地位。职业发展教育应该面对所有学生,并成为核心课程的一部分,应该由专业的职业发展教育工作人员来提供,并为这些工作人员创造深造和再学习的机会。[①]

三、澳大利亚职业发展教育政策

澳大利亚制定了《职业发展纲要》,对职业成熟程度、职业发展教育的内容、考试及评估等方面做出了具体规定。还开设了职业和个人发展课程,内容包括正确评价自己的能力、潜力、需要和志向,培养自控和自助能力;制订

---

① 刘欢.英、美、澳初中物理教材中职业生涯教育内容比较研究及启示[D].武汉:华中师范大学,2018.

个人未来发展计划;将职业和劳动力市场信息渗透到各学科中,使课程内容与日常生活密切相关,培养学生的研究思考能力及正确的生活态度等。① 近些年来还采取了一系列的政策以加强学生的职业辅导,如颁布了《学校教育国家战略的阿德莱德宣言》、总理的青年道路行动计划报告《通往未来的足迹》,各州或联邦就业教育培训部签订了《前行协约》以使所有学生明确自己的发展方向。

为了使生涯辅导实践与国际接轨,澳大利亚吸收、借鉴了国外的一些职业辅导政策。如《澳大利亚职业发展蓝图》就是借鉴加拿大的《加拿大生活/工作蓝图设计》和美国国家职业信息统筹委员会的指导方针改编而成的;同样,澳大利亚版《真实的游戏》也是国际合作的结果。这些国家层面上的政策极大地推动了该国职业辅导的开展,使各类职业辅导制度化、系统化。同时,在推进职业发展教育的过程中,除颁布法令保障其顺利实施外,政府还提供了大量的资金支持。②

四、澳大利亚职业发展教育实施机构

澳大利亚有一个联邦制的机构,主要的政府职责分配给联邦、六个州和两个领地。州负责学校教育、联邦负责提供资金支持。每个州都有自己制定课程的权力。州还有立法权,包括向私人的职业发展教育机构分配课程。提供雇佣服务是联邦的职责,但有些州也会提供雇佣服务。

职业辅导包括在中小学、大学和学院、培训机构、公共雇佣服务、公司、志愿或社区部分及私人机构所提供的服务。许多职业辅导服务还是集中在学校,由州领导管辖。职业发展教育和培训体系,尤其是技术与继续教育学院(TAFE)和大学也有生涯辅导服务。联邦雇佣服务已经以合同制的形式交给私立的机构。澳大利亚职业辅导领域中私立部分所占的比例比某些OECD国家高。

澳大利亚职业发展教育主要在中小学进行,大学或继续教育学院也提

---

① 林雪治,王敏.大学生职业生涯发展教育立法现状及对策研究[J].吉首大学学报(社会科学版),2015,36(S1):199-201.
② 刘要悟,陈鹏.澳大利亚高校生涯辅导实施状况及其启示[J].湖南师范大学教育科学学报,2013,12(04):103-107.

供职业发展教育。私立的职业发展教育服务机构通过竞标,签订合同,也可以提供职业发展教育。

许多联邦、州和领地机构都为人们开展与发展职业服务,但是没有一个机构是专门为人们整个生命历程提供职业信息、辅导、咨询服务而存在的。

澳大利亚职业辅导服务的主要协调机构是教育、雇佣、培训和青年事务委员会(Ministerial Council On Education, Employment Training And Youth Affairs, MCEETYA),它把教育部、雇佣部、培训部和青年事务部在联邦政府层面、州层面的档案集中在一起。1998年,它的国家职业小组颁布一系列职业发展教育和咨询服务原则,它把这些原则看作是"将在帮助人们成为终身学习者,在工作、学习之间转化,并能适应一个新的不断变化的境况中起到一个关键作用"。1999年,MCEETYA发布了一系列学校教育目标《阿德莱德宣言》,宣言中包括所有离校者应该"具备与雇佣相关的技能、把工作环境、职业选择和路径作为职业发展教育与培训、继续教育、雇佣和终身学习的一个基础,并对职业发展教育与培训、继续教育、雇佣和终身学习有一个积极的态度"。

澳大利亚教育、科学、培训部(The Department of Education, science and training)在全国都能使用的职业信息、辅导、咨询服务提供政策、财政、项目发展方面扮演了重要角色。澳大利亚雇佣和工作关系部(The Department of Employment and Workplace Relations)负责管理公共雇佣服务,也在提供基于职业的劳动市场信息中发挥了重大作用。

福利部(Center link)是传播服务的入口,通过这个入口能够访问由教育、科学、培训部所管理和赞助的服务。

澳大利亚国家培训委员会(Australian National Training Authority)负责职业发展教育与培训(VET)的政策构想和财政支持。它建于1994年,是一个有企业董事会的联邦法定当局,旨在加强全国对于职业发展教育和培训的关注,它由联邦、州和领地中负责政策领域的部长组成。

国防部队招募组织(The Defense Force Recruiting Organization)向对澳大利亚国防部队中的职业感兴趣的公民提供辅导和信息。

家庭和社区服务(family and community services)负责提供社区服务,如为满足残疾者能被雇佣的需要所提供的社区服务。

澳大利亚政府委员会是澳大利亚最高的跨政府论坛,由联邦总理、州总理、领地首席部长和澳大利亚地方政府协会主席组成。它的职责是发布、发展和指导有全国意义的政策改革,这些政策改革也需要澳大利亚政府的合作。

五、澳大利亚职业发展教育项目的组成要素

职业发展教育通过一些教育项目来使学生获得知识、技能和态度的发展,来帮助他们有效地应对未来的职业选择及其他人生抉择。一个综合性的职业发展教育项目包括以下部分:

(一)自我意识活动(self awareness)

自我意识活动是让学生识别自己的个人属性,如身体特征、智力特征、情感特征、技能以及兴趣和价值观等,挖掘他们的个人属性与能够有效参与到不同的人生、工作境况中所需要的技能之间的关系,评价那些对他们在不同的人生境况或工作境况中学习造成影响的策略和条件。

(二)机遇意识活动(opportunity awareness)

机遇意识活动就是让学生调查、探索、体验大量的工作以及这些工作中所蕴含的各种各样的路径。这些活动包括让学生体验、研究不同的工作环境,给予学生调查一系列职业及教育、培训的机会,让学生分析大量工作中历史性的变化。

(三)决定学习(decision learning)

决定学习即学习如何做出决定的活动,让学生探索其他人是如何做出决定以及对一个人做决定的过程有影响的因素、确定适合自己的决策风格和策略、生成自己的一系列与职业相关的选择。

(四)过渡学习(transition learning)

过渡学习涉及学生应付新形势所需要的意识和技能,不管这些新形势是否是学生渴望遇见的。过渡学习活动包括让学生识别他们一生中可能遇到的在他们人生规划内外所发生的人生、工作的转变,让学生探索其他人如何应对转变,从而发展一些技能来有效地管理一系列可预见及不可预见的转变,如解决问题的技能,构建人际关系网络的技能。

由此可见,一个全面的职业发展教育项目要使学生能够参与到一系列

认识自我、认识职业、做出决定、管理人生转变的活动,从而做出与职业相关的恰当的决定并有效地管理人生中的变化。①

六、澳大利亚大学职业发展教育的实施

作为一个自治的机构,每一个大学都自主决定提供给学生职业发展辅导。事实上,所有的大学都有各自的职业服务,但其职责和来源不同。有些是单独的服务,有些是与个人咨询项目相融合。大学愈来愈重的财政压力已经使大部分服务的资金减少。因此,它们在寻求一些传递服务的更为划算的途径。许多大学已经建立了自己的网站,并更多地通过电子形式来提供它们的服务。一些大学把它们的服务以收费的形式提供给使用者,而不是它们的学生。对于应聘人员来说,他们最好具有研究生学历水平的职业辅导资格,但研究生学历并非是必需的。

一些大学已经引入了学分制职业发展教育管理课程,如皇家墨尔本理工大学、莫道克大学、埃迪斯科文大学。其他一些大学也提供更短期的、不为修学分的课程。相当多的大学在与课程相关的发展方面已经引入了档案体制,与中小学引入的档案体制平行,这个体制不仅要求学生记录他们正在学习的内容,而且还要记录通过这些学习所获得的与工作相关的能力。学校可以通过截屏材料或者是电子版材料,在班级层面上开展对于这个过程的支持。生涯服务明显地参与到发展与执行这些举措的过程中。

澳大利亚毕业生生涯协会(The Graduate Careers Council of Australia)集中提供大学生涯服务,其中包括提供信息资源。这个协会也执行由联邦政府拨款的年度毕业生目的地调查。这些调查数据不仅对生涯辅导有用,同样也被一些大学用以课程发展评论上,这些都会提高在制度框架下生涯服务的重要性。

"起作用的职业"(careers that work)是维多利亚州皇家墨尔本理工大学生涯管理和雇佣单元的一个创新课程,它通过背景课程(context curriculum)来提供。背景课程占4个学分,是皇家墨尔本理工大学为使所有大学生参与跨学科选修课程而采取的一个举措。

---

① 陶倍帆.澳大利亚职业生涯教育研究[D].上海:华东师范大学,2014:12-14.

"起作用的职业"这门课程也通过一个为期13周的集中性项目来进行,该项目由皇家墨尔本理工大学为澳大利亚本土及国际项目提供,并且已经在马来西亚和新加坡实施。

"起作用的职业"这门课程是为了帮助所有学生发展对于自己的认知和理解,对于多种多样的工作的认知和理解,能够分析、计划和执行职业决定,并能管理工作中的转变。学生要去调查21世纪工作的性质,包括判断劳动力市场的发展趋势、影响职业和工作的历史性的、社会性的要素,还要了解有关的工作和立法方面的理论。学生要依据当前的价值观、兴趣、能力形成职业发展规划,并确定他们还需要了解的内容,才能够做出关于工作的决定。寻找工作策略的技能是通过简历撰写、面试技巧和网络化的方式发展起来的。按照学生对课堂活动的贡献、有关工作和职业进程的论文和研究报告,以及一个职业文件夹(包含了详细职业规划及简单工作的申请和简历)来对他们进行评价。皇家墨尔本理工大学职业发展教育课程的成功使得其他大学(如莫道克大学等)引入了与"起作用的职业"相似的其他课程。①

七、职业发展的蝴蝶模型

由于时代进步以及研究者的不懈努力,职业发展的混沌理论问世后又不断衍生和扩充,职业发展的蝴蝶模型(the butterfly model of careers)便产生于此。"蝴蝶模型"源自20世纪60年代美国著名气象专家洛仑兹(Lorenz)发现的第一个混沌吸引子(chaotic at tractor),因形状与蝴蝶相像,洛仑兹将其命名为蝴蝶吸引子(butterfly at tractor)。见图6-1。

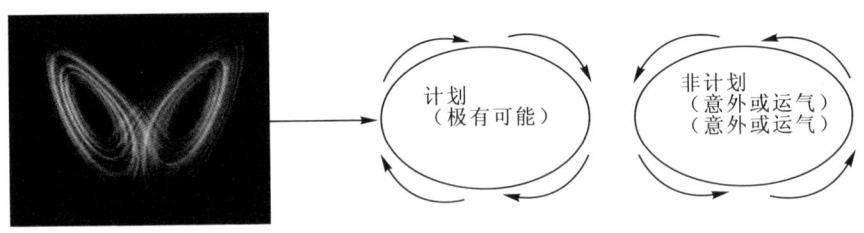

图6-1 蝴蝶模型的演化图

① 陶倍帆.澳大利亚职业生涯教育研究[D].上海:华东师范大学,2014:12-14.

蝴蝶吸引子左边像一个同心圆,运动到一定时候会突然跳到图案右边,接着又返回——"稳定性"与"内在不确定性"纠缠于其中。蝴蝶模型与洛仑兹蝴蝶吸引子类似,在它的轨道上没有起点也没有终点,图6-1中的箭头预示着运动的必然性和突变即将发生的可能性。同时,通过关联计划(planned)和非计划(unplanned),蝴蝶模型强调对极有可能(稳定性)和意外(内在不确定性)事件的处理,这在本质上与蝴蝶吸引子相同。在澳大利亚,职业生涯蝴蝶模型应用的对象主要是10年级学生,也在个人咨询中应用,包括一些具体的操作步骤和操作图。[①]

(一)操作步骤——课堂型

(1)在一张学习单上,要求学生描绘出他们设想的自己一年、两年、三年和五年后的生活和工作情况;

(2)学生将步骤1中提到的工作和生活计划做成卡片;

(3)学生拿到一些包含可能发生的事件的"机会卡片"(由教师提前准备);

(4)学生讨论这些事件发生的可能性;

(5)学生列举一些生活中关于计划和偶然的例子,如某个家庭成员的职业路径或一些他们父母相遇的故事;[②]

(6)教师在白板上展示蝴蝶模型图,大家一起讨论它的事实真相;

(7)学生或个人或成对或组成小群体,用一些他们亲身经历或臆想的情况循着圆圈的线条填充模型:在模型左边圆圈12点钟位置上,学生填写一个他们计划好的终极目标(见图6-2);在3点钟位置上,要求学生填写此时起3年后计划取得的成果。在6点钟位置上,填写此时起6年后计划取得的成果,在9点钟位置上填写此时起9年后计划取得的成果;接着,要求每个学生从小纸盒中抽出一张机会卡片,并读懂它;在模型右边圆圈6点钟位置上,要求学生填写这件事情(指中机会卡片中的事件);要求学生考虑这件事对他们的计划产生的影响,并把这种影响填写在模型右边圆圈12点钟位置上;然后,要求学生沿着"机会圈"逆时针运动,在中间与计划圈相遇;在相遇

---

① 唐振华,刘珊珊.澳大利亚职业生涯教育的"蝴蝶模型":介绍及启示[J].职业技术教育,2011(32):92-95.

② 刘鹏志,金琦.蝴蝶模型在生涯教育课中的应用[J].中小学心理健康教育,2018(06):17-19.

的位置,要求学生并靠着原始计划填写修改的3年后的计划;尔后,要求学生在左边6点钟位置填写修改的6年后的计划,在9点钟位置填写修改的9年后的计划;待以上诸项完成,教师应鼓励学生领会原始计划与修改计划的差异之处(以及有时与原始计划相比,修改计划的进步之处)。①

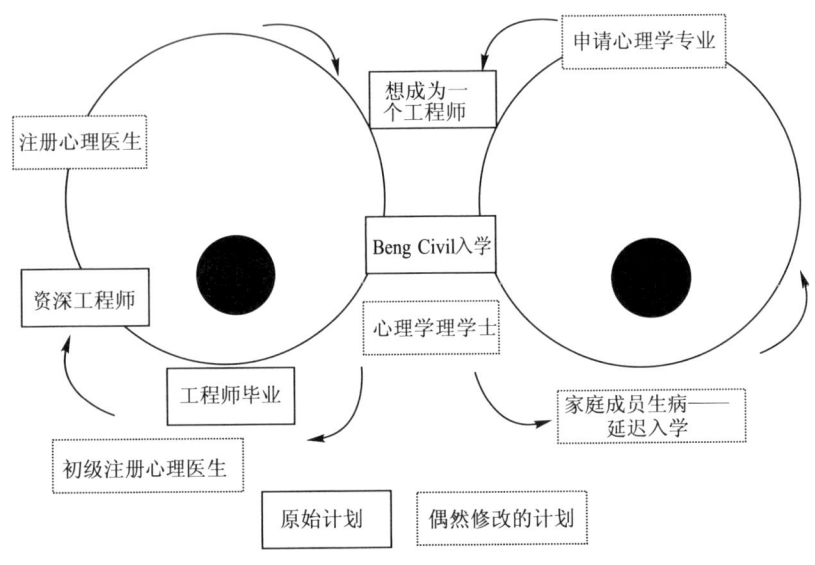

图 6-2 蝴蝶模型的实际工作案例

(二)评析

1. 设计与实施过程中"学生本位"思想的贯穿与融合

从整个过程的设计看,职业发展的蝴蝶模型结合了多种教学方法,如讲授法、讨论法、案例法等,全体学生在教师引导下积极参与教学活动。与此同时,采取目标分解的方式交互运用基于自我目标的和随机抽取的案例填充蝴蝶模型图,既让学生发挥主观能动性有意识思虑未来发展,又使其在学习中树立起关注"意外"事件的意识,为成功规划自我生涯起到良好的铺垫作用。②

---

① 华德仁.基于内外因和混沌理论的大学生创业教育双循环发展模式探究[J].职教通讯,2014:52-54.

② 唐振华,刘珊珊.澳大利亚职业生涯教育的"蝴蝶模型":介绍及启示[J].职业技术教育,2011(32):92-95.

2. 职业发展教育微观领域的延展与推进

一方面,职业发展的蝴蝶模型因借鉴了生涯混沌理论的核心框架,吸收了它的要素内涵,同时又兼备着蝴蝶模型独有的特征,一定程度上丰富和延展了职业发展教育理论。另一方面,它的操作图和具体步骤给职业发展教育教师及学生提供了一种新的实践导向,用以通往理解那些复杂晦涩、准确反映现代职业世界的生涯混沌理论之路,推进了职业发展教育混沌理论在学校层面职业发展教育领域(职业发展教育在宏观上包括社会层面与学校层面的生涯教育,单就学校层面而言只是职业发展教育的一个微观领域)的发展。

3. 传统职业发展教育方式的挑战与革新

绝大部分传统的职业发展教育只强调职业的确定性、稳定性、有序性,而忽略职业的不确定性、动荡性、无序性,且坚信对未来的长久规划能促使我们积极前进。这种方式阐释静态、线性的职业世界尚可,但在急速变化的环境中,面对不按固定逻辑和既定路线发展的现代职业世界显然已力不从心。职业发展教育的蝴蝶模型将对"极有可能"(the likely)的事件与"意外"(the contingent)事件的规划和关注结合,将职业发展的目的性和突创性有机联结,运用整体论和辩证法思想,统一有序和无序、稳定和动荡、确定和意外,摆脱了严格的因果观和实证主义还原论的桎梏。

此外,职业发展的蝴蝶模型还有如下特点:第一,课堂的设计与实施对教师要求非常高,教师要熟练掌握职业发展的混沌理论、蝴蝶模型的相关知识;除引导学生配合外,还需及时将课程的结果转化成其学习的内在动机,以满足后续职业发展教育学习的需要。第二,理论基础比较深奥,操作程序较为烦琐;同时,教师提前准备好的待考虑的偶然事件可能不具典型性,超过学生阅历所及。第三,整个操作流程缺少学生自我总结、自我表达的环节。[①]

---

① 唐振华,刘珊珊.澳大利亚职业生涯教育的"蝴蝶模型":介绍及启示[J].职业技术教育,2011(32):92-95.

八、澳大利亚职业发展教育的主要特点

(一)早期性

澳大利亚职业发展教育的早期性主要表现在两个方面:

一是职业发展从中小学就开始。大学的职业辅导是中小学职业辅导的延续,需要有一定基础。澳大利亚在小学、中学阶段就设有职业发展教育课程和生涯辅导活动,向学生介绍不断变化的职业市场及社会需求,指导学生有针对性地选定升学或就业目标。学生升学时,学校提供多种心理测验帮助学生了解自己的兴趣爱好、能力和人格特征等,并为学生报考合适的学校和学科提供参考意见,这为今后大学生的生涯规划起到了启蒙作用。

二是职业辅导从大学生入学就开始。这不仅能帮助大学生在学习过程中确定明确的职业目标和职业规划,还能使他们在校期间不断调整自己的行动并学会适应、学会决策,以更好地达到自己的职业目标。[①]

(二)全面性

从辅导对象看,澳大利亚的职业发展教育不仅面向本科生,也面向研究生及留学生;不仅面向即将毕业的学生,也面向入学新生和毕业后两年的学生及已工作的校友。从辅导内容看,不仅涉及面试技巧、简历撰写等,还通过个人辅导帮助学生明确职业目标,确定潜在的职业兴趣,进行课程选择;不仅给毕业生提供全职工作信息,还为在读生提供兼职、假期工作、临时工作及实习机会等。从辅导方式看,不仅有讲座、小组研讨会,还有个人咨询辅导;不仅可进行非预约的短时指导,还可接受预约个人指导;不仅提供图书馆资源,还提供在线的视频、音频资源以及校友的"人脉资源"。

(三)网络化

澳大利亚高校基本实现了职业辅导的网络化。有关职业规划的视频、音频等资料非常健全,学生从学校生涯中心的网站上可以非常清楚地了解该中心职业辅导的每一个细节并依此确定自己需要的服务。对于需要预约的服务可以在线进行预约,有些咨询可在网上直接进行。这些都使得职业

---

① 刘要悟,陈鹏.澳大利亚高校生涯辅导实施状况及其启示[J].湖南师范大学教育科学学报,2013(12):105-109.

辅导更加快捷、方便、灵活、有效,真正体现了职业辅导"以生为本""重在服务""讲求实效"的精神。

(四)协同性

澳大利亚高校的职业辅导并不单独依靠生涯中心,而是围绕职业发展中心,其他部门也参与其中并相互协调合作进行。例如,许多高校的职业发展中心与档案部门联合对学生、毕业生及校友的推荐信、信用档案等资料进行管理;校友会也与职业发展中心合作加强学校、校友与招聘单位之间的联系,校友关心并参与对在校生的指导,而校友会里校友的培训及一些职业辅导方面的服务也可由职业发展中心负责。再如,有些高校对学校工作人员的职业辅导由职业发展中心与人力资源部门共同进行,学校人力资源部门为学校工作人员提供职业发展的机会,职业发展中心则为学校工作人员提供这些服务的宣传并组织相应的培训或指导。①

(五)针对性

澳大利亚高校的职业辅导注重对学生的个人辅导,根据辅导对象的特点及其所遇到的具体问题给予有针对性的辅导。主要表现为:

一是利用各种心理测评工具指导大学生对自己的兴趣、爱好、人格特征等进行科学的测量和评估,②并对自己进行合理的角色定位,以帮助学生更好地进行职业生涯规划;

二是对不同的对象提供不同的服务,如给大一至大三的学生提供职业探索服务,③给毕业生提供就业指导,给留学生提供留学、兼职、升学信息,给校友提供职业信息,为学校工作人员提供挖掘潜能的工作,等等;

三是为特殊群体提供专门的生涯服务,有些大学有专门为残疾学生提供的职业探索辅导、就业服务指导等,有些大学还为留学生提供跨国工作信息,并开展专门针对留学生的职业辅导。④

---

①③ 刘要悟,陈鹏.澳大利亚高校生涯辅导实施状况及其启示[J].湖南师范大学教育科学学报,2013,12(04):105-109,103-107.

②④ 陈鹏.美、加、澳三国大学生生涯辅导的实践及对我国的启示[D].长沙:湖南师范大学,2010.

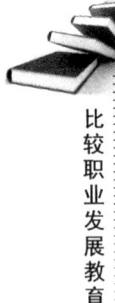

第二节 加拿大职业发展教育

加拿大地广人稀,但政府对教育非常重视,人均教育经费全球第一,每年的教育经费投入占国内生产总值的7.1%,超过所有发达国家。

一、加拿大职业发展教育政策及机构设置

(一)职业发展教育政策

1994年,加拿大的《学校走向工作机会法案》增加生涯探索、与工作相关的学习和其他与学校职业发展相关的活动,以加强加拿大在国家层面上给予职业发展教育的重视,这在《工作/生活蓝图》(Work/life blueprint)一书中得到了较为充分的体现。据记载,近些年来加拿大教育部也制定了一些政策与计划,主要指向职业指导、职业辅导和学校向工作过度的紧迫性。如B.C省在20世纪90年代实施了一项名为《职业与个人计划》(Career And Personal Planning,CAPP)的综合职业辅导计划,目前,该计划已较为成熟,并取得了良好效果。安大略省(Province of Ontario)也于1999年实施了一项职业辅导与职业发展教育的计划政策《从选择走向行动》(Choices into Action),提供了进行职业发展教育与职业指导的一些措施和方案。[①]

(二)职业发展教育机构设置

加拿大全国性的职业指导机构是加拿大指导和咨询协会,每个学区设有学校委员会,管辖本地区的中小学,学校委员会中设有职业指导部负责指导各学校的职业指导工作。在加拿大,学校设有专门的生涯中心,并提供专门的场所,配有专职和兼职的职业辅导人员。

二、加拿大职业发展教育课程设置

(一)加拿大安大略省中学的《职业发展教育与指导》

加拿大安大略省目前所实施的中学《职业发展教育与指导》来自1999年和2000年安大略省教育部分别制定的两个课程政策文件:9、10年级《职

[①] 陈鹏.美、加、澳三国大学生生涯辅导的实践及对我国的启示[D].长沙:湖南师范大学,2010.

业发展教育与指导》课程指南和 11、12 年级《职业发展教育与指导》课程指南。2004 年,该省教育部又增补了 10、12 年级《职业发展教育与指导开放课程(草案)》,与前面的课程加起来共分作七大项目。① 如表 6-1 所示。其中,9 年级的《学习策略:在中学获得成功的技能》主要探究学习策略,教会学生改善学习策略以提高他们的学习成绩,尤其是读写算、交流与规划能力等。10 年级的《职业生涯研究》主要探究学生在中学后的各种学习选择;《发现职场》主要是让学生通过在学校、社区的实际经历以及对工作场所的参观、体验形成对工作的理解,找到自己感兴趣的职业。11 年级的《设计你

表 6-1　加拿大安大略省 9—12 年级《职业生涯教育与指导》

年级	课目名称	课目类型	课目代码	学分	先决条件
9	学习策略:在中学获得成功的技能	开放	GLS1O	1.0	无
			GLS1O(特殊教育)		校长推荐
10	职业生涯研究	开放	GLC2O	0.5	无
	发现职场	开放	GLD2O	1.0	无
11	设计你的未来	开放	GWL3O	1.0	10 年级的职业生涯研究
	领导与同伴支持	开放	GPP3O	1.0	10 年级的职业生涯研究
12	高级学习策略:在中学后获得成功的技能	开放	GLS4O	1.0	10 年级的职业生涯研究
			GLS4(为有 IEP 的 12 年级学生修订)		校长推荐
			GLS3O(为有 IEP 的 12 年级学生修订)		校长推荐
	驾驭职场	开放	GLN4O	1.0	无

注:IEP 指 Individual Education Plan(个人教育计划)
资料来源:加拿大安大略省《职业生涯教育与指导》

---

① 赵金香.从外在规划到自我规划[D].曲阜:曲阜师范大学,2013.

的未来》是为学生进入中学后的工作、教育或培训做准备;《领导与同伴支持》是培养学生的领导能力与合作能力。12年级的《高级学习策略:在中学后获得成功的技能》是让学生学会评估并通过一定的技巧提高自己的学习效果。① 另外,学生需要考察有关就业以及中学后教育或培训的学习要求,并为之制订发展计划。《驾驭职场》要求学生通过真实的工作体验,探索感兴趣的职业,并制订今后的规划,同时还要考察平稳地转移到中学后目标所需的资源与支持。

(二)课程理念

加拿大安大略省教育部将"职业发展教育与指导"课程置于核心地位,中学教育阶段的课程均是围绕着学生未来的职业发展而展开。虽然该课程的名称是"职业发展教育与指导",但并不是一种简单的有关职业的教育。② 他们认为,职业发展教育是个长期的过程,不但包括职业,而且还包括了个人在一生中,无论是工作、家庭还是社区中需要承担的各种角色。所以,职业发展教育的课程理念是使学生了解自己、了解职业、了解社会以及了解自身在各种社会角色中所应承担的责任。因此,这是一种广义的职业发展教育理念,它与我们在"全时期"(指从基础教育开始到职业生涯教育结束的整个时期)职业发展教育的课题中对职业发展教育的定义是一致的,即:职业发展教育是有目的、有计划、有组织的培养个体(或当事人)规划自我职业发展的意识与技能,发展个体综合职业能力,促进个体职业发展的活动,是以引导个体进行并落实职业发展规划为主线的综合性教育活动。②

(三)课程目标

加拿大《职业发展教育与指导》的总体目标是:通过一系列的学习,使学生在未来职场中能够游刃有余,获得幸福、成功的人生。为达到这一目标,不同的科目还设有不同的目标。如《发现职场》和《驾驭职场》两个科目的课程目标是:

(1)工作与学习的基本技能:培养学生发现在各种职业中获得成功所

---

①② 贾万刚.美、加两国"全时期——早期"生涯教育课程的比较研究[J].基础教育,2012,9(2):32-37.

② 王珺.高职院校职业规划与就业指导教育全程化体系的构建研究[J].长春教育学院学报,2015(31):153-155.

需的基本技能,并能积极学习和发展这些技能。

（2）个人管理:培养学生与他人合作以及工作任务的规划与组织方面的技能。

（3）机遇的探索:培养学生发现信息的技能。

（4）为变革做准备:培养学生另外五个科目的解决问题和制定决策的能力。

总体课程目标是:①学习技能;②个人的知识与管理技能;③人际的知识与技能;④机遇的探索;⑤为变革做准备。

（四）内容设计

加拿大安大略省"职业发展教育与指导"的课程内容设计是根据学生的年级,由低到高,在不同的阶段配备不同的教学内容。见图6-3。

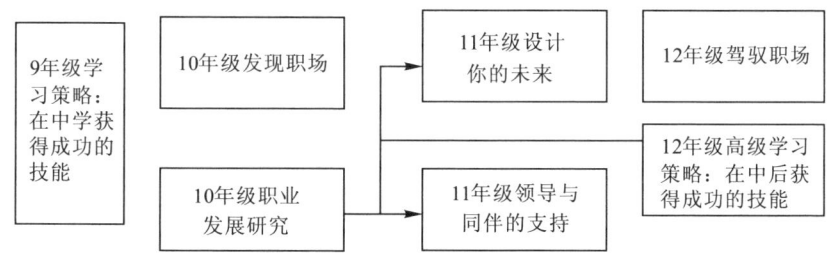

图6-3　不同教育阶段的课程内容

（五）教学方法

加拿大"职业发展教育与指导"的教学方法包括个别辅导、直接辅导、简介指导、经验性学习、合作性学习、角色扮演、案例分析、苏格拉底对话法以及探究式学习等。比如经验性学习,强调学校与社区的联系,学生有机会在一些工作环境中,①通过与雇主和雇员的互助获得相关经验,将所学应用到课堂及其他环境中,并评估自己取得的进步。此外,探究式学习的使用也很普遍。整个教学过程的重点在于学生的探究,教师只是以间接指导的身份出现。这种方法既发展了学生的创造力也发展了学生的人际交往能力。

---

① 贾万刚.美、加两国"全时期——早期"生涯教育课程的比较研究[J].基础教育,2012,9(2):30-35.

三、"现实的系列游戏"的内涵与目标

(一) 含义及目标

"现实的系列游戏"(the real game series,简称 RGS),是一种为 K-16(从小学到大学)层次的学生设计的生涯指导课程,该课程能够在教室和群组的场景下进行互动式、体验式的学习,由六个创造性的生涯游戏活动组成,分别为六个不同年龄和年级的学生量身定制了不同的游戏。该游戏强调团队互动,教师、学生父母、员工、雇主也可参与进来。相比较传统生涯指导活动,"现实的系列游戏"作为生涯指导活动具有灵活性、趣味性和挑战性的特征。学生可以在安全的教室环境下扮演一些成人角色,通过游戏,学生逐渐获得对学校课程与未来生活和工作机会关系的新的理解。因此,现实系列游戏的基本目标是将成人的现实工作世界用一种有意义的方式带给不同年龄和年级的学生,增加学生对学校经验和未来生活以及工作关系的理解,最终使学习者得到良好的教育。

(二) 内容

1.现实的游戏系列 1(the play real game):3—4 年级

该游戏向 3—4 年级的学生介绍基本的生活以及工作概念和词汇,让学生扮演成人的角色,在各种成人角色中创建社区,为自己和他人寻找工作,一起工作去实现有价值的目标。在角色扮演的娱乐中,学生学到了社区价值、团队工作的乐趣和责任、能力发展的重要性以及教育跟职业选择之间的相关性。

2.现实的游戏系列 2(the make it real game):5—6 年级

该游戏让 5—6 年级的学生通过进入到一次成人工作的模拟旅行中,来增强团队合作重要性的理解,每个学生扮演成人角色,每个角色都有独特的个人历史,学生要组建研究和发展创新项目的公司,随后作为结果呈现到观众面前。通过该系列游戏让学生了解工作的重要性,认识到每一个职业目标的实现都有许多不同的方式。

3.现实的游戏系列 3(the real game):7—8 年级

该游戏为 7—8 年级的学生提供机会去探索成人的现实生活,如税收、生活消费、工作环境和突发情况等。扮演成人角色的学生被随机地分配到某个职业角色中并且去理解学校活动与职业选择、生活方式和收入间的关系。通过深入探究各自扮演的角色,学生们学会了如何管理时间和财务并且看到了在生活方式、社区生活和终身学习间做出平衡的重要性。游戏的最后,学生将意识到工作满意感在生活中是要优先考虑的,并且逐渐认识到职业生涯选择对于未来的重要性。

4.现实的游戏系列4(the be real game):9—10年级

该游戏向9—10年级的学生展示一个人的职业生涯是如何建构的,始于童年,涉及生活的每个领域包括家庭、朋友、教育、娱乐活动和生活方式的选择、社区生活以及劳动力市场变化。当学生扮演一名有经验的在多种就业、未就业以及家庭背景下的成人工作者时,学生将会逐步理解通用能力、自我知识、终身学习和职业发展教育的重要性。[1]

5.现实的游戏系列5(the get real game):11—12年级

该游戏为11—12年级的学生呈现了广泛的职业选择机会,当学生试图去实现选择的职业目标时,让学生模拟面向未来的学校到工作的转变,为了让学生现实地探索职业目标实现的可能路径,指导者会向学生们提供更深层次的现实信息,如高等教育、多种工作培训形式、工作经历、见习或者当学徒、服兵役、志愿者和社区工作、企业家和自主创业等。学生在游戏过程中学会了如何管理时间,如何综合考虑各种职业选择因素,如何界定目标和列出行动计划以及如何将自己更好地呈现在一次求职面试中。

6.现实的游戏系列6(real times,real life):成人阶段

该游戏帮助成人学习者透视自己的生活愿景,消除负面的自我意象,如失业,其目的是让成人开始自信地规划职业。学习者要扮演工作者的角色,学会理解职业发展中的变化是不断的也是不可避免的,发展一种对现代劳动力市场的理解,并且学习在一个领域获得的技能如何迁移到另一个领域中去。学习在团队中如何工作,学习如何评估自己的现状,产生现实性的行

---

[1] 王华.加拿大"现实的系列游戏"生涯指导课程及其启示[J].中小学教师培训,2014(8):64-66.

动计划和知道如何获取帮助。①

(三)"现实的系列游戏"的效果评价

"现实的系列游戏"发展至今已有十多年的历史,目前在加拿大的学校教育领域得到了广泛的应用,并逐渐将其作为学校职业发展教育实施的重要组成部分,取得了不错的效果。国际上很多国家的研究者也对该游戏的有效性进行了大量的应用研究。罗伊(Rowe)(2009)对"现实系列游戏"的相关文献进行了分析,认为该游戏为教师帮助学生提高职业生涯管理能力提供了有价值的工具。大量的实证研究也支持了这一论断,认为这种角色扮演的体验式学习对学生了解工作世界知识以及增强学业成就和未来角色的关系理解有重要影响。多米特(Dim mitt)(2007)的研究还发现,使用过"现实系列游戏"的学生在学业成就测验成绩上有显著性提高。在澳大利亚有超过100所学校参与了试点项目,从参加者的反馈情况来看,得到了大量积极的反馈。学生、教师、父母的反馈是非常积极的,正如一位教师所说:"现实的系列游戏让学生们预知了未来,这对学生们的未来生活方式和职业选择会有直接影响,同时对学生在学校学习的积极性也有积极影响。"学生也对相应活动做出了反馈:"现实系列游戏让自己意识到成长比想象的困难。"甚至学生父母也对该项目报有热衷,认为该游戏让学生认识到了学校学习对于未来成功的重要性,让学生明白要实现梦想,就必须沿着梦想的道路努力学习和工作。总之,现实的系列游戏为学生提供了一个职业发展建构的环境,让不同年龄的学习者能够看到未来成人的生活和工作世界,尤其是对于那些认为学校学习与未来生活和工作缺乏联系的学生来说,这一生涯指导课程更具有重要的意义。②

在加拿大,高校大学生的工作实习或合作教育不同于我国高校学生的专业实习,加拿大大学生的工作实习或合作教育是针对工作探索进行的,有两种形式,一种是学校有单独的部门负责,另一种是在就业指导中心作为就业指导的一部分。实习得到政府的资助,通过补贴雇主的方式来进行。有的学校学生也出少部分资金用于学校联络费用。学生参加工作实习,一方

---

①② 王华.加拿大"现实的系列游戏"生涯指导课程及其启示[J].中小学教师培训,2014(8):64-66.

面探索个人对职业的适应能力,另一方面为就业作铺垫,抉择是否到实习单位就业。学校对学生申请工作实习是否批准也是有严格的条件限定的,要求学习成绩在 B+以上,在个人品格方面要有合作精神,工作认真负责。一般要由专业教师推荐和面试考核等。学生的工作实习计划和准备是按照完整的程序在专业教师的帮助下进行的,也就是就业指导的环节。学校对工作实习的学生进行跟踪考察,到实习单位同雇主讨论学生的表现。实习结束,根据考察情况和雇主的鉴定判定实习是否合格。按着实习次数和时间,有的发单独的实习证书,有的在毕业证书上加注实习经历。雇主在用人方面很看重学生的实习经历和表现。[①]

四、加拿大职业发展教育的特点

(一)职业发展指导贯穿高中和大学阶段

在高中阶段,就有文、理、工、医、商、艺等大类,学生在高中一年级就接受专业职业咨询顾问的指导,[②]然后根据兴趣爱好选择大学的专业方向。在大学阶段,加拿大大学与学院协会要求大学、政府与私人部门共同合作致力于大学生就业能力的提升。如大学应该培养学生具有劳动力市场所需要的综合技能;大学应该咨询产业、政府及行业委员会,以确保将准确可靠的劳动力市场信息传递给学生,从而利于学生进行职业决策;[③]政府应该提供核心资助,以使大学能持续开发所有学科领域毕业生所需要的技能组合等。

(二)职业发展教育人员专业化水平高,服务意识强

加拿大高校从事职业发展的人员专业化水平很高,如咨询师要求具有教育学、心理学、咨询学或相应的人文社会科学的博士学位,而且有一定工作经验,指导教师或管理员也要求具有人文社会科学背景的硕士学位。[④] 加

[①] 张福喜.日本、加拿大高校毕业生就业指导考察报告[J].河北职业技术师范学院学报(社会科学版),2003(3):6-11.

[②] 胡元聪,黄晓梅.职业生涯规划实践的国际比较及我国的改革方向探析[J].教育与职业,2008(5):32-34.

[③] 王秀芝,罗嘉珂.欧美高校提升大学生就业力:模式、措施及启示[J].现代教育管理,2013(5):120-124.

[④] 于伟.西方高校解决大学生"就业难"问题的理念、对策及启示[C]//青年就业问题与对策研究报告——中国青少年研究会优秀论文集(2004).中国青少年研究会:中国青少年研究会,2004:8.

拿大高校的就业指导服务意识非常强,其主要的职能和任务包括:根据毕业生个人兴趣和特长,帮助学生确定就业意向,建立职业目标;对毕业生进行技能评估,发掘其潜在的技能,帮助毕业生把在专业学习和课外活动中所积累的经验转化为工作技能;为毕业生提供职业发展教育,使毕业生有能力不断谋求更适合自己的职业岗位;进行求职技能培训;为学生联系实习单位,创造实习机会;搜集和提供就业信息。

第三节　新西兰职业发展教育

新西兰在2017年发布的《全球未来教育指数》榜单上排名世界第一,因其有强有力的政策支持、雄厚的教育投入、优越的教学环境和社会经济环境。这与其良好的职业发展教育密不可分。

一、国家层面的政策支持

(一)《国家行政纲领》

2004年修订的《国家行政纲领》(National Administration Guidelines, NAGs)是属于新西兰教育部颁布的《国家教育目标》(National Education Goals, NEGs)下针对教育行政相关事务的纲领性文件,主要用于规范各类学校行政职务与活动。后者将执行到2023年1月。

纲领共分六部分,其中第一部分第f项(NAG.1.f)规定:"学校董事会(包括从校长到教职员),应该为所有学生提供合适的职业发展相关信息和指导,尤其对即将毕业而无法顺利就业的学生应该给予并加强针对性的指导工作。"

(二)《新西兰学校中的职业发展教育与辅导》

职业发展教育在新西兰政府中受到高度重视,新西兰教育部于2003年发布了《新西兰学校中的职业发展教育与辅导》(Career Education and Guidance in New Zealand Schools)这一纲领性文件,详细地规定和说明了职业发展教育开展的内容、目标、实施手段以及评价等多个方面内容。该文件指出,开展职业发展教育是学校工作者必须尽到的责任,同时也是学校教育的必要构成部分,职业发展教育应该被完整地融合到学校教育当中,成为学校整体工作的一部分。2009年,新西兰教育部结合教育审查办公室(Education Review Office,ERO)2006年发布的《学校职业发展教育与指导的质量》报告(The Quality of Career Education and Guidance in Schools)修订并颁布了该纲领性文件的最新版。该新版本借鉴《新西兰课程》文件(the New Zealand Curriculum)中提出的1~13年级学生应该掌握的五个关键能力,分别是自我管理能力、人际交往能力、社会参与以及贡献能力、思维能力、语言文字能力,将这五种关键能力作为新西兰学校职业发展教育的目标。[①]

二、职业发展教育的相关项目

新西兰从1996年开始在学校中实行职业发展教育,并得到各方的大力支持,例如教育部发布的《新西兰学校中的职业发展教育与指导》文件;此外还有一系列的相关服务资源以及工具。近年来针对职业发展教育实施的主要项目有以下几个:

(一) 规划生涯(designing careers)

2005年,"规划生涯"这一实验项目开始在75所学校内展开,为期一年半。该项目的重点主要是提供对10年级学生生涯教育的支持,同时为那些有可能尚未对深造学习或者工作岗位做好准备便离开学校的学生(student at risk)提供更细致深入的支持。10年级的学生由于接近义务教育的结束阶段,即将就读高中,面临着全国教育成绩证书(NCEA)的科目选择,因此被选取作为本次实验项目的主要涉及对象。

这一项目包含的主要内容如下:

为教师提供职业发展教育有关内容的支持以及教学资源;为10年级学生提供学习经验以及生涯规划;为11、12、13年级中那些有必要的学生提供个性化的职业指导(由负责职业发展教育的顾问直接为学生进行指导)。

在职业发展教育项目中提供这样一系列的定向规划辅助,主要是为了让学生更好地将当前的决策与将来的职业发展方向结合起来充分考虑。该项目还要求学生应该至少每年更新一次自己的规划,使其与当前的职业指导内容保持连贯与一致,同时,这一做法对于学生来说也有以下的好处:了

[①] 李彬龙.新西兰生涯教育标准研究[D].上海:华东师范大学,2014.

解终身学习以及了解职业发展教育的过程;充分利用好 NCEA 中的机会,以及在高等教育中可供选择的课程;在离开学校时能拥有使得他们成功过渡到学习进修、培训或者就业的规划。

该实验项目的影响超出了原先的预料,除了学生,项目对参与其中的工作人员也产生了广泛的影响,包括他们对职业发展教育的认识和态度。他们都对这次实验项目的价值和影响做出了积极的报道和回应。

从新西兰教育审查办公室的报告来看,此项目带来的积极影响有:学校为 10 年级学生所提供的职业发展教育变得更好;加大了对部分有需要学生的支持力度;提升了职业发展教育在学生与教师中的形象和影响力;为其他年级职业发展教育的开发提供借鉴与经验;促进了学校中参与职业发展教育团队的发展。

除了肯定带来的积极效应,教育审查办公室在相关的评价报告中也指出该实验存在的部分问题。例如在规划阶段未给出清晰的成果指标;缺乏一些基础的数据来进行有力的自我回顾与评价;缺乏清晰的责任与义务的描述;并未提高家长在其孩子职业发展教育过程中的参与度;对于毛利学生、太平洋族裔学生或者有特殊需求的学生并未提供相应的针对性项目。

(二)创建出路,构建人生(creating pathways and building lives,CPaBL)

该项目在 2007 年由新西兰教育部倡议和发起,力求创建一种全校参与的职业发展教育方式。根据所处区域、学校类型、招生规模等一系列标准,教育部在全国范围挑选了 100 所中等学校来参与。在"规划生涯"这一项目成功的基础上,CPaBL 将其目标确定为通过一种全校参与的方式,在职业发展教育中融入可持续的系统与实践,使得提供给学生的职业发展建议更为有效。CPaBL 可以理解为是"规划生涯"项目的改进版,在保持原项目对学生的职业过渡提供支持这一行动的同时,也根据从项目实施后的评价与回顾中获得的相关经验来开发全校性的职业发展教育实施方式。

1.CPaBL 项目的原则

新西兰职业发展服务中心(Career Services,现更名为 Career New Zealand)为这一项目制定的指导原则强调,利用一种协同合作的方式来强化职业发展教育的支持基础,强化校园中的职业发展文化。具体来说,主要包

含以下四个重点原则:

(1)彼此共享职业发展知识与技能,这种共享是指所有参与职业发展教育的人员间的共享,包括专业人员或者相关责任人,并且是全国性学校间的共享。这些知识与技能主要是针对学校的政策与规划、职业发展教育项目、学生个人规划、有特殊需求的学生(例如毛利人、太平洋族裔、难民以及移民);

(2)在所有相关的职业发展教育活动中,所参与的团队必须有明确而清晰的领导者;

(3)在校内开展职业发展教育应采取预先规划的方式,包括对实施过程、评价过程、可获得资源的持续性都要有所考虑顾及,同时还应该对学生的成果以及特定学生的需求有额外的关注;

(4)使家长、家庭参与进来,并与社区建立良好的联系。

2.CPaBL 项目的内容

CPaBL 的核心是希望摒弃传统职业发展教育中以职业顾问为中心的方式,并尝试寻找一种新的实施职业发展教育的方式。从规划生涯实验项目实施的经验可以看出,单凭职业顾问日复一日地为学生提供辅导,是无法将职业发展教育提升至全校环境中实施的。具体来说,CPaBL 项目主要包括以下内容:

(1)每所学校都要完善一个额外的数据信息档案,档案内详细记载学生的成果及其当前的职业发展活动。这一档案以后能作为该项目进行回顾与评价的基础数据并成为今后学生需求分析的基础。

(2)每所学校应该与学校支持服务系统及职业服务系统共同开发出它们之间的专业支持协议,协议包含一系列项目的规划成果,并会在项目推行的过程作为动态文件来进行回顾和检阅。

(3)在对学生的需求分析以及结合自身环境、具体情况来设计职业发展教育方案的基础上,学校应对其职业发展教育规划进行开发,对其全校参与的职业发展教育方式有全局性的表述,并加以实施。

(三)中等—高等对接办法(the secondary - tertiary alignment resource,STAR)

STAR 项目是从 1996 年开始由新西兰教育部为学校提供的独立于国家

课程以外的资助计划,帮助高年级学生顺利地完成从高中向高等教育或工作领域的过渡。具体内容包括:工作体验式学习,计学分的职业、教育和培训课程,超出13年级常规课程内容的高等教育资格认证,以及介绍高等教育和工作体验的短期入门课程等。学生通过 STAR 等学校项目可以获得各种发展机会,上大学并不是唯一的出路,选择职业发展教育或参加国家提供的多种就业项目也能有很好的发展前景。①

除了上述几大项目之外,还有政府实施的"入门计划"项目(gateway),把工作实习作为课程内容,让11至13年级的中学生有机会接受工作实习训练。参加这一项目的学生除获得辅以课堂授课的工作实习机会外还可按新西兰国家资格评审制度接受评核。②

三、学校中职业发展教育的实施

(一)学前以及基础教育阶段

职业发展教育在学前阶段并未正式开展,但教育部提出的学前教育课程目标包含有"探索世界"这一项,鼓励孩子积极地感受自然、社会、世界和身边的实物。幼儿园内提供仿真的电磁炉以及微波炉等家用电器或设备,孩子可以借助这些设备初步体验生活以及掌握一定的相应生活技能。

基础教育方面,学校会开设数量众多与技术、职业相关的课程。例如,某些学校在技术活动教室内配有钻头和车床等机械工具,供学生自己动手进行学习和操作。此外,还有经济、社会研究、电影制作、烹饪等各种体现出典型职业特色的选修课,帮助学生了解主修科目之外的知识领域以及职业发展途径。学生完成职业类课程,不仅能获得学分,还可以获得社会认可的资格证书,对于他们将来进入社会走上工作岗位大有裨益。除了课程之外,学校还会举行职业博览会等诸如此类的活动,帮助学生了解更加丰富的职业信息,为他们做出职业发展决策提供帮助和指导。

在职业发展的过程中,若学生在关键阶段或者是面临抉择和困惑的时候,可以向学校中的职业顾问求助。一般情况下,要成为职业顾问,学校里

---

① 朱凌云.新西兰中小学生涯教育的特点与启示[J].外国教育研究,2013(40):22-28.
② 李彬龙.新西兰生涯教育标准研究[D].上海:华东师范大学,2014.

的教师必须经过专门的培训学习并获取相应的资格证书。

(二)高等教育中的职业发展教育

在高等教育阶段,职业发展指导融入学生的必修课程中,学校有专门的就业辅导中心帮助学生更好地就业以及管理其职业。例如,就业辅导中心会帮助学生分析寻找更适合其个人发展的行业领域,并就此提出建议;安排介绍学生到相关行业机构,协助学生搭建属于自己的成功之路。当面临就业抉择时就业辅导中心会为学生提供相关信息及实质意见。此外,学生通过就业辅导中心还可以学习简历和求职信的写法参加校内举办的职业研讨会,学习面试技巧,以及作为雇员所拥有的权利和义务。①

四、新西兰高等教育职业发展标准框架②

高等教育阶段的标准框架与前两阶段的形式一致,核心依然是学生的职业管理能力,而外部输入的三个维度则分别为学生参与、雇主与行业参与、高等教育组织参与,见图6-4。

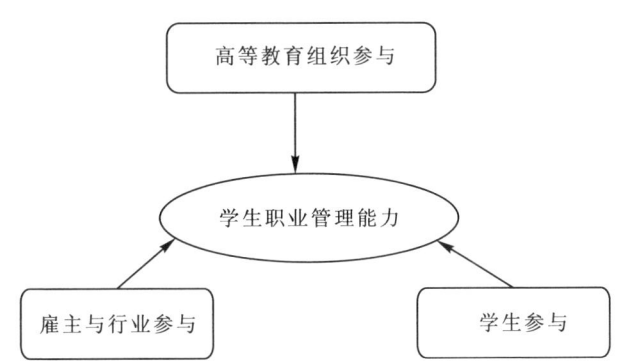

图6-4 新西兰高等教育职业发展标准框架

(一)学生职业管理能力

对高校学生而言,要进一步发展生活、工作和学习的自我管理能力,他们需要有效的、针对各自文化的职业发展项目和服务的支持。职业管理能力使得学生能够做出合理的职业决策以及学习选择,发现自身潜能,完成他

---

①② 李彬龙.新西兰生涯教育标准研究[D].上海:华东师范大学,2014.

们的学历,成为国家经济、社会的好公民以及贡献者。有良好职业发展素养的学生能够清晰表达出他们独特的能力,并展现出对终身学习的适应力、信心和坚定。该维度的指标见表6-2。

表6-2 职业管理能力的指标

指标	学生职业管理能力
1	学生拥有强烈的自我意识,包括他们的身份、语言、文化,与他人的关系,发展的潜能。他们能够确认自身的社会以及文化影响,以及如何与经济和社会互动。学生能够考虑、分析并应用以上能力到当前以及将来所追求的生活中
2	学生能够发现、评价生活、学习、工作中出现的机会,并采取相应行动。能够意识到地区、国家和全球经济的变化以及这些变化对他们生活、学习和工作的影响
3	学生做出明智决策,并落实灵活的生活、学习和工作规划;对变化能够适应并做出响应。当面临困难和阻碍时能够找到替代的方案,生活、学习和工作环境发生变化时有能力去适应
4	学生能够清晰地表述他们的个人和市场身份,这些身份反映了他们的价值观、技能、受过的训练、知识以及兴趣所在,并且在他们与外部世界(包括可能的雇主、网络、线上空间等)的交流中有明显的体现

(二)雇主与行业参与

雇主以及行业的参与,对于学生职业管理能力的发展、帮助他们做好高等教育后进入工作领域的准备,是必不可少的。高等教育组织应该与雇主以及行业之间建立并加强彼此间清晰、开放的沟通交流。全组织范围内有计划性、策略性的方法途径对于雇主和行业的参与很有必要,而这又需要健全的信息系统作为支撑,以供学生、组织人员以及雇主使用。具体指标见表6-3。

表6-3 雇主与行业参与

指标	雇主与行业参与
1	雇主、行业以及高等教育组织展开合作,确保有效的参与策略得以实施。这其中包括正式协议、良好的合作关系,使得各方尤其是学生能够取得互惠的成果
2	学生能够参与到与其学习相关的工作项目以及事务中,能够获得当前的行业信息,以拓展其职业能力并为将来工作做好准备

(三)学生参与

高质量的职业发展信息系统、项目和服务能增加学生参与程度,帮助学生发展其自我管理能力,顺利完成从高等教育到工作环境的过渡。具体指标见表6-4。

表6-4 学生参与

指标	学生参与
1	有统一、协调的职业发展项目和服务,使得学生有效切实地参与其中。它们为所有学生提供了一系列的机会,让学生在高等教育阶段得以发展以及展示他们的职业管理能力。在学生的整个高等教育学习过程中,这些项目和服务的相关信息可以在每个学生各自的在线职业档案中获取
2	生涯发展信息系统、项目以及服务通过数据分析、回顾和评价等方式来加以发展和提升;通过引入新的途径和条件来满足学生明确、具体的职业发展需求
3	项目与服务积极地使学生、家庭家族、社区参与其中,为学生提供支持。有不断发展的网络,作为学生"相互学习、知识产生以及知识管理的源泉"
4	职业发展信息系统对学生的参与提供支持,这些系统能够方便地被当前以及后续的学生、员工、雇主以及当地社区来获取和使用;系统应是与时俱进的、有相关性的,并且定期进行评审,以确保通用性

(四)组织参与

高等教育组织内部应该富有职业发展文化氛围,这一点对于组织和学生取得成果来说非常关键。有效的领导和积极的氛围是保证学生成功转型或过渡的必不可少的资源。组织内应该有清晰的战略以及规划,通过一种全组织参与的方式,将职业发展适当地整合到组织架构中去。具体指标见表6-5。

表6-5 组织参与

指标	组织参与
1	积极、坚定的领导,知悉实践的情况,为学生职业管理能力的发展积极推动组织的政策与规划,并将这一切都整合到组织的项目与服务、信息系统、雇主参与策略和报告中
2	有计划的、战略性的团队方式来进行职业发展实践。这一团队与组织内的高层管理团队有直接的联系,并包括至少一名的职业发展专家来实现一系列职业发展项目和服务的整合。职业发展人员的角色定位以及相应的职责都有明确的规定。注意到个别组织没有建立特定的职业发展部门,这种情况下他们应关注如何提供高质量的职业发展项目以及服务
3	组织提供职业信息管理和专业资源,来确保项目和服务能满足所有学生的特定职业发展需求。组织充分利用其研究能力并与伙伴组织进行合作,提升项目与服务,促进学生成果。职业发展资源应该有策略地加以利用,以此确保成功的学生成果

五、新西兰职业发展教育的特点

(一)生涯健康成长是职业发展教育的中心

在衡量新西兰职业发展教育质量的过程中,学生的生涯管理能力始终是关键指标。其他的维度都是围绕这一指标进行设计的。此架构使学校对学生进行生涯规划指导的整个过程都能贴近学生的真实生活、学习与未来工作。以学生的生涯健康成长为中心还体现在对学生生活生存能力的重视上。2007年新西兰教育部颁布的《新西兰课程》中,强调学生需要掌握的五种核心能力：自我管理，关心，参与和贡献，以及思维与运用语言、文字、符号的能力。相应地，学校的职业发展教育结合新课程要求，强调学生自我管理能力，基于自我认知树立适宜的个人目标并严格地去实现目标，发现和挖掘学生自身的潜能。

（二）特别关注少数民族和弱势群体学生

新西兰拥有多个民族，由于历史的原因，移民比较多，教育层次参差不齐；土著居民发展不平衡，学生呈现出文化差异性。因此，在职业发展教育中，必须为不同民族的学生群体提供适合他们需要的职业发展教育方案。新西兰的新课程改革也数次强调教育平等，要求尊重所有民族的文化传统，并对所有地区给予相同的教育支持，尤其要对弱势群体给予更多的保护和支持。在职业发展教育评价标准中特别关注来自毛利土著居民与太平洋岛屿居民的适龄学生及其他特殊群体，如贫困学生、残疾学生、学习障碍学生等，让他们享受同等的生涯规划辅导，帮助他们顺利完成从学校到生活、工作或升学的转换。

（三）多方参与职业发展教育评价标准制定

职业发展教育评价标准制定并不是由政府单方面决策强加给学校的，而是为学校提供一个评估的框架，供学校参考。每所学校在开展职业发展教育质量评估前，一般都要召集重要的利益相关者，如学校董事会、校长、学校资深管理人员、评估专家、生涯规划与指导专家、教师等相关人员参与，共同细化评估的指标体系、权重和内容等。此外，在学校提供的职业发展教育项目与服务体系中，鼓励学生家长、社区、雇主以及各行各业的人员参与，充分发挥利益相关者的角色。这些都为职业发展教育的开展提供了诸多帮助，也给了学校相互借鉴的样板。

思考题：

1. 澳大利亚职业发展教育的主要特点表现在哪几个方面？
2. 澳大利亚职业发展的蝴蝶模型的核心内容是什么？
3. 加拿大职业发展教育的课程特色有哪些？
4. 新西兰职业发展教育标准框架所涉及的外部输入维度包含哪些指标？

推荐读物:

1.吕红.澳大利亚职业教育课程质量保障研究[M].北京:外语教学与研究出版社,2011.

2.杨燕燕.加拿大安大略省职业生涯教育与指导课程述评[J].比较教育研究,2005(12).

3.张妍.加拿大维多利亚大学职业发展教育分析及启示[J].生涯发展教育研究,2016(01).

4.覃川,戴格崴.启航:2013中国—新西兰职业教育论坛文集[C].青岛:中国海洋大学出版社,2016.

国外论文导读与阅读(一):

导读:职业发展的国际最佳实践:文献综述

作者:乔治·理查德(George V. Richard)

近年来,在不断变化的劳动力市场中,人们面临对工作的不断选择,反复决策。因此国家很有必要在个人生涯内为其提供职业发展服务。职业发展理论早在20世纪初就存在了。但直到最近三四十年,才对职业咨询和指导的有效性进行研究。虽然研究发现职业咨询是有效的,但针对职业咨询的具体组成部分的研究仍然有限,实施职业指导服务的研究更为有限。职业发展已经成为许多国家政策发展的重要组成部分,因为它对劳动力市场有潜在影响。本文简要回顾了与职业生涯规划项目(或最佳实践)发展相关的研究文献。这些研究涉及元分析研究、国际政策制定、职业发展项目的效果以及职业发展指南和标准的制定。这些研究有助于形成最佳职业规划和职业指导的框架。尽管职业发展领域现在已接近百年,但是令人惊讶的是,对这一主题的研究如此之少。希望未来有更多的研究,提供更多的全球视角来实现职业发展和指导服务。

文章来源:

George V. Richard .International Best Practices in Career Development:Review of the Literature[J]. International Journal for Educational and Vocational Guidance (2005) 5: 189-201.

国外论文导读与阅读(二):

导读:利用参与式行动研究掌握一所新西兰大学职业发展框架的实施情况

作者:戴尔·福尔比什(Dale S. Furbish),罗宾·贝利(Robyn Bailey),大卫·特劳特(David Trought)

新西兰教育部要求所有中学提供就业服务,但新西兰高等教育机构的职业服务没有这种任务规定。因此,新西兰各高等教育机构的职业发展服务的结构十分不同,高等教育标准为所有高等教育院校提供指导,以确定其职业服务的质量和全面程度。高等教育标准的总体目标是发展学生的职业管理能力。在本文中,采用参与式行动研究方法来研究这一过程。本次研究由三位经验丰富且职业发展背景各不相同的成员组成。研究的目的是新西兰一所大学的商法系建立职业服务时,采用高等教育标准,为新的职业发展服务提供了一个机会。

参与式行动研究的结果显示:首先考虑制定实施职业规划和政策的战略,这是组织参与标准的子类别,组织参与下的另一个子类别是组织方法,还有平等。具体而言,平等要求制定战略满足马奥里(新西兰土著人)和帕西菲卡学生的职业发展需要,他们是新西兰的目标公平群体。此外,研究还考虑了国际学生的特殊职业发展需要,这些学生在商学院和法学院的招生中占有相当大的比例。组织参与标准包含许多子类别,以员工资格和领导力为目标;组织参与的另一个分类侧重于职业发展信息管理和分配的专业资源,以确保课程和服务满足所有学生确定的需求。信息管理是该研究认为目前配置不足的一个方面。研究认识到,有关学院学生的职业计划和职业需求的信息既没有系统地收集,也没有记录下来。组织参与标准的最后一个子类别说明需要将研究整合到职业服务中。该研究将这一子类别确定为职业和就业中心的优势,认为PRP项目本身就是一个研究。

文章来源:

Dale S. Furbish, Robyn Bailey, David Trought. Using Participatory Action Research to Study the Implementation of Career Development Benchmarks at a New Zealand University[J]. International Journal for Educational and Vocational Guidance, 2016(16):153-167.

(节选的英文原文见附录7)

第七章　我国职业发展教育

本章要点：
1. 我国职业发展教育课程产生的基础；
2. 我国职业发展教育的课程特点；
3. 国外职业发展教育对我国的启示。

第一节　我国职业发展教育的相关政策

一、新中国成立前我国职业发展教育概况及出台政策

1927年，国民政府成立后，鉴于日趋严重的社会失业问题，教育部门吸纳大批进步教育家的意见与建议，将职业指导工作视作解决失业问题和发展国民生计的重要手段。1928年5月，在第一次全国教育会议上，与会专家一致认为，要解决大批青年学生的失业问题，必须积极开展职业指导，使学生学会求职的方法，并获得适宜的职业。会议通过了《设立职业指导所及励行职业指导案》，该案不仅要求各级学校在学生修业期最后一个学年对学生进行职业指导，并在全国各大学及中学设职业指导部，而且决定由大学院拟定程序，会同有关各部，通令各省设立职业指导所。1930年9月，全国职业指导机关联合会成立，它以研究各机关共同的职业指导问题为宗旨，旨在推动职业指导在全国的扩展。1933年7月，教育部又颁布了《各省市县教育行政机关暨中小学施行升学及职业指导办法大纲》，令各省市县教育行政机关组织其所属小学从五年级起，初中、高中分别从二年级起实施升学及职业指

导,并详细规定了各级教育行政机关和中、小学实施升学及职业指导的主要任务和工作。大纲的颁布,标志着职业指导工作开始走向法定化和制度化的阶段。1935年11月,教育部又专门制定颁布了《各省市教育行政机关设置职业指导组暂行办法》,责令"各省市教育行政机关应斟酌实际需要情形,设置职业指导组",并详细规定了各省市教育行政机关所设职业指导组的组织机构、工作范围及工作手续等事宜。此后,职业指导工作逐渐受到社会与各级教育行政部门的重视,各地职业指导机构和职业指导团体迅速增多,职业指导的理论研究范围不断拓宽,实践领域日益广泛,职业心理测验得到加强,职业指导工作向着更加社会化、科学化的方向发展。但1937年后,由于我国抗日战争和国内战争时期的内忧外患等诸多原因,国家无力深入进行职业指导研究以及具体的实施职业指导。①

二、新中国成立后我国职业发展教育概况及政策

1949年,中华人民共和国成立以后,由于实行计划经济体制的原因,人员统包统分,职业选择和人员流动的余地极其有限,我国的职业指导工作中断了。

十一届三中全会以后,我国经济体制逐步由计划经济向社会主义市场经济体制过渡,随着经济体制变革,就业制度发生了根本变化,逐渐形成用人单位和劳动者双向选择、合理流动的就业机制,为职业指导提供了良好的发展机遇。② 1989年原国家教委、原人事部印发了《高等学校毕业生分配制度改革方案》,贯彻了近四十年的高校毕业生由国家统包统配的就业制度终于被改革的利剑击破。随后,清华大学、上海交大等院校开始进行毕业生就业工作改革试点。后期陆陆续续全国许多高校都开始对应届毕业生进行就业指导,1995年5月,原国家教委办公厅颁发了《关于在高等学校开设就业指导选修课的通知》,各地高校逐渐根据本校情况开设了就业指导课。③ 2000年10月,北京市学联等单位发起在北京大学、清华大学、中国人民大学等8所首都高校组织开展"2000年大学生职业生涯规划"活动,受到大学生

---

① 谢长法.近代中国职业指导的历史进程[J].教育与职业,2002(10):45-47.
② 刘武昌.中国高等院校职业指导的历史演变[J].现代企业教育,2014(10).
③ 王伟.我国职业指导研究现状的分析与评价[D].南京:南京师范大学,2011.

的普遍欢迎,标志着现代意义上的大学生职业生涯规划教育的正式兴起。①

进入21世纪以来,职业指导工作越来越受到重视,并由以高校为主体逐渐扩展到整个社会,创业也逐步加入到职业发展教育模块中。2002年教育部在《关于切实做好普通高等学校毕业生就业工作的通知》中明确提出"各省(自治区、直辖市)人民政府和各高校要尽快建立并完善高校毕业生就业指导服务机构,在场地、经费、人员等方面给予充分保证。高校要按一定的师生比配备专职的工作人员,以适应数量迅速增加的高校毕业生的就业工作需要"。2003年教育部提出,"要加强毕业生就业指导,将就业指导课作为学生思想政治教育的重要组成部分,并纳入日常教学"。② 2007年12月,教育部办公厅印发《大学生职业发展与就业指导课程教学要求》,明确制定了职业指导的教学大纲,要求高校必须开设就业指导课程,实现了大学生职业生涯规划教育,实现了从"鼓励和提倡开展"到"必须开展"这一重大转变。另外为了与课程配合,各高校还辅助进行了职业演讲、参观、调查、个别谈话、角色扮演、职业生涯规划大赛、网上招聘、供需见面会等活动,极大地促进了职业指导的深入开展,唤醒了学生自主规划未来职业的意识,也有效促进了高校毕业生的充分就业。③ 当高校就业指导工作如火如荼展开时,应对时代发展的要求,大学生创业被融入职业发展教育内容中来。2012年8月1日,教育部办公厅下达关于印发《普通本科学校创业教育教学基本要求(试行)》的通知,规定本科高校必须将"创业基础"课纳入必修。④

新时期,职业发展教育不仅仅局限在高等教育领域内,而是逐渐向中小学渗透。2015年8月,《河南省普通高中生涯教育课程指导纲要(试行)》通知要求,各级教育行政部门要充分认识开展普通高中生涯教育的重要性和必要性,积极将生涯教育纳入本地普通高中课程体系,结合本地实际,制订切实可行的实施方案;要指导学校加强生涯教育课程教师队伍建设,探索并

---

① 徐婕.大学生职业生涯规划教育研究[D].扬州:扬州大学,2012.
② 罗群,董红祥.高等教育大众化背景下的大学生职业生涯教育模式演变[J].淮南师范学院学报,2010(10).
③ 孔夏萌.近代中国职业生涯教育30年:回顾及前瞻[J].职教论坛,2013(13):92-96.
④ 吕莹莹.高校创业型人才培养体系研究——基于创业型大学的考察剖析[D].杭州:浙江工业大学,2014.

完善生涯教育教师培养制度,认真做好生涯教育教师遴选、培训工作,建立一支专兼职相结合的生涯教育教师队伍;要结合本地实际,积极整合学校、社会和家庭教育资源,开发组建本地互动式、体验式生涯教育学习实践基地,为学生搭建生涯体验和学习实践平台,构建理论和实践相结合的生涯教育课程体系。① 各级教科研部门要加强对生涯教育课程的研究,组织相关专家和教研员与学校开展"一对一"结对指导,及时解决课程实施过程中遇到的困难和问题。《浙江省教育厅关于加强普通高中学生生涯规划教育的指导意见》中也指出,"开展高中生涯规划教育是贯彻选择性教育思想,促进学生全面而有个性发展,实施素质教育的重要组成部分"。虽然仅有河南省、浙江省少有的几个省市开始进行初高中生涯发展教育,但其趋势必将势不可挡。②

第二节　我国职业发展教育课程

一、大学生职业发展教育课程产生的基础

作为一门非传统课程,它的产生和发展既有坚实的理论基础也有多样化的现实基础,同时也在我国就业形势的变化中持续开展教学理论和教学实践探索,并通过实施改革,逐步提升课程质量。

(一)职业发展教育课程产生的理论基础

本课程的理论基础主要来源国内外的理论成果。

一是我国的传统文化。我国传统文化作为展现民族特质的文化形式,博大精深、历史悠久,这对职业发展教育课程产生了潜移默化的作用;

二是马克思主义的全面发展理论。马克思主义的全面发展理论是本课程的理论支撑点和理论基石,培养人的全面发展的主要方式是教育,而本课程就是关注和致力于引导和帮助大学生规划自己的职业发展问题,因此要在马克思主义全面发展理论的指导下构建有中国特色的大学生职业发展

---

① 胡紫薇.基于SWOT分析的新高考中学地理学科营销策略[D].南昌:江西师范大学,2018.
② 王小平.浙江省高中生涯规划教育现状调查[J].教师教育论坛,2019,32(02):24-27.

教育；

三是社会主义核心价值观。党的十六届六中全会首次提出社会主义核心价值观,在经济新常态背景下,以社会主义核心价值观为指导,鼓励和引导学生在个人职业选择中以正确的世界观、人生观、价值观为导向,在学习、成长和职业实践中科学合理地规划大学生活,职业发展是符合社会发展客观需要的；

四是西方发达国家系统的职业发展理论。这包括20世纪初美国的弗兰克·帕森斯提出的"特质因素论"、施恩的职业生涯周期理论、戴维斯和罗奎思提出的职业适应理论等,之后舒伯将"职业指导"发展成为"职业生涯教育",完善了当今西方发达国家生涯辅导的理论基础。[①] 同时也影响了我国的职业发展教育。

(二)职业发展教育课程建设的现实基础

丰富的国内外实践奠定了职业发展教育课程的现实基础。

1.西方国家职业发展教育的兴起

自20世纪初美国学者帕森斯提出"职业指导"的问题之后,全球开始关注大学生职业发展教育,西方国家开展实践探索和研究,经过一百多年的发展,历经了就业指导、职业指导、职业生涯教育的发展历程,在实践中逐渐建立并不断完善一套系统的职业发展教育模式。随着我国就业问题的日渐突出,高校就业指导工作越来越引起重视,职业发展教育课程在高校的开设也成为理所当然。

2.我国就业制度的变革

高校毕业生就业制度的变革为就业指导的开设提供了实践基础,随着经济体制的改革,我国高校毕业生就业的方式从有计划的分配转变到自主择业。高校在就业制度改革初期,由于缺乏就业指导相关课程的开设以及积极的引导,致使高校毕业生和市场经济条件下的人才配置方式的要求不匹配,在某种程度上影响了高校毕业生的就业质量。

---

① 刘筠.大学生职业发展教育课程产生和发展问题研究[J].中国大学生就业,2016(04):54-60.

3. "新常态"带来的新挑战和新机遇

我国经济进入新常态,首先给大学生就业创业带来新挑战。当前,我国经济发展方式进入"三期叠加"的新常态,国内经济下行压力进一步增大,2015年大企业岗位需求明显减少、中小民营企业同比没有大量增加的趋势,加之高校的培养结构与市场需求存在一定的结构性矛盾,毕业生和家长的就业观念和就业心态趋向传统等问题,使得就业形势愈加复杂严峻。其次经济新常态给大学生就业创业带来新机遇。从总体上看,我国经济发展的基本面没有改变,经济运行仍然处于合理区间,仍然呈现缓中趋稳、稳中有进势头,经济运行内在动力仍然比较强劲;随着"一带一路"等重大国家战略的实施,西部地区企业快速发展,用人需求增长较快,东部和中部地区增幅相对平稳。

4. 大众创业万众创新的新要求

2014年国务院推出促进大众创业、万众创新的政策。目的是通过实施这一政策,推动我国经济结构调整、打造发展新引擎、增强发展新动力,大力实施创新驱动发展战略、促进经济社会转型升级。为此,国家、地方政府配套出台了一系列政策措施,推动大众创业、万众创新走向深入。但现在面临的突出问题就是高技能人才、创新创业型人才明显不足,高校毕业生的社会适应性和创新创业能力不足,这需要我们加大力度开展适应新形势的职业发展教育、就业引导和创业扶持等工作。①

二、我国大学生职业发展教育课程的发展阶段

我国的高校就业指导课程开设始于20世纪90年代,主要原因是随着高校毕业生人数的急剧增加和大学生就业问题的突出,国家和地方的教育部门和高校开始重视此项工作,以制定政策为抓手,力图推动课程的发展,就业形势发展的新要求也在促使课程进行改革和完善。②

(一)课程尝试开设阶段

这个阶段在高校毕业生工作进入供需见面与双向选择时期,原国家教委在1990年、1995年和2003年先后出台专门的文件,对各高校提出"有条件有

---

①② 刘筠.大学生职业发展教育课程产生和发展问题研究[J].中国大学生就业,2016(04):54-60.

计划开设就业指导课"的建议,制定"建议高年级学生开设就业指导选修课纳入思想政治教育课程体系"的政策。① 这一时期,高校职业发展教育的主要内容为对毕业生的就业指导,由于当时毕业生就业形势并没有像近些年这样严峻,因此这项工作虽已为各大高校所关注,但并没有受到足够的重视。

(二)课程规范开设阶段

2007年以来,伴随着我国高等教育大众化,进入劳动力市场进行职业搜寻的大学生数量与日俱增,高校毕业生就业矛盾也日趋凸显。2007年12月,教育部办公厅关于印发《大学生职业发展与就业指导课程教学要求》的通知明确提出,从2008年起提倡所有普通高校开设职业发展与就业指导课程,并作为公共课纳入教学计划,贯穿学生从入学到毕业的整个培养过程。② 2009年国务院办公厅发文,明确要求全国高校"以必修课的形式开设就业指导课",随后教育部办公厅也下发了课程教学要求,对高校开设的课程提出明确要求。而且随着人才的评价标准改变、经济的转型、我国人才战略的转变、高校毕业生就业形势愈加严峻等,都使社会、政府、高校和毕业生本人对此项问题开始高度关注。③ 已经开展职业发展教育实践,许多高校将职业发展教育课程纳入学校课程体系,列入教学计划,为大学生搭建职业生涯咨询与服务的平台。

(三)课程改革和完善阶段

按照要求,我国高校普遍以公修课和选修课的形式开设了职业发展教育课程,在帮助高校毕业生科学规划职业生涯,明确职业发展方向,提高自身就业能力方面开展了有效地工作,基本能够实现课程教学目的并取得一定的效果。就高校来说,客观认识学校的办学定位,立足现实,结合实际,认真分析新常态下大学生的职业发展需求及实现的思路和方法,发展和完善大学生职业发展教育模式,改革和完善课程体系,提升课程的教学效果,有效的引导和帮助学生提升职业素质和就业竞争力尤为必要。④

---

① 刘筠.大学生职业发展教育课程产生和发展问题研究[J].中国大学生就业硕士论文,2016(04):54-60.
② 陆学彬.中国劳动力市场制度变迁:2001-2010[D].北京:中国人民大学,2011.
③④ 刘筠.大学生职业发展教育课程产生和发展问题研究[J].中国大学生就业,2016(04):54-60.

三、大学生职业发展教育的课程体系

2007年教育部印发了《大学生职业发展与就业指导课程教学要求》。目前,该《教学要求》是高校开展职业发展教育应遵循的重要文件和教育主管部门对其进行监督管理的主要依据。

(一)课程性质

高校的职业发展教育课程开始成为公共课纳入常规的教学活动计划,不再以选修课的形式进行课程设置,引导高校和大学生对职业发展教育这门新兴学科加以重视,帮助高校和大学生端正对大学生职业发展教育课程的学习态度,激发高校大学生对学习这门课程的学习兴趣,从而帮助大学生树立科学的职业目标,实现其职业价值。①

(二)课程设置

要求国内各高校结合本校实际情况,严格遵照《教学要求》规定的课程时间设置安排。教育部文件要求在整个大学期间,关于职业发展教育的相关课程不得少于38学时。《教学要求》以明文规定来保障大学生职业发展教育的课程执行,在一定程度上彰显了政府对大学生职业发展教育课程的重视。并提出了三种课程设置模式作为参考:第一种是开设一门涵盖整个大学生涯的职业发展教育课程。即高校根据本校实际情况和学生特点,在本校学制生涯中开设围绕"职业生涯发展"相关的课程,包括理论类课程或实践类活动等,加强大学生对职业生涯发展教育的认知。第二种在大学期间开设两门课程,如"职业生涯与发展规划"与"就业指导"。这是现阶段大部分高校的课程设置模式,据走访观察发现,大部分高校在大学生一年级下学期或二年级上学期开设"职业生涯与发展规划",在大三下学期开设"就业指导"课程。第三种是开设三门课程,课程安排"职业生涯发展规划""职业素养培养与提升"和"就业创业指导"。这种课程安排模式仅在一些对职业发展教育重视度较高的高校得以实践,课程的设置安排属于"渐进式",易被大学生所接纳,同时能够较好地实现该课程的教学目标。② 具体表现为:

---

① 张星晨.职业社会学视域下我国大学生职业发展教育研究[D].沈阳:沈阳师范大学,2014.
② 张星晨.职业社会学视域下我国大学生职业发展教育研究[D].沈阳:沈阳师范大学,2014.

1.清华大学模式

主张开发课程模块,模块中包括若干门短、平、快的课程,课程就像一种工业产品,针对不同情况的大学生提供不同的产品,缺什么补什么。如有的学生反映面试中不会沟通,就把他们组织起来上"沟通训练",有的学生对自己缺乏全面认识,就针对他们开设"自我探索",有的学生想出国深造,就给他们提供"留学指南"。整个模块包括6~9门课,基本上按照职业生涯发展过程中可能出现的问题来设立课程,属于问题式教学,每门课程记1个学分。

2.复旦大学模式

主张开设一门课程,各年级学生均可以选修,课程名称为"生涯规划与就业指导",2个学分32个学时。课程主要内容包括:生涯规划的基本理论,自我探索,职业社会认知,生涯决策,大学生涯发展规划的制订与实施,职业素养与职业发展,就业形势与政策,就业中的心态管理。①

3.武汉理工大学模式

主张分层开设多门课,分别是"大学生涯规划与职业发展"和"大学生求职技巧",前者针对大一学生,记2个学分32个学时,后者针对大三下学期、大四上学期的学生,1个学分16个学时。条件成熟时再针对研究生开设"职业生涯管理与开发"。

(三)课程目的

(1)"大学生涯规划与职业发展"课程目的主要是帮助大学生树立大学阶段的个人发展目标,规划和实施个人职业发展规划,激发和调动学生主动学习、自觉发展的内在原动力,从根本上提高大学生的就业竞争力和职业发展能力。首先是要学生进入大学就树立适合个人发展的目标,这个目标既包括适合学生自己的职业发展长期目标,更要着眼于大学阶段的短期发展目标。其次是帮助学生培养两种意识,一是就业主体意识,二是职业生涯规划意识。大学生在大学阶段就应该学习有关职业生涯规划的基础知识和理论,为自己的职业发展确定明确的目标,科学地选择适合自己发展的职业,为实现个人的职业发展目标做出大学阶段的学习计划,并制定详细的实施方案。培养大学生职业生涯规划意识的目的,就是让大学生树立个人的职

---

① 张正武.大学生全程化职业生涯规划教育研究[D].济南:山东大学,2009.

业发展目标,制定大学阶段实现个人职业目标的学习与能力培养规划,培养终身学习的观念。①

(2)"大学生就业指导课程"课程目的主要是帮助大学生了解当前的就业形势,进行科学合理的职业定位,培养和训练大学生的求职技巧,提高大学生的表达和沟通能力,增加大学生的公关礼仪知识,通过教学提高学生的就业能力,实现顺利求职。②

(四)教学模式

高校职业发展教育课程是一门集职业发展理论知识的传授、职业素质的培养和职业活动的实践等于一体的综合型应用学科。它既有知识的传授,也有技能的培养,还有态度、观念的转变,是集理论课、实务课和经验课于一体的综合课程。在教学过程中,既要有专业就业指导教师对就业理论的讲授,就业知识的传授,同时还需要具有丰富的职场经验的成功职业人、校友等进行专题讲座,将理论知识与实践相结合。教学上可以采用讲授与场景模拟训练相结合,利用典型案例、情景模拟、社会调查等方法。在教学过程中可利用丰富的现代资源,利用先进的测试工具如职业测评、心理测评等可以帮助学生充分了解自我、分析自我,进而做出合理的职业生涯规划。②

(五)课程内容

"要求"将课程内容分为六部分,第一部分是引导大学生建立生涯和职业意识;第二部分是帮助大学生制定职业发展规划,主要是在社会宏观就业环境下,通过课堂分析国家最新出台的就业文件政策和相关职业领域的最新职业趋势,以及不同地域对大学生就业的具体指导意见和优惠政策,避免大学生在择业过程中进入求职误区,引导大学生对职业社会环境有正确的认知;第三部分是提升大学生的职业素质和就业能力,尤其是职业道德、职场的团队协作能力等;第四部分是对大学生的求职择业的过程指导,主要包括求职择业的形象设计、求职简历设计和求职过程中的谈吐等;第五部分是帮助大学生适应职业和稳定职业;第六部分是对大学生的创业指导教育。但就该要求所提出的课程内容来看,学科内容设计多以理论和概念居多,对

---

①② 李玉红.大学生职业生涯规划研究——提升就业竞争力[D].武汉:中南民族大学,2007.
② 陶胜男.辽宁省硕士研究生职业发展教育与就业指导课程建设研究[D].沈阳:沈阳师范大学,2013.

该课程的实践部分没有做出具体的课程内容设置安排,甚至部分课程内容板块安排顺序也不是较为合理。①

(六)课程评价

我国各高校大学生职业发展课程评价方法,主要包括以下几个方面的内容。

(1)大多数高校开设的职业发展课程都是在课程结束或者一个学期结束时进行评价,有少数高校采用形成性评价并取消期末考试,即在课程各个阶段对学生进行评价,如北京大学的选修课大学生职业生涯规划、上海商学院的必修课职业生涯规划与管理。

(2)课程评价的方式为开卷,无论是采用终结性评价还是形成性评价,都是采取开卷的形式,学生根据自己的实际情况作答。

(3)课程评价的主要内容包括,终结性评价为主的高校是让学生递交职业生涯规划、撰写自荐信或简历等提交报告的形式,少数还会涉及案例分析和针对就业政策等的简答题。形成性评价为主的高校主要以学生的出勤率、课堂表现、课堂活动参与、课业完成情况等作为学生最终的课程成绩。

四、大学生职业发展教育课程特点

大学生作为社会的特殊群体,他们的生存和发展受到方方面面的关注,影响着社会的发展和稳定,因此对大学生的职业生涯指导不仅仅是人职匹配这一结果。从高等教育的角度而言,通过职业发展课程的学习,可以帮助和引导学生树立正确的人生理想和择业观念,提高自身的职业素质和职业能力;从学生自身的角度而言,该课程是帮助学生更好地认识自我、认识社会环境,分析自身的优势和不足,不断地完善自我,处理好自我与职业的关系,制定出切合实际的职业生涯规划;从学校的角度而言,职业生涯指导是学校的一项常规工作,是学校培养优秀人才,推进学生就业,提高学校社会影响力的重要抓手之一,大学生职业发展课程是高校职业发展教育的主要方法之一,为学生实践实训奠定了基础,是对职业测评与职业咨询的补充和衔接。经过十几年的实践和探索,我国大学生职业发展课程形成了自己的特点和模式,就目前的发展趋势看,大学生职业发展课程具有以下几个鲜明

---

① 张星晨.职业社会学视域下我国大学生职业发展教育研究[D].沈阳:沈阳师范大学,2014.

的特点。[1]

（一）课程分阶段进行

大学生职业发展教育是从大学一年级开始一直延续到学生大学毕业的,因此大学生职业发展课程也就不同于一般的基础课和专业课,放在一个学期内或一个学年内就讲授完成,针对不同阶段有所侧重,低年级侧重对自我的探索和大学学习生涯的短期中期规划,二、三年级对职业环境的认识、中高年级侧重对学生就业能力的提升和就业政策的了解。从目前的情况来看,不少学校已经将大学生职业发展课程全程化,比如东华大学以新生入学职业发展启蒙教育为起点,八次主题教育为主线,个体辅导贯穿始终,职业发展课程"大学生生涯规划与职业发展",面向低年级学生,大学生成功就业训练课程面向高年级学生;复旦大学的职业发展课程设有生涯发展规划,针对低年级和高年级分别进行就业指导;上海商学院职业生涯规划与管理分为起始阶段(本科第一学期)、实践阶段(本科第二到第五学期)、后期阶段(本科第六学期)。

（二）学生是课程的建构者,教师是引导者

大学生职业发展课程的主要目的是教会学生掌握分析自我和探索社会的方法和技巧,调动学生的积极性和主动性,促使他们对自己未来的生涯发展做出决策和行动,教师在这里更主要的任务是一个引导者而不是传授者,需要针对学生不同的特点采取不同的教学方法和教学内容,对学生进行个性化的指导和帮助,因此学生是这门课的构建者。

（三）弹性的课程评价

大学生职业发展课程是指导学生探索自我,探索社会的一门课程。每个人的成长经历、性格特点、对未来的期望等都是不一样的,同一个人在不同的阶段对自我的规划也是不同的。因此对于大学生职业发展课程而言,无论是终结性考核还是形成性考核,都是没有标准答案的。它不同于一般的基础课,比如数学是有固定的解题步骤和标准答案的。如要求学生完成未来5年的职业生涯规划,每个学生根据他的性格、经历、志向会有不同的答案,而且这个答案是随着对自我和环境探索的深入不断变化的。再比如简

---

[1] 高洁静.大学生职业发展课程评价初探——从真实性评价的角度[D].上海:华东师范大学,2010.

历的制作,不同人的简历肯定是不一样的,即便是同一个学生针对不同的单位和岗位,也是有所侧重的,不是一成不变的。因此,弹性的评价体系是要引起我们高度关注的。①

第三节　国外职业发展教育对我国的启示

借鉴国外职业发展教育的经验,我国在开展职业发展教育时应注意以下六个方面:

一、树立正确的人才观

国外的职业发展教育是以现代人才观为理论基础的。知识经济时代脑力与体力劳动紧密融合,凡是在职业发展中能成为优秀劳动者的都是人才,相信人人都能成才,鼓励人人成才,造就各级各类人才,使整个社会形成宝塔型的、结构合理的人才"集合体",是职业发展教育的出发点和归宿,也是职业发展教育能够推行的认识基础和舆论氛围。社会分层是客观存在,分工不同是社会需要,在各个层次、各种职业、各自岗位的优秀劳动者都应得到社会的尊重,教育不能只为培养和选拔"精英"服务,而要以提升国民素质,使全体受教育者成人、成才、成功为目标,这是实施人才强国战略、构建和谐社会的必然要求。②

二、加强职业发展教育法制化

20世纪70年代,美国政府实施了"职业发展教育"的拨款计划,要求在普通教育中开展相关的职业发展教育课程,普通教育与职业发展教育不再是两条平行线,要将两者结合起来。③ 美国曾两次专门以政府法案的形式改革职业发展教育,分别是20世纪70年代的《生计教育法案》以及90年代的《学校—就业法案》(School—To—Work)。这意味着美国建立了从职业认识到职业选择的完整职业指导体系,使学生能主动地进行自我选择和未来的

---

① 高洁静.大学生职业发展课程评价初探——从真实性评价的角度[D].上海:华东师范大学,2010.
② 谷峪.日本社会转型期的职业技术教育——兼谈对我国职业技术教育发展的启示[D].长春:东北师范大学,2006.
③ 徐婕.大学生职业生涯规划教育研究[D].扬州:扬州大学硕士论文,2012.

人生规划,对于促进学生的有效职业选择有重要意义。韩国为了在短期内迅速推进学校职业指导工作,曾出资在全国46个地区建立起覆盖初中、高中和高校的"职业指导模范学校",试图为其他学校职业指导工作的开展提供榜样和示范①。英国制定了一些相关法令,社会相关各部门要为学生熟悉各种职业提供便利条件。日本也制定了一系列相关的政策、法规,推动学校与企业等社会组织共同配合实施。另外,学校内部也要建立相关制度,通过选修课程、综合实践课程等实施职业发展教育,建立职业发展教育评价机制,遵循全面原则、绩效原则与连贯性原则,让学生能学习到系统的职业发展教育技能②。

三、注意职业发展教育的早期性和全程性

1994年,美国联邦政府教育部和劳工部推行校外锻炼计划,该计划适合1年级至12年级的所有学生,目的是帮助学生通过一定阶段的社会实践,在接受高等教育前就能初步了解职业世界,了解未来职业的需求方向和不同职业对员工的素质要求。在小学阶段,学校不定期地邀请用人单位的负责人给小学生普及职业的基本知识,介绍社会上有哪些岗位,具体岗位需要什么样的人才,并安排小学生进行一定的社会实践;在中学阶段,学生要进行为期1至6个月时间不等的实习,获得一定的工作经验,进入大学前的实践情况都会被记入档案。我国大部分高校的大学生职业发展规划教育只针对毕业生,对低年级学生关注得较少,而美国高校的就业指导工作从学生一入校就开始,贯穿整个大学发展,以增强学生的择业能力。就业指导中心在大学新生刚入校时,就对学生开展职业发展教育,帮助学生了解社会需求和市场情况;第二年,指导学生科学客观地分析自身能力、兴趣、个性、爱好等,并积极参与各类职业活动,选择和自身匹配的专业;第三年,鼓励学生积极参加社会实践,了解社会的人才需求和各类职业的能力需求,帮助学生更好地认识所学专业;最后一年,教授学生如何撰写简历、求职书,帮助学生锻炼面试技巧,为学生收集就业信息,组织学生参加各类招聘会。③

---

① 陆小玲.国外高校职业发展规划教育对我国的启示[J].教育探索,2011(3).
② 葛鑫,李森.国外中学职业发展教育对我国的启示[J].教育探索,2008(9).
③ 徐婕.大学生职业生涯规划教育研究[D].扬州:扬州大学,2012.

四、重视教师专业化建设

职业发展教育是一项专业性很强的工作,辅导人员必须具备专业的知识和技术,能够通过各种途径提供有效的服务,这就要求每位职业发展教育教师具备较高的素质和能力。[1] 美国对职业发展辅导、咨询从业人员的要求颇高,一般要求其具有心理学、教育学等与辅导、咨询相关学科硕士以上的学历以及由全美发展协会颁发的专业职业发展辅导人员资格认证证书,并且要求具备一定的工作经验。[2] 虽然日本学校从事职业发展教育工作的老师有专兼职之分,但主体是一支具有相应学历、层次与岗位职责分明的专职队伍。所有工作者都持证上岗,长期从事特定领域的工作,不仅经验丰富,而且业务的系统性较强[3]。

我国职业发展教育的开展,尚缺乏必需的一定数量质量的师资队伍。所以,建设一支强有力的师资队伍是开展职业发展教育工作的当务之急。从长远的观点出发,职业发展教育人员的培养必须坚持系统化、专业化的原则,使培训人员掌握职业发展教育的基本要领和专业知识。全面提升职业发展教育教师的研究能力、组织能力、管理能力与指导能力,使他们逐步成为职业发展教育的"专家"。职业发展教育教师应该具备相关的职业发展教育理论,比如帕森斯的人职匹配理论等。同时,教师要掌握基本的心理辅导方法,指导学生了解、认识自我,寻找适合自己特点的人生规划。为了尽量使职业发展教育能覆盖到更多的人、发挥更大的作用,辅导人员需要使用心理测量工具了解学生的性格特征和能力倾向,进行有针对性的指导。因此职业发展教育人员需要有一定的心理学基础或者需要和心理咨询人员密切配合,以有效开展职业发展教育工作。[4]

职业发展教育教师的培养,可以采取多种培养方式,如组织聘请专家,对准备从事职业发展教育管理与实践工作的人员培训;在有条件的师范院校开设职业发展教育专业或创建职业发展教育系;选派人员去国外接受培训等方式。尽快培养大量合格的职业发展教育师资,是职业发展教育顺利

---

[1] 卓念.中美两国普通中学职业生涯教育比较研究[D].兰州:西北师范大学,2009.
[2] 陈禹.人力资源开发背景下美国高校职业生涯教育研究[D].长春:东北师范大学,2011.
[3] 吕显然.日本职业发展教育研究及启示[D].青岛:青岛大学,2014.
[4] 卓念.中美两国普通中学职业生涯教育比较研究[D].兰州:西北师范大学,2009.

实施的重要保障。其中在高校开设职业发展教育专业可以从源头上解决职业发展教育的师资问题,是最基本的也是最重要的途径。

五、注重职业发展教育服务机构建设

任何一项工作都要通过一定的组织机构来组织实施。设立专门的组织管理机构才能从体制上保证职业发展教育在整个教育体系和学校教育中的重要地位。教育行政部门应设立职业发展教育指导机构,负责指导下级机构和各学校开展职业发展教育工作,同时为学校、家长和学生提供有公信力的职业发展信息和帮助,以及负责培训专业教师等。学校职业发展教育有其自身的特殊性,应作为学校教育的相对独立的部分,建立专门的组织机构、配备专业人员负责开展,才能保证其功能的发挥。为此,有必要建立国家、地方、学校三级职业发展教育工作机构。学校一级的组织是职业发展教育工作的基层单位,一切职业发展教育的计划目标最后都需要通过学校才能够得到落实,因此要特别加强学校中的职业发展教育机构建设,保证在学校中有专门机构、专人负责职业发展教育工作的实施。学校也要高度重视职业发展教育的开展,把职业发展教育的组织与实施列入学校的工作计划,放在与其他教学同等重要的位置,并从学校实际出发积极组织落实。①

六、增强课程开发力度

"课程问题,在任何一个教育体系中总是居于中心地位。"课程是实现教学目的进而实现人才培养目标的重要载体。独立地开设职业发展教育课程,重点向学生讲解职业生涯规划、职业生涯与人生、职业与社会等方面的基础知识和基本理念,培育学生进行职业生涯规划的意识与能力。通过实施职业生涯教育课程,保证职业生涯教育有计划、有目的、有组织地进行。但职业生涯教育的特性决定了课程不应该局限在课堂上,形式多样的授课方式和校内外的互动将激发学生的兴趣,开阔他们的眼界,提高职业发展教育的有效性。②

在美国,每所高校都有一批关系密切的机构、单位和企业,它们是高校大学生参加社会实践的基地,通过组织各年级大学生的实习、见习等活动,

---

①② 卓念.中美两国普通中学职业生涯教育比较研究[D].兰州:西北师范大学,2009.

提高学生的社会适应性和实践操作能力,帮助他们更好地了解职业世界和社会需求。为了拓展就业渠道,提高毕业生的就业率,美国高校就业指导服务机构会主动和用人单位联系,建立双方良好的合作关系,组织各种招聘活动,为学生和用人单位之间搭建沟通桥梁,增加双方互相选择的机会。美国高校就业指导中心在开展相关工作时非常注重激发学生的创新意识,培养他们的自主创业精神和运用知识解决实际问题的能力,力求把高等学校办成"创业者的熔炉",因此美国大学生的创业活动起步较早,取得了很大的社会反响,并且推动了整个社会的创新能力。麻省理工学院是美国的重点院校,根据其在1999年所做的调查,该校的毕业生已经创立了4000个公司,在美国高校中遥遥领先,学院也成为美国高校真正的"创业者的熔炉"。该校从1990年以来,师生平均每年新建150个公司,雇佣上百万工人,创造了可观的销售额,对麻省甚至整个美国的经济发展都起到一定的推动作用。大学生自主创业是当代大学生就业的新方式,不仅帮助他们顺利就业、实现职业理想,还能为社会减轻就业压力,推动社会的稳定和经济的繁荣,因而大学生自主创业已经成为大学生职业辅导的新课题。①

思考题:

1. 我国职业发展教育课程产生的基础是什么?
2. 我国职业发展教育的课程特点有哪些?
3. 国外职业发展教育对我国有哪些经验启示?

推荐书目:

[1]黄炜.大学生职业发展教程[M].北京:科学出版社,2011.

[2]朱德全.职业教育统筹发展论[M].北京:科学出版社,2016.

[3]顾静.让人生出彩——大学生职业发展教程[M].北京:高等教育出版社,2014.

[4]张华东.大学生职业发展教育与就业指导[M].北京:科学出版社,2017.

[5]李春举.大学生职业发展与高校创新创业教育研究[M].北京:中国纺织出版社,2017.

---

① 徐婕.大学生职业生涯规划教育研究[D].扬州:扬州大学,2012.

国外论文导读与阅读:

导读:职业发展课程和教育成果:职业课程有所作为吗?

作者:杰米·汉森(Jamie M. Hansen),亚伦·杰克逊(Aaron P. Jackson),泰勒·佩德·森(Tyler R. Pedersen)

该论文旨在研究职业发展课程对教育成果的影响。这项研究比较了两组本科生:一组成功完成了职业发展课程和一组未参加职业发展课程的学生。分别对这两个小组的毕业率、毕业时间、课程提取和累积平均成绩(GPA)进行了比较。该论文的主要内容分为两部分。

第一部分介绍了研究设计。研究收集了从2000—2007年的学生样本,其中:完成职业发展课程的学生样本作为实验组;没有参加职业发展课程的学生样本作为参照组。研究中的自变量是职业课程,因变量包括毕业率、毕业学分等。

第二部分是结果分析和结论。结果显示两组在毕业率方面没有显著差异。然而,结果表明准实验组和对照组之间在毕业学分(课程参与者毕业时获得的学分多于非课程参与者)和累积GPA(课程参与者毕业累积GPA高于非课程)方面存在统计学显著差异。

文章来源:

Jamie M. Hansen, Aaron P. Jackson, Tyler R. Pedersen. Career Development Courses and Educational Outcomes: Do Career Courses Make a Difference? [J]. Journal of Career Development, 2016:1-15.

(节选的英文原文见附录8)

参考文献

[1] 庞春敏,张伟民,劳汉生.基于"盖茨比标准"的生涯教育改革:英国新一轮生涯教育改革与启示[J].外国中小学教育,2018(10).

[2] 魏雪杉.高职院校大学生职业成长互助生态圈的研究[D].桂林:广西师范大学,2018.

[3] 郦娅萍."立德树人"视角下的职校生职业生涯规划研究[D].南京:南京师范大学,2018.

[4] 周凌.英国现代高等教育发展对我国"双一流"建设的启示[J].中国高教研究,2017(11).

[5] 王小玲.诊所式教学模式下大学生职业生涯规划课程教学探析[J].陕西教育(高教),2017(09).

[6] 李蕾,陈鹏.发达国家职业启蒙教育的经验与启示[J].职教论坛,2017(21).

[7] 胡凤麟.基于美英两国经验的民办高职院校职业生涯发展课程研究[J].新课程研究(中旬刊),2016(10).

[8] 杨昕.高校就业指导管理体系构建问题研究[D].保定:河北大学,2016.

[9] 孟可可.英国普通中学生涯教育研究[D].上海:上海师范大学,2015.

[10] 苏敏,赵国平,隋立国.中英职业教育人才培养方案的比较与思考:英国华威学院幼教专业调研报告[J].中国成人教育,2015(08).

[11] 程青曼.南京医科大学低年级医学生职业生涯规划教育现状及对策研究[D].南京:南京医科大学,2014.

[12] 邓宏宝.国外高校职业生涯教育课程开发与实施研究[J].学术论坛,2013,36(12).

[13] 邓宏宝.国外中学生涯教育课程实施:经验与启示[J].外国中小学教育,2013(10).

[14] 张益民.发达国家大学生职业生涯规划研究与启示[J].学理论,2012(22).

[15] 仇道滨.英国高校"职业管理技能"培训体系的特点及其启示[J].中国青年政治学院学报,2012,31(01).

[16] 季振宇.义务教育背景下职业教育理念的渗透[J].职业技术,2010(12).

[17] 杨思帆.国外学生人生规划教育的若干特点与启示[J].教育与考试,2010(02).

[18] 卓念.中美两国普通中学职业生涯教育比较研究[D].兰州:西北师范大学,2009.

[19] 李晓涛.英国普通中学职业指导研究[D].重庆:西南大学,2009.

[20] 谌启标.英国职业指导的组织结构、框架体系和政策走向[J].职教通讯,2005(11).

[21] 侯立军.英国高等教育的现状和发展趋势分析[J].南京财经大学学报,2005(05).

[21] 荀澄.德国中小学的教育体制[J].天津师范大学学报(基础教育版),2008(12).

[22] 方伟.中国大学学术管理法律关系及立法完善研究[D].北京:北京大学,2005.

[23] 马陆亭.德国高等教育的制度特点[J].教育研究,2002(10).

[24] 孟浩.中国研究生招生制度变革研究[D].上海:华东师范大学,2009.

[25] 李祖德.德国高等教育制度对中国西部高校发展的借鉴作用[J].青海大学学报(自然科学版),2003(04).

[26] 黄日强.政策因素对德国职业教育的促进作用[J].世界教育信息,2006(07).

[27] 黄翠芳.中国职业教育纳入免费义务教育的必要性研究[D].武汉:华中科技大学,2012.

[28] 侯捷.论就业制度对我国大学生就业的影响[D].武汉:华中科技大学,2006.

[29]肖松涛.中德就业指导比较探析[J].电子世界,2012(12).

[30]李望云.基于产业发展的武汉东湖高新就业现状与人才培养策略建议[J].武汉职业技术学院学报,2015(12).

[31]施晓轩.大学生就业服务机构的比较研究[D].杭州:浙江师范大学,2012.

[32]毛立红.发达国家大学生公共就业服务供给机制的经验与启示[J].行政管理改革,2012(11).

[33]王萌.美国、日本、德国大学毕业生就业中政府作为的研究及启示[J].外国教育研究,2012(01).

[34]高嘉勇.德国高校课程设置与可雇佣性研究[J].天津市教科院学报,2008(08).

[35]高震华.德国高校"关键能力"培养研究及其启示[J].教育与职业,2015(05).

[36]陈文.德国高校创业教育特点及启示[J].学校党建与思想教育(高教版),2012(10).

[37]李建强.普通高中实施职业生涯教育的探索[D].杭州:浙江师范大学,2007(10).

[38]黄晓梅.我国大学生职业生涯规划综合实施机制探析[J].中国成人教育,2010(01).

[39]王曦.普通高中职业生涯规划教育现状的调查研究[D].北京:北京师范大学,2012.

[40]胡元聪.职业生涯规划实践的国际比较及我国的改革方向探析[J].教育与职业,2012(02).

[41]黄雄英.安徽省高校毕业生就业指导队伍现状研究[D].合肥:合肥工业大学,2007.

[42]陆海英.德国经验与中国借鉴:高校就业机制的发展与方向[J].教育评论,2016(05).

[43]王林.高校就业指导队伍建设研究[D].北京:北京师范大学,2008.

[44]刘小玲.新形势下大学生就业心理制度模式研究[D].南昌:南昌大学,2006.

[45]武晓红.德国大学生就业服务体系对我国高校就业指导工作的启示[J].亚太教育,2015(03).

[46]赵峰.高校就业指导工作体系及相关问题研究[D].南昌:南昌大学,2009.

[47]白娟娟.人力资本理论视角下对德国大学生就业服务体系的研究[J].武汉职业技术学院学报,2018(09).

[48]劳晓芸.大学生职业生涯发展教育工作研究[J].思想理论教育,2006(06).

附 录

附录1

Career Development and Its Practice: A Historical Perspective
(节选)

The use of the term career development as descriptive of both the factors and the processes influencing individual career behavior and as synonymous with intervention in career behavior (e.g., the practice of career development) is relatively recent. As professional vocabulary evolves across time, so do the form and substance of career interventions and those to whom they are directed. At the beginning of the new millennium, this article reviews the legacy of the 20th century and considers selected theoretical and practical issues likely to be prominent in the practice of career development in the decades immediately ahead.

The term career development, as used in the title of the National Career Development Association, had increasingly come, at the end of the twentieth century, to describe both the total constellation of psychological, sociological, educational, physical, economic, and chance factors that combine to shape individual career behavior over the life span (Sears, 1982) and the interventions or practices that are used "to enhance a person's career development or to enable that person to make more effective career decisions" (Spokane, 1991). Thus, inherent in the current usage of the term career development are two sets of theories, or conceptual categories, one that explains the development of career behavior across the lifespan and the other that describes how career behavior is changed by particular interventions.

This perspective about the contemporary use of the term career development is important simply to establish that terms, like professions, evolve. They are historical creations, the shape, substance, and labeling of which reflect social, political, and economic change. Indeed, the term career was rarely used before the 1960s and the term development was rarely used before the 1950s. When the two terms were combined, they tended until the late 1960s to be described as vocational development or vocational psychology, not career development.

Against this context it is useful to consider the antecedent events that have led to the focus of this special issue: the practice of career development. Historical references to career development practice are more likely to use terms like vocational guidance or counseling or career guidance or counseling, rather than career development practice, but all of these terms flow from the same roots.

Historical Perspectives

In this millennium issue of The Career Development Quarterly, it is useful to acknowledge that if one believes in evolution, rather than revolution, as the origin of career development practice, then the seeds of the future exist in the past and in the present. In such a view, the practice of career development in the twenty-first century will build on, be distributed more evenly across the world, and refine much of what has been learned and implemented in the twentieth century. If one discounts the interesting accounts (Dumont & Carson, 1995; Williamson, 1965) of the origins of career development practice that can be traced far into antiquity to demonstrate how various societies have helped persons choose their work, or, more likely, allocated work to people based on their class or caste, one can conclude that the theories and techniques that constitute current approaches to the practice of career development are primarily creatures of the late nineteenth and early twentieth centuries.

Factors Influencing the Emergence of Vocational Guidance

The rise of what was first identified as vocational guidance in the United States in the late nineteenth and early twentieth centuries was directly associated with major shifts from a national economy that was primarily based in agriculture to an economy that was, as part of the industrial revolution that was spilling over from Europe to the United States, increasingly based in manufacturing and industrial processes. As the latter occurred, urbanization and occupational diversity increased, as did national concerns about strengthening vocational education and responding to the needs for information about how persons could identify and access emerging jobs. By the late 1800s, particularly in urban areas, such information was so differentiated and comprehensive that families or neighborhoods could no longer be the prime sources of occupational information or of the allocation of jobs; other more formal mechanisms, including rudimentary forms of vocational guidance, began to emerge in schools, in settlement houses, and in community centers.

A major factor in the rise of vocational guidance was the accelerating movement of large numbers of immigrants from nations with poor economic opportunities coming to the United States seeking new live sand options; a parallel phenomenon was occurring as people in the United States were migrating from rural to urban areas, spurred by the urbanization of jobs, particularly in the concentrations of plants in major cities making steel, furniture, automobiles, and other large capital goods.

Cast against the processes of industrialization, urbanization, and immigration were many other issues that affected the development of vocational guidance. These issues included concerns about appropriate education for children and effective placement of adults into a rapidly changing occupational structure, about effective methods of distribution of immigrants across the spectrum of available occupations, and about the way to bridge the gap between schooling and the realities of the adult world. At the beginning of the twentieth century as at its end, many voices were raised in behalf of educational reform, arguing that schools were too "bookish," too college oriented, and with insufficient vocational education.

Other issues were also pervasive at the turn of the twentieth century. Among them were concerns about how to address changing family structures, the increasing proportion of girl sand women entering the workplace rather than confining themselves to homemaking, diminished extended kinship systems, child labor, and the shifts in child rearing practices that were emerging in relation to migration and the consuming force of the industrial revolution. Moreover, as the social reformers and human rights activists were advocating, there was an emerging moral imperative that opposed child labor and argued that workers in the burgeoning economy of the early twentieth century needed to be seen not as the chattels of employers, not as property to be consumed and cast aside, but rather as persons of dignity with a right to determine their own destiny.

By any analysis, it is clear that the heritage of career development practice in the United States is rich, complex, and responsive to the social, political, and economic forces shaping the national context. Observers in and out of the professional ranks of career counselors and specialists in career guidance have reinforced the notion that the theories and practices that undergird and stimulate career development practice do not exist in a vacuum. Although, in any period of social change, the force of certain personalities as articulators and visionaries, who advocate what needs to be done to convert ideas about career guidance or other processes into action, is critical, the historical moment−the political and social conditions−must be right for the seeds of change to take root and flourish. The last quarter of the nineteenth century and the first quarter of the twentieth century were such times.

One of the important chronicles of the rise of vocational guidance in the United States (Brewer, 1942) identified four conditions that were seen as major influences: the division of labor, the growth of technology, the extension of vocational education, and the spread of modern forms of democracy. Other observers elaborated on the connections between the rise and redirection of vocational guidance and counseling during the past 100 years and the effects of particular political or social phenomena−legislation, national crises, shifts in social values,

the civil rights and women's liberation movements, and economic conditions.

Cremin (1964), a historian of education, contended that one of the associated outcomes of the Progressive Education movement in the late 1800s and the first 50 years of the twentieth century was the beginning of the guidance movement, particularly its emphasis on vocational guidance. He, like others, contended that the social reformism of the urban settlement workers was directly involved in the beginning of vocational guidance during the first years of the twentieth century and its subsequent implementation in the schools of Boston and other cities. Cremin argued that social reformers of the time believed

[n] ot only that vocational counseling would lead to greater individual fulfillment; but that people suited to their job would tend to be active in the creation of more efficient and humane industrial systems ... [therefore] the craft of vocational guidance would serve not only the youngsters who sought counsel, but the cause of social reform as well.

Cremin further contended that the effort to develop a science of education, also at the heart of the progressive movement, was reflected in the major interest in tests and measurements that grew up in the United States immediately after the turn of the twentieth century. According to Cremin, it was in this context that "the idea developed of the guidance worker as a trained professional, wise in administering and interpreting scientific instruments for the prediction of vocational and educational success"

Cremin's (1964) analysis of the impact of the Progressive Education era on vocational guidance and counseling is but one of the interesting interactions between educational reform and the rise of vocational guidance. Stephens (1970), also a historian, has argued that "the vocational education movement was an educational response to the general reform movement spawned by the industrialization of American". More to the point of the origins of vocational guidance are Stephens's observations that

[t] o many leaders of the vocational reform movement ... it was apparent that vocational education was but the first part of a package of needed educational reforms. They argued that a school curriculum and educational goals that mirrored

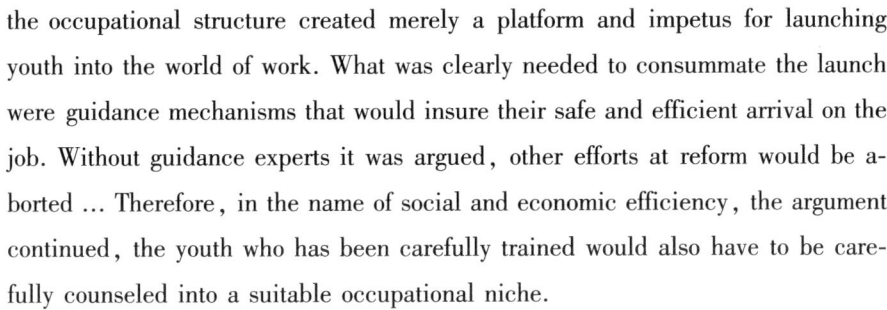

the occupational structure created merely a platform and impetus for launching youth into the world of work. What was clearly needed to consummate the launch were guidance mechanisms that would insure their safe and efficient arrival on the job. Without guidance experts it was argued, other efforts at reform would be aborted ... Therefore, in the name of social and economic efficiency, the argument continued, the youth who has been carefully trained would also have to be carefully counseled into a suitable occupational niche.

These analyses of the array of forces that shaped and defined the original antecedents to contemporary approaches to career guidance, career counseling, and to the practice of career development could be repeated from other vantage points. They would include extended discussions of persons and events that made significant conceptual and empirical contributions to the evolution of career development and its related career interventions. To do so would affirm the general applicability of Borow's (1964) observations that the history of vocational guidance teaches two lessons:

(1) The growth of the movement must be evaluated against the Zeitgeist. Without an appreciation of the prevailing social and intellectual temper of the times, the interpretation of episodes in the sweep of professional history remains incomplete and often distorted; (2) Progress flows from seemingly small beginnings.

The Emergence of Vocational Guidance

The period to which the citations of Borow(1964), Brewer(1942), Cremin (1964), and Stephens (1970) spoke is considered the founding period of vocational guidance in the United States. It is the period when Parsons, generally conceded to be the father of the vocational guidance movement and, indeed, the architect of the vocational counseling process, wrote his classic book Choosing a Vocation, posthumously published in 1909. Trained as a civil engineer and a lawyer, Parsons spent most of his life dealing with social reform among the excesses of the free enterprise system as he saw them and the debasement of human nature, which he considered a result of the management of industrial organizations. He was at various times involved with activities of the settlement

houses that had grown up in central Boston and in other cities along the northeastern seaboard.

Parsons in the later years of his life turned the focus of his attention to industrial education and vocational guidance in response to his feeling that too many people, especially the immigrants from Europe, were being wasted, both economically and socially, because of the haphazard way they got into the specialized world of the factory. Like so many others of his time, Parsons attacked the public schools for their specialization in book learning and advocated that "book work should be balanced with industrial education; and working children should spend part time in culture classes and industrial science" (Stephens, 1970).

It was in response to the questions and issues inventoried here-those dealing with human dignity, the effective matching of persons and jobs, educational and social reform-that the early models of vocational guidance and vocational counseling were created. The early vocational guidance procedures were seen as methods, both practical and humane, to help persons to be matched with the needs of the occupational structure in ways that both preserved the order and the rationality of such choices and the power of persons to make decisions about job options available to them rather than to be coerced or forced into whatever was immediately available. However, at the beginning of the twentieth century, although there was important research taking place about the measurement of individual differences and other counseling - relevant processes in university laboratories in Europe and the United States, there was essentially no scientific basis or theory on which to build models of vocational guidance or counseling. The practice of career development was emerging, but not yet career development theory.

To compensate for the lack of theory and applicable science-and the tools that counselors have come to depend on in career development practice (e.g., tests, dictionaries of occupational titles, The Occupational Outlook Handbook)-persons of conceptual genius in Europe and in the United States developed techniques and insights that began to create a knowledge base on which vocational counseling could be built.

Exemplary of such persons was Alfred Binet's work in France on intelligence testing; Spranger's work in Germany on types of personalities in relation to different types of jobs; Munsterber's research in Germany on occupational choice and worker performance; the work of Jesse B. Davis and Eli Weaver in the United States on the educational and career problems of students; and, perhaps the preeminent contribution: the three step paradigm of Parsons that guided the development of vocational guidance for at least the first 50 years of the twentieth century. Parsons, as part of his vision of the process, coined the term vocational guidance. In general, Parsons saw vocational guidance as a one-on-one process, which he also called "vocational counseling" (Cremin, 1964; Parsons, 1909). In his concern about developing techniques by which school children, adolescent school leavers, and adults could come to true reasoning about jobs available to them, he proposed a tripartite set of concepts as a frame of reference for the use of techniques by a counselor. His classic three-step design included the following:

First, a clear understanding of yourself, aptitudes, abilities, interests, resources, limitations, and other qualities. Second, a knowledge of the requirements and conditions of success, advantages and disadvantages, compensation, opportunities, and prospects in different lines of work. Third, true reasoning on the relations of these two groups of facts. (Parsons, 1909)

The techniques readily available for Parsons (1909) to use to implement his three-step process were limited. As a result, Parsons had his counselees read biographies and interview workers to learn about working environments and the occupational structure. In the absence of standardized tests of aptitudes or interest inventories, or directories of information about jobs or occupations, Parsons emphasized counselor observation of client characteristics and the coaching of the client in comprehensive self-study and in study of industrial opportunities available. He used extensive lists of questions for client self-study and sharing with the counselor. He offered techniques to assist clients to be introspective about their own likes and dislikes, successes and limitations, and to talk with the counselor about how to engage in true reasoning (decision making) related to the informa-

tion they had. Although it is rarely noted, Parsons was expressly inclusive of, and tailored approaches to, both young men and young women. He assumed that many, but not all, of the vocational techniques he used were of equal value to boys and girls and men and women, and he provided special attention to information about industries open to women and how these positions could be accessed. He also provided statistics about occupations in which both men and women were employed as well as those that employed primarily men. Some of the techniques Parsons pioneered are still used today, and some are incorporated into more sophisticated interventions for counselor use.

Although the history of the twentieth century has included fleshing out Parsons's model, adding steps to it (Salamone, 1988), providing scientific bases to each of the steps—identifying and measuring individual differences, documenting differences in occupational content and activity, and clarifying the elements of the decision-making process—the century's achievements go beyond the important contributions of Parsons's paradigm. Other theorists and practitioners have created an array of career development theories and practices that effectively intervene in the facilitation of career development, job choice and entry, work adjustment problems, unemployment, and underemployment. Still other theorists have advocated the differential perspectives and needs of women and men as well as of persons in racial and ethnic minority groups for career guidance (Gilligan, 1982; Leong, 1995; Pierce, 1933). As a result, the possible recipients of vocational guidance have become increasingly comprehensive in the range of problems that they present and in their ages and settings rather than being primarily adolescents in schools or settlement houses, as was true at the beginning of the twentieth century. Nevertheless, Parsons's paradigm continues to be a remarkable milestone in the evolution of career development practices.

Although there is much more that can be said about the important forces that shaped vocational guidance in the decades spanning the nineteenth and twentieth centuries, given the spatial limitations here, it is necessary to fast forward to the middle of the twentieth century to capture the growing conceptual changes that have shaped the final 50 years of the twentieth century. For a decade-by-decade

compilation of major events shaping contemporary forms of career development practice, the reader is invited to examine the article later in this special issue titled "Selected Milestones in the Evolution of Career Development Practices in the Twentieth Century" (Herr & Shahnasarian, 2001).

......

Changing Definitions of Vocational Guidance

In addition to the important role of federal legislation, a subset of major importance in affecting the practice of career development during the latter half of the twentieth century was the rise of theories of career development and the related redefinition of vocational guidance. A major milestone occurred in 1950, when Hoppock, then president of the National Vocational Guidance Association, observed that the traditional view of vocational guidance was "crumbling" (Hoppock, 1950). In 1951, following on Hoppock's observation, Super recommended that the traditional definition of vocational guidance that had stood since 1937 be revised. The 1937 definition stated that vocational guidance was "the process of assisting the individual to choose an occupation, prepare for it, enter upon it, and progress in it" (Super, 1951). The definition proposed by Super (1951) and adopted by the National Vocational Guidance Association defined vocational guidance as

[t] he process of helping a person to develop and accept an integrated and adequate picture of himself [sic] and of his role in the world of work, to test this concept against reality, and to convert it into a reality, with satisfaction to himself and to society.

The latter definition changed the focus of vocational guidance from a concentration on what is to be chosen to increasing attention on the characteristics of the chooser. In the process, it diminished the emphasis on matching individual to job and on the provision of occupational information at a particular point in time. Instead, it emphasized the psychological nature of vocational choice, accented the developmental influences on career behavior across the lifespan, blended the personal and vocational dimensions of guidance into a whole, and elevated the importance of self-understanding and self-acceptance as the evaluative bases to

which occupational and educational alternatives should be related.

Super's (1990) theoretical conceptions in the 1950s through the 1990s emphasized a life-span approach to career development, which describes changing career tasks and concerns in each of a series of life stages: growth, exploration, establishment, maintenance, and decline. He addressed both similar and different career patterns exhibited by men and women related to such physical and social phenomena as sex stereotyping, socialization, biological differences, and the opportunity structure. He made explicit the interaction of career development and personal development, the differential salience or meaning of work, how life roles and work roles affected individual career patterns, and the processes and elements related to career maturity and career adaptability.

During the 1950s and the 1960s, and subsequently, other major theories of career development were created and tested. The career theories of Roe (1956), Holland (1966), Krumboltz (1979), and others spawned additional paradigms of career behavior, based on interdisciplinary perspectives such as the psychodynamic effects of child-rearing practices on the development of occupational interests, the role of behavioral style or personality type as the major influence in career choice, and the role of unique learning experiences reinforced by unfolding life events that affect individual preferences. The work of Roe, of Holland, of Krumboltz, and of Super (1957, 1990) led to the development of a large array of new assessment instruments (e.g., the Self-Directed Search, the Vocational Preference Inventory, the Adult Career Concerns Inventory, the Career Maturity Inventory, the Values Inventory, the Career Beliefs Inventory) and counseling interventions that operationalized the constructs embedded in the career theories. Theory building continued throughout the ensuing years of the twentieth century as had the creation of new tests and career interventions.

Of particular importance to theory building during the last quarter century of the twentieth century was the growing attention to the career development of women and of minority populations. Among such contributions are those of Astin's (1984) four constructs that address the possibility of gender differences in degree of career behavior rather than kind: motivation, sex role socialization, the structure of opportunity, and work expectations; the work of Betz and Hackett (1986) in examining the effects of level and strength of self-efficacy related to women's entrance into and performance in career-related processes; Farmer's (1985) analyses of influences on aspiration, mastery, and career commitment for men and women and her studies of diversity and women's career development from adolescence to adulthood (Farmer & Associates, 1997); Gilligan's (1982) efforts to describe women's sex role development leading to differences in the sexes in their expressions of intimacy and identity in relation to career behavior; and Hansen's work with her colleagues on creating career development curriculum designed to reflect the changing roles of young men and women in the workplace and in other life roles (Hansen & Minor, 1989) and her model of Integrative Life Planning (Hansen, 1997); and the work of Leong (1995) in describing the influences on career behavior of culturally different populations.

As the work of theory building and the legacy of ongoing work on individual differences, learning and development, trait-and-factor approaches, personality typologies, and interest measurement were assimilated into more comprehensive sets of constructs during the 1950s, 1960s, and 1970., the language of vocational guidance and vocational counseling was subtly replaced by terms like career guidance and career counseling (Crites, 1981; Gysbers & Moore, 1971; Herr & Cramer, 1996; Wrenn, 1964) and by the emerging notions of the practice of career development. Assessment instruments were sometimes refined and renamed (e.g., the Vocational Maturity Inventory became the Career Maturity Inventory) and older theoretical models were reconceived and wedded to new constructs (e.g., trait-and-factor approaches seen as person-environment fit; (Chartrand, 1991). The name of the National Vocational Guidance Association was changed to the National Career Development Association in 1985, suggesting that earlier views of the process of career development as the object of career interventions became instead synonymous with the practice of career development.

The latter decades of the twentieth century demonstrated the importance and the effectiveness of the practice of career development across a wide range of career issues, settings, and populations (e.g., Campbell, Connel, Boyle, & Bha-

erman, 1983; Herr, 1997; Holland, Magoon, & Spokane, 1981; Hoyt, 1980; Oliver & Spokane, 1988; Spokane & Oliver, 1983). These decades also witnessed a consolidation of what is known about career behavior and how it can be used to guide planned programs of career interventions. In this sense, the practice of career development rests upon a legacy of concepts and practices that were developed and refined throughout the twentieth century (Herr, 1999; Savickas, 1999).

Insights Into the Future

Although it is not possible to be exhaustive in a brief retrospective view of the history of the practice of career development, it is clear, nevertheless, that there were major social, political, and economic changes throughout the twentieth century to which career theories and practices have been addressed. The history of the practice of career development is a record of conceptual growth and practical effects that is very positive in its contributions to individual purpose and productivity and to the economic health of the nation. However, this legacy of achievement is not yet complete.

Many of the questions and issues that precipitated the rise of vocational guidance and counseling in the late nineteenth and twentieth centuries, as the world began its transformation from a primarily agrarian economy to an industrial economy, are present in new guises as the nations of the world engage in the transformation from an industrial to a global, information-based economy. In the emerging world of the present and the future, career guidance and counseling, the practices of career development, are being constantly challenged to find new paradigms and new scientific bases as the important questions of individual choice and dignity are cast against a new and emerging set of questions that reflect the characteristics of a world occupational structure that is in considerable flux; that is increasingly affected by the pervasive influence of advanced technology on workplace procedures that reduce the need for worker's physical strength and increase their needs for knowledge and intellectual strength; and in which the opportunities to work, the language of work, the educational requirements to do work, and the organization of work are changing throughout the world. These conditions at the beginning of the twenty-first century are giving rise to such trends as the following.

Growth in the Practice of Career Development as a Worldwide Phenomenon

The practice of career development, career guidance and career counseling, and the other forms of career intervention were neither the same nor at the same level of development across the world at the end of the twentieth century. However, in the twenty-first century, the practice of career development is likely to be more comprehensive in scope, more evenly distributed and accessible, and more indigenous as nations increasingly identify how the practice of career development will best meet their needs.

Such national and cultural tailoring of the practice of career development to political, economic, and demographic characteristics will increase dramatically in the next several decades. So will the career theories and interventions that are invented and implemented in nations that differ substantially in their levels of educational and economic development. As such, career guidance, career counseling, and the practice of career development will become worldwide phenomena.

The Practice of Career Development as an Instrument of Individual Human Dignity

In a world that continues to struggle with conflicting desires to either degrade or enhance human dignity, assaults on human dignity continue to occur as a function of economic and workplace issues. They include the rise of, and the persistence of, high rates of unemployment in many nations; the permanent dislocation of persons from jobs because their skills are inadequate or because there are insufficient jobs; the procedures that bar people from work or occupational mobility because of ageism, racism, or sexism; the diminished feelings of personal identity and self-worth, affiliation, mastery, and economic independence that accompany organizational downsizing, unemployment and underemployment; the substitution of technology for people or the placing of persons in toxic work environments to produce economic gain. In these conditions, the practice of career

development, among its other outcomes, serves as a mechanism to provide hope to people, the affirmation of their individual dignity and worth, and the support to establish new career directions. Without feelings of dignity and hope, it is unlikely that any individual can attain his or her full potential as a human being. Without personal dignity and hope, it is difficult to grant these things to others, to take personal responsibility for one's actions, to gain a sense of agency or self-efficacy, or to find alternatives to violence as an appropriate strategy to gain what one seeks.

The Practice of Career Development as an Instrument of Personal Flexibility

In the twenty-first century, career counselors and other career guidance specialists will be increasingly expected to assist persons to identify and learn the skills by which they can be more effective in planning for and choosing jobs, in making effective transitions and adjustments to work, in working cross-culturally and cross-nationally, and in managing their own careers and career transitions effectively. Scholars in the United States and in other regions of the world have argued that changes in the way that work is organized are resulting in new concepts about careers that are qualitatively different from the concepts that had prevailed through much of the twentieth century. New notions of career in many nations include such implications as

the changes taking place in the structure of employment opportunities mean a widening diversity of career patterns and experiences ... more and different sorts of career transition will be taking place. One consequence may be that in the future more men will experience the kind of fragmented careers that many women have experienced. (Arnold & Jackson, 1997)

More people will be working for small and medium-sized employers, and there will be more people who are self-employed ... they highlight the need for lifelong learning and an appropriate strategy for career guidance to support people especially during career transitions ... (Arnold & Jackson, 1997)

In a similar fashion, Hall and Associates (1996) speak to the rise of "protean careers." Accordingly,

People's careers increasingly will become a succession of "ministages" (or short cycle learning stages) of exploration-trial-mastery-exit, as they move in and out of various product areas, technologies, functions, organizations, and other work environments.

This protean form of career involves horizontal growth, expanding one's range of competencies and ways of connecting to work and other people, as opposed to the more traditional vertical growth of success (upward mobility). In the protean form of growth, the goal is learning, psychological success, and expansion of the identity. In the more traditional form, the goal was advancement, success and esteem in the eyes of others, and power.

Although it is not clear what proportion of the workforce will be affected by "new careers," personal flexibility in such contexts means that people in the twenty-first century need to know how to change with change, accept ambiguity and uncertainty, negotiate job or career changes multiple times in their working lifetimes, be able to plan and act on shifting career opportunities, develop technical and social skills as well as an ability to understand how and why such skills are used, modified, and supplemented, and to have the motivation to be career resilient-to persist in the face of change and unplanned-for problems and difficulties.

Career Counselors Will Take on Expanded Roles

Career counselors will increasingly take on roles as planners, applied behavioral scientists, and technologists as they tailor their career practices to the settings and populations that they serve. In addition to the role of the counselor or specialist in the practice of career development as one who seeks to keep hope alive in his or her clients, such professionals will increasingly assume other technical roles. As the twentieth century laid the base for the scientific knowledge of career behavior and documented the effectiveness of career interventions that facilitate or modify career behavior, the twenty-first century will undoubtedly witness major growth in knowledge related to the processes and techniques that work most effectively to resolve certain career problems with particular populations (e.g., women and men, the affluent and the poor, majority and minority members) under specific conditions. Much of the new information in the field will come from cross-national studies and indigenous research in nations across the world. The expanded knowledge base in the theories of and the practice of career development will require career counselors, in their role as applied behavioral scientists, to become experts in how to facilitate positive career development across the lifespan and in its applications to particular settings and populations.

Flowing from a role as applied behavioral scientist, the career counselor of the twenty-first century will have an expanded role as a planner of structured programs. As is increasingly true in the present, among the major practices of career development will be the provision of workshops, modules, structured group programs, psychoeducational approaches, and career guidance curricula specifically planned to facilitate the types of career knowledge, skills, and behaviors that lead to personal flexibility and personal competence.

Furthermore, the career counselor of the twenty-first century will routinely be a technologist, able to plan and apply the use of computer-assisted career guidance systems, the Internet, CD-ROMs, and virtual reality approaches to experiencing possible work environments, games, self-assessment, international databases about educational and occupational opportunities, and other forms of technology to complement individual or group approaches to the practice of career development. Although the base for such roles had been initiated in the twentieth century, in the decades immediately ahead technology will be a core element of the practice of career development.

Conclusion

This article discusses in skeletal form the heritage that undergirds the practice of career development in the twenty-first century. The view here is that the early decades of the twenty-first century will witness a refinement of the conceptual perspectives and scientific knowledge that shaped career counseling and career guidance in the twentieth century. However, it is expected that the acceleration of the worldwide availability of career guidance and counseling in an international economy will be accompanied by a theoretical and research base that will develop from nations around the globe that are committed to developing their own indigenous models and practices of career development, rather than adopting those models and practices that originated in North America or Europe.

In such contexts, new theoretical and practical issues will continue to arise. They will include ensuring that the practice of career development is delivered in ways that are cost-effective and efficient; research that is devoted to understanding more fully the career behavior of the poor and the less educated; understanding more fully the pluralistic value and belief systems about the centrality of work among other life roles that dominate in different societies; career practice-career problem interactions; gender and racial factors in career behavior; methods of coaching and mentoring to stimulate career motivation and resilience that will bridge the chasms of despair, stress, and confusion that frequently accompany career transitions, poor person-job fit, underemployment or the loss of work; and new theories of work and practices of career development that address the growing number of temporary employees and persons unable to find permanent institutional employment around the world. As affirmed by the history of the twentieth century, the importance of the practice of career development in the twenty-first will grow as a worldwide, sociopolitical force designed to facilitate the economic health of nations and the purpose and productivity of individuals.

文章来源:

Edwin L. Herr. Career Development and Its Practice: A Historical Perspective [J].The Career Development Quarterly(March 2001 · Volume 49):196-211.

附录2

Career Learning and Development: A Social Constructivist Model for the Twenty-first Century
(节选)

Background, context and calls for new models

In response to the constantly changing nature of work in globalised marketplaces and the impact this has on the lives of individuals, there have been calls for new models, better suited to illuminate the role of career development than traditional matching models. In Section 8 of the Skills Commission's Report (2008) "Inspiration and aspiration: Realising our potential in the 21st century," a number of experts in the UK were consulted to gain their views on the models currently in use and the following comment from the report summaries these:

Professor Bimrose said that in various forms, the matching model has remained the dominant influence on guidance since the model's formulation in the first decade of the 20th century. She and other experts said that there is an urgent need to recognise that the matching model is flawed. Professor Bimrose described the matching model as "a hundred years out of date" and Gareth Dent, former Head of Advice and E-services at University for Industry (UFI), argued that "it is important that we move beyond this approach."

The Skills Commission's (2008) report goes on to examine the problematic nature of the matching model including its suitability for a more stable time when the labour market was less complex, when people made a career decision at the start of their working lives and often did not then need to review it later in life. It also discusses the desire of many to be flexible, rather than have a career for life and to make autonomous decisions, rather than be matched to a career by an outsider. The section concludes with the strongly worded recommendation in relation

to information advice and guidance (IAG) in the UK: We "must recognise that IAG is often provided using outdated delivery models and that IAG services will become increasingly irrelevant unless this changes".

For the majority of the previous century the work of career practitioners involved making an assessment of the individual in relation to occupations in order to seek a good match between the two. This can be seen as falling within the positivist paradigm, where the objective reality of a career for life, to which a person could be matched, was sought. It is important to emphasise at this point that there is no doubt that traditional approaches, such as trait/factor matching (Parsons, 1909), have aided those in career guidance and development for many years. However, there is also a need for new approaches that fit twenty-first century life; otherwise, theory runs the risk of being seen as outdated at best and irrelevant at worst.

In the later part of the twentieth century, the notion of a job for life was called into question for a number of reasons including economic recessions, the impact of globalization and information and communications technology (ICT), which served to create constant and rapid change in people's experiences of career (Collin & Watts, 1996). The need for people to navigate a pathway through lifelong learning and work grew in prominence. For example, Savickas (2000) asserted that people needed to be "managers of their own work lives" and become more "self-directed to flourish in the postmodern information age". Rational, positivist traditions began to be rejected in favour of constructivist approaches, where the client is an active participant in the process of constructing their career, for example through narratives (cf., McMahon & Patton, 2002, 2006) and life designing (cf., Savickas et al., 2009). In describing constructivism, Patton and McMahon (2006) asserted that it "is directly derived from the contextualist worldview; the 'reality' of world events is constructed 'from the inside out' through the individual's own thinking and processing". These individuals are described as living within open systems that interact constantly with their environment.

Young and Collin (2004) analysed the ambiguity caused by the often inter-

changeable use of the terms constructivism and social constructionism. They offer the following definitions for clarity. Constructivism "focuses on meaning making and the constructing of the social and psychological worlds through individual, cognitive processes" and social constructionism "emphasizes that the social and psychological worlds are made real (constructed) through social processes and interaction" (Young & Collin, 2004). Patton and McMahon (2006) accepted Young and Collin's suggestion that the terms constructivism and social constructionism be combined under the term "constructivisms". However, the term constructivisms is problematic for two reasons. First, it assumes that all career development from a constructivist viewpoint happens "from the inside out." Second, its singular focus on the individual is highlighted as a clear weakness by Young and Collin (2004) and by Colley (2007). Where career is concerned, it is clear that many approaches continue to give much greater emphasis to the individual. As Blustein, McWhirter, and Perry (2005) asserted, "Vocational psychology is still dominated by a worldview that implicitly values autonomy and individualism".

The origins of career learning and development (CLD)

The concept of CLD emerged during the process of writing An introduction to career learning and development 11—19 (Barnes et al., 2011). The overall aim of the book is to provide a source of support and guidance in order to enable those who plan, develop, and deliver career learning to do so effectively. Whilst carrying out research for the book, including discussions with teachers, it became clear that many programmes of careers education in schools continue to focus on activities, such as writing a good CV and techniques for succeeding in job interviews. These are activities that help people to get a job, or to gain entry into a college or a university when they leave school. Career is viewed from a narrow, positivist orientation as "What I do when I leave school?" often as a result of some form of matching process. After reviewing the literature concerning recent theoretical developments, the authors began examining the ways in which programmes of careers education could move forward in order to begin to prepare people for a more uncertain future.

Living in a complex world, where change is constant and the future of career becomes more and more difficult to predict (Bloch, 2005), a model focusing on what people can achieve next, rather than the job or course they will get when they leave school, appears appropriate, indeed vital, for careers work. Alongside this, there is the need to help people to develop the skills to manage change and, in particular, to cope with challenging and unexpected circumstances. Constructivism as a paradigm posits that learning is an active process, where the learner builds his or her knowledge in an ongoing way and actively constructs or creates his or her own subjective representations of reality. In contrast to the positivist paradigm, knowledge and truth are not absolute, but are created through activity and processes of social interaction.

In her research with students applying for university courses, Bassot (2006) began to explore the application of Vygotsky's zone of proximal development (ZPD) to career guidance practice. Vygotsky's (1978) work formed one of the foundations of constructivism, and he defined the ZPD as "the distance between the actual developmental level as determined by independent problem solving and the level of potential development as determined through problem solving under adult guidance or in collaboration with more capable peers". Wood (1998) later defined it as "the gap that exists for an individual child (or adult) between what he is able to do alone, and what he [sic] can achieve with help from one more knowledgeable than himself". Two facets of the ZPD are particularly worth noting. Firstly, people learn best those things that are within their ZPD (or proximal to them) rather than outside of it (or at a distance). Secondly, interactions with others enable the individual to achieve more than they could have achieved alone. The focus of learning in the ZPD is on what the learner can achieve next. Learners are supported in the process of constructing new knowledge, and this support is gradually reduced until the ultimate aim of independence is achieved: What learners can do with help today, they will be able to do alone tomorrow. In relation to issues of career, the positivist notion of "What I will do when I leave school?" is replaced by learning in the ZPD that focuses on "What I will do next?" as career is constructed throughout the changing life course.

As a result of discussion and critique the concept of CLD and the bridge model was developed. This model is presented here and offers an integration of a number of recent theories (or singular ways of understanding or explaining behaviour) to illustrate the vital continuing role that CLD has to play in maintaining the link between education (and lifelong learning) and work in its broadest sense. At the heart of the metaphor of the CLD bridge are the necessary tensions that allow it to carry out its essential functions.

文章来源：

Barbara Bassot. Career learning and development: a social constructivist model for the twenty-first century[J].Int J Educ Vocat Guidance (2012) 12:32-35.

附录 3

My System of Career Influences: Responding to Challenges Facing Career Education
（节选）

A major challenge facing the field of career psychology is to reinvigorate its theory and practice to be more responsive to 21st century needs and to forge closer links between theory and practice (Savickas, 1993, 2003). Constructivism has emerged as an influential force in this regard with its underlying tenets responsive to theoretical and practical issues driving the need for reinvigoration (McMahon & Patton, 2006; Patton & McMahon, 2006). Career education is a field of practice within career psychology that also faces the need to reformulate and constructivism has a potential role to play in this reformulation. However, constructivism itself faces the challenge of being more developed theoretically and philosophically than practically (Reid, 2006) and its influence is less evident in the field of career education (Collin & Watts, 1996; Gibson, 2000).

The present article examines these challenges facing career theory and practice within the field of career education. It describes a constructivist theory, the Systems Theory Framework of career development (STF; Patton & McMahon, 1999, 2006), and its related career assessment tool, the My System of Career Influences (MSCI; McMahon, Patton, & Watson, 2005a, b), as a response to these challenges.

Several authors have drawn attention to a range of challenges facing career education if it is to be responsive to the career development needs of young people in the 21st century (e.g., Amundson, 2006; Gibson, 2000; Gysbers, 1996; Gysbers & Henderson, 2006; Patton & McMahon, 1999, 2006). In general, these challenges relate to the roles of career development practitioners and students in school settings and to the nature of career education itself. Amundson argues that, in order to be effective, career development practitioners need to broaden their knowledge base and also the range of interventions they use.

Traditionally, career education has been narrowly focused on subject choice and career choice at specific points in the secondary school years which has prescribed its content. In this way, career education has been reactively structured to maintain a focus on the content rather than the processes of career development, resulting in calls for more holistic approaches to career education that are located within the broader context of lifelong guidance (Van Esbroeck, 2002) and the overall career development of the individual. Thus a reformulation of career education is emerging. Specifically, there have been calls to cast this reformulation within a learning framework (Collin & Watts, 1996; Gysbers, 1996; Law, 1996) and to incorporate approaches of constructivist theory (Gibson, 2000; Miller, 2004; Patton, 2005; Patton& McMahon, 2006).

This theoretical reformulation is consistent with challenges that have been identified for career education. For instance, Gysbers and Henderson (2006) suggest that career education should stimulate a "career consciousness" in school students that enables them to understand, visualise, and plan for the dynamic of their own life career development. This goal of career education is suggestive of constructivism's focus on individuals as active agents in the context of their lives who create their own careers (Gibson, 2000; Patton & McMahon, 2001). The construct of active agency would require the development of dynamic and narrative approaches (Amundson, 2006) that suggest different roles for career development practitioners and also for school students. The former role becomes more facilitative than didactic, and the latter role emphasises active rather than passive participation in learning. All of this places a greater focus on the process than the content of career education learning (Patton, 2005; Patton & McMahon, 2001).

The implications of constructivism as a theoretical base for career education require that career education is student focused, holistic and contextual in its approach. Fundamental to constructivist approaches is the notion of story or narrative. The telling of their stories enables students to search for meaning in their career development and, in so doing, reflect on where they are and who they are becoming (Gibson, 2000; Gibson, 2004). Gysbers (1996) argues that students need to be afforded the opportunity to systematically explore their personal attributes in relation to the contextual influences that impact on them. Schools can provide such an opportunity as part of the system of influences on the career development of students (McMahon, 1997; Patton & McMahon, 1999, 2006) and, specifically, career education can enable schools to secure a place in that system of influences (McMahon & Patton, 2002).

The systems theory framework of career development

The Systems Theory Framework (STF) of career development (McMahon & Patton, 1995; Patton & McMahon, 1999, 2006) is a metatheoretical account informed by the constructivist worldview that bridges theory and practice through the development of a qualitative career assessment instrument, the My System of Career Influences (MSCI; McMahon, Patton, & Watson, 2005a, b; McMahon, Watson, & Patton, 2005). While other theoretical approaches such as Savickas's (2005) career construction theory and the Social Cognitive Career Theory of Lent, Brown, and Hackett (2002) also acknowledge the broader context and processes of career development, the STF is "one of the first approaches to attempt to embed school based career education within a theoretical framework which included the individual and the context" (Patton & McMahon, 2006). While Patton and McMahon (1999, 2006) discuss the STF's theoretical application to school settings within the context of a learning framework, the present article explores the MSCI as a practical tool that can be used in career education.

The STF is a holistic framework that demonstrates both the content and the process influences on career development. Content influences demonstrate the holistic nature of an individual's career development by describing personal qualities and characteristics intrinsic to individuals, as well as contextual influences such as the people and organisations with whom they interact, and the society and environment in which they live. Process influences demonstrate the dy-

namic nature of career development and include recursiveness (the interaction between influences), change over time and chance. The STF is organised as a series of interconnecting systems of influence on career development, specifically the individual system, the social system, and the environmental-societal system, all of which are set within the context of past, present and future. In this way, the STF recognises the process of career development, that is, the changing nature and interaction of these influences.

Central to the STF's description of content influences, the individual system includes a range of intrapersonal influences such as gender, interests, age, abilities, personality, and sexual orientation. Because individuals do not live in isolation, the individual system is part of a much larger contextual system comprising the social system and the environmental-societal system. The social system includes family, educational institutions, peers and media with which the individual interacts. Both the individual and the social systems occur within an even broader system, the environmental-societal system. The environmental-societal system includes influences such as geographical location, socioeconomic circumstances, political decisions and globalisation.

The STF's description of process influences emphasises recursiveness, change over time and chance. These influences are illustrative of the dynamic nature of career development and the interaction that occurs within and between systems. Recursiveness, the interaction between influences, relates to the way in which an influence can introduce change into one part of the system which results in change in another part of the system thus demonstrating multidirectional and nonlinear interaction. Not all influences will be planned, predictable or logical as unexpected or chance events such as accidents, illness, or natural disasters may profoundly influence career development. Further, all of the content and process influences are set within the broader context of time. Invariably, the nature and degree of these influences change over time. In addition, the past influences the present, and together, past and present influence the future. Fuller descriptions of the STF and its assessment tool, the MSCI, are available in the literature (e.g., Patton & McMahon, 1999, 2006; McMahon, Patton & Watson, 2005a, b).

My system of career influences

The STF has stimulated the development of a qualitative career assessment instrument, the My System of Career Influences (MSCI; McMahon, Patton, & Watson, 2005a, b), through which students may engage in a sequential reflection of their systems of influence and, through this reflection, to meaningfully create their own career stories (McMahon, Patton, & Watson, 2004). The MSCI serves as a map that guides students through a step-by-step process of visually representing, elaborating, and reflecting on the holistic pattern of influences on their career development. In this way, a better understanding of the uniqueness, wholeness and interconnectedness of career development is facilitated for students and their school career development practitioners.

The MSCI is a booklet of twelve pages that each provides brief information, instructions and examples, and a place where reflections can be recorded. This guided process begins in the first section of the booklet with the student's present career situation in which the student reflects on occupational aspirations, work experience, life roles, previous decision-making and support networks. The next section of the booklet mirrors the construction of the STF in that students diagrammatically identify and prioritize their influences by *thinking about who I am* (the individual system), *thinking about the people around me* (the social system), *thinking about society and the environment* (the environmental-societal system), and *thinking about my past, present and future* (the context of time). For each of these systemic influences examples are provided from which students can select or to which they can add their own. The summation of students' reflections on their influences is guided by a page titled *representing my system of career influences*. These reflections are then represented diagrammatically on a chart titled *my system of career influences*. Finally, on a page titled *reflecting on my system of career influences*, students reflect on the insights gained through a guided process and complete my action plan on a subsequent page.

Using the MSCI as a career education activity in the classroom becomes a collaborative activity in which the school career development practitioner is a facilitator who encourages a process that is meaningful to students who are recog-

nised as active agents in the process of constructing their career stories. McMahon, Patton and Watson (2005a) suggest in the MSCI Facilitators' Guide that the MSCI be embedded in a more extensive career learning process which includes preliminary and

follow-up activities. In particular, these authors provide case studies that introduce students to systemic thinking and the language of career development and recommend

that these be completed prior to the MSCI activity. They also provide a case study that introduces the concept of lifelong career development that can be used on completion of the MSCI. Additional supplementary activities are also included in he Facilitators' Guide.

McMahon, Patton and Watson (2005a) suggest that in a classroom setting the MSCI activity is best conducted as a series of lessons of 30—40 min, each of which focuses on a section of the booklet. For example, the first lesson would focus on the student's present career situation. The second lesson could focus on the individual, social, and environmental-societal systems, that is *thinking about who I am*, *thinking about the people around me*, *thinking about society and the environment*, *and thinking about my past, present and future*. A summative exercise in this lesson would be for students to reflect on these influences

using page seven, titled representing my system of career influences, and to represent

their summation diagrammatically on a chart titled *my system of career influences*. In the third and final lesson based on the MSCI, students are provided with an opportunity for *reflecting on my system of career influences*. This leads them to *create my action plan*. Page 11 of the booklet provides an opportunity for students to revisit their MSCI at a future time by completing *my system of career influence*—2.

文章来源:

Mark Watson, Mary Mcmahon. My system of career influences responding to challenges facing career education[J].Int J Educ Vocat Guid (2006) 6:160-163.

附录 4

Donald Super's Contribution to Career Guidance and Counselling in Japan
（节选）

Influence on the theoretical frame of reference for school career guidance

In order to clarify Dr Super's contributions to school career guidance in Japan a historical overview of vocational (career) guidance would be helpful (Watanabe, 1989). It was in 1915 that the concept of vocational guidance was initially introduced into Japanese society from the United States of America (Irisawa, 1915). Five years later, vocational counselling centres for teen-aged workers were established in Tokyo and Osaka by each department of labour under municipal governments. In 1927, the Ministry of Education recommended that elementary and secondary schools provide pupil and student assistance in occupational and educational choice and placement. From 1930 till 1945, school vocational guidance took on the role of labour force distribution for wartime.

It is a historical fact that the American occupation forces restructured the Japanese education system in order to conform to the American concept of democracy. Under the School Education law of 1953, school guidance and counselling were introduced as instruments of national policy designed to democratise the educational opportunities for secondary students. With this political impetus, and through the efforts of visiting American counselling and educational psychologists who gave lectures to Japanese professors in related fields in the 1950s, "... the system and organisation of school guidance and counselling were established in every secondary school throughout the natio" (Watanabe, 1989). However, the function of vocational guidance did not change for 40 years. The primary model used was the matching model, focusing on how to choose one "best fitting" job or

occupation in the transitional period from school to work.

The Teachers' Manuals for Vocational Guidance, prepared by the Ministry of Education from 1947 to 1962, demonstrate how Dr Super's theoretical frame of reference for school career guidance in Japanese secondary schools shifted their focus from the dominant job matching model to the career model. For example, in the Teachers5 Manual for Vocational Guidance of 1947, school vocational guidance was defined as a process to help students in choosing an occupation, preparing for it, and finding appropriate placement (Monbusho, 1947). The Manual revised in 1949, redefined school vocational guidance as a process to help students in finding and utilising their own potentials through provision of appropriate occupational training, and to assist them in acquiring the life experience needed for leading a rewarding life, both personally and as a member of society.

The influence of the vocational development approach became evident in the 1961 edition of the Manual. In this edition, the Ministry of Education, Sciences, Sports and Culture introduced the new term of career guidance and counselling, instead of vocational guidance. They also recommended that secondary school authorities implement a systematic and longitudinal career guidance program intended to help every student develop abilities of selfunderstanding, decision-making, life-planning, and action-taking to be able to adjust in the career options he or she decides to pursue. Though the Teachers5 Manual had been revised four times by 1990, this particular recommendation remained unchanged.

It is important to indicate that although Dr Super's theory was recognised and accepted as the main theoretical frame of reference for the secondary school career guidance system (Watanabe &Herr, 1993), it was not put into practice. This is due partly because most Japanese professionals admired Dr Super as the greatest theorist and researcher of vocational psychology but did not identify him as the greatest counselling psychologist. As a result, Dr Super has had enormous influence on ideas but, until recently, not on behaviour. Therefore, since no practical education program has been provided for executing the developmental concept in schools, most guidance teachers could not shift the model of their activities from person-job matching to career development.

Since the committee that designed the latest school reform, which started in 1995, emphasised a teacher guidance function as well as counselling skills, the Japanese Ministry of Education, Science, Sports and Culture asked for a new practical model of career guidance to be developed. It was suggested that "the competency-based new model for a career guidance program through elementary to high schools" (Watanabe-Muraoka, 1999) should be adopted. This model was constructed on the basis of findings acquired through field studies. The author (Watanabe - Muraoka, 1999) concluded that Dr Super's formulation of life stages and tasks of career development (Super, 1992) would be the best theoretical frame of reference for this new model. A systematic education program for teachers to enable them to implement the new model is currently being developed.

Influence on the theoretical framework for career counselling of adult population

The current drastic and rapid socio-economic and demographic changes in Japanese society provided the context to verify that Dr Super's theory is rooted in the real world and has universally high value. In addition to socio-economic and demographic changes, the employment environment has substantially changed since 1990. "First, the unemployment rate has been rising and many Japanese enterprises have been making efforts to restructure their business... Second, traditional Japanese employment practices, such as the lifetime employment system and the seniority wage system, are also changing" (JIL, 2000). These environmental changes have resulted in the diversification of individual value systems, behavioural and attitudinal changes toward their career and life, as well as changes in career patterns and career paths of workers (Watanabe &Herr, 1993). It appears that the recent changes in both the inner-personal and outer-career worlds of Japanese youth and adults have enhanced the value of developmental and career counselling as well as crisis intervention.

Career counselling, using a matching model, was recognised for forty years as an important approach for those youngsters who go to work after leaving schools even after career development theory was introduced. However, under the circumstances mentioned above, every generation of male and female, young and old

workers is facing increased difficulty in thinking about their own future plans and in taking personal responsibility to manage their own careers. Accordingly, there is no doubt that the person-job matching model is a limited response that needs to be bolstered through more comprehensive assistance for workers and helping professionals in developing career problem solving and planning skillsrelated to choosing and managing future career pathways and balancing work and other life roles.

Under these situations, three groups of Japanese adults are identified as in particular need of career counselling. One group is women who try to reenter the labour market. Another is older workers. The third is persons in mid-career who were unexpectedly discharged asaresult of the restructurmg of enterprises. Most of the non-traditional clients of career counselling seek professional help not only in order to seek immediate employment, but also to plan for a future in which they can find self-fulfilment.

Through her career counselling practice, and on the basis of a survey of more than 200 women participants in career-planning seminars (21st C. Vocational Foundation, 1999), the first author has found that Dr Super's "The Life-Career Rainbow: A life-span, life-space approach" (Super, 1990) is the most applicable and rewarding approach with respect to re-entry women, mid-career job seekers, and older workers (Watanabe &Masaki, 1993). Embedded in this approach, the Life-Career Rainbow is a graphic tool that assists these persons to analyse the forces affecting their career patterns, life roles, and the potential conflicts or integration among them.

In order to examine the applicability of Dr Super's formulation of career development in adulthood and late adulthood, Okada (2000) conducted research using the case study approach. As his subjects, he chose three mid-career businessmen who were in the stage of maintenance according to Super's formulation of career development (ages of 40, 49 and 53). They were also identified as fulfilling such conditions as being successfully promoted up the career ladder of a large-scale enterprise and being recognised and respected as models of career success by colleagues and their employers. Their qualitative data were collected by three-hour videotaped interviews as well as by a set of questionnaires on their career histories. Okada found that all three subjects showed such characteristics as time perspective, mastering exploratory behaviour and skill, decision-making competency, reality oriented behaviour, open-minded, good human-relation skills, and warm consideration and basic trust of subordinates and colleagues. Further, the three subjects indicated that they had experienced transitional crises between the ages of 25 and 30, 40 and 45, and early 50s and had finally overcome them. These findings indicated that Dr Super's postulates (1990) on the elements of career maturity at mid-career were applicable to these Japanese men. The construct of career adaptability (Herr, 1997; Super&Knasel, 1981) seems to be appropriate to describe their career behaviour in adulthood.

There is other research (Matsumoto et al., 1997), which also supports Dr Super's theory. This research aimed to clarify the relation between the career behaviour that takes place in the process of mandatory retirement and adjustment in post-retirement life, using 108 retired males aged between 50 and 59. Path analysis with three independent and 10 intermediate variables showed that life planning skills and psychological distance between individual and organisation as well as positive self-esteem were variables that most influenced post-retirement life for these persons.

文章来源：

Agnes M. Watanabe-Muraoka, Thomas-Aquinas Takeshe Senzaki, Edwin L. Herr. Donald Super's Contribution to Career Guidance and Counselling in Japan [J]. International Journal for Educational and Vocational Guidance (2001)1: 99-106.

Career Education for Young People Rationale and Provision in the UK and Other European Countries
（节选）

The rationale for career education

We are in the middle of a major historical transformation in our concepts of work and of career. The language used to describe the new era varies: a post-industrial era, a post-modern era, a new information age. Our concept and methods of career guidance are being remodelled as part of this transformation. The concept of career education is a key element within this remodelling.

Now, the traditional model of career is fragmenting. This process represents a "careerquake" (Watts, 1996a): a shaking of the foundations of traditional structures, but with the opportunity to build new and more robust structures in its wake. There are two main reasons for the change: the impact of new technology and of globalisation of markets. The result is that organisations have to be prepared to change much more regularly and rapidly than ever before. They are accordingly seeking more compact, more fluid and more flexible forms, and are less and less prepared to make long-term commitments to individuals.

The result is a profound change in the psychological contract between the individual and the employer: their perceptions of the obligations each has to the other. The traditional contract was a long-term relational one, based on security and reciprocal loyalty: this has largely broken down. Now the contract tends increasingly to be a short-term transactional one, based on a narrower and more time-limited exchange. Even where the relational contract survives, it commonly involves exchanging relative job security for greater task flexibility. Either way, therefore, it has to be constantly renegotiated (Herriot & Pemberton, 1995).

This requires individuals to take more responsibility for enacting their own career development, improvisationally but purposefully, on a lifelong basis (Arthur et al., 1999). Security, is argued, lies not in employment but in employ ability: accumulating skills and reputation that can be invested in new opportunities as they arise (Kanter, 1989). In this "risk society" (Beck, 1992), individuals have to construct their own work identity, on an ongoing basis, as part of a reflexive process connecting personal and social change (Giddens, 1994).

These transformations require a new model of career. Career needs now to be redefined, as the individual's lifelong progression in learning and in work. Viewed in these terms, it is potentially available to all.

If this potential is to be realised, career guidance has a critical role to play. But it needs to be remodelled. Instead of being viewed as a single event, focused on choosing a career, it should be seen as a continuous process, helping individuals to construct their career. This process should start early in schools, should continue through the now often extended period of transition to adult and working life, and should then be sustained throughout adult and working life. This should be parallelled by a move to a more open professional model, with the concept of an expert guidance specialist working with clients in a psychological vacuum being replaced or supplemented by a more diffuse approach in which a more varied range of interventions is used (including, for example, curriculum programmes, group work, computers, and other media) and more attention is given to working with and through networks of other individuals and agencies (for instance, involving parents, supporting the guidance roles of teachers and supervisors, and making use of voluntary and community agencies). Underpinning these changes should be a greater emphasis on the individual as an active agent, rather than a passive recipient, within the guidance process. Studies of guidance service have demonstrated that changes in all these respects are visible across Europe (Watts et al., 1988; Watts et al., 1994).

Career education is a crucial part of this model. Its aim is to help individuals to develop the knowledge, skills and attitudes they require in order to make the decisions and transitions that will determine the course of their career

development in other words, in order to manage their career. To some extent, such knowledge, skills and attitudes develop naturally as part of social maturation (Super, 1957). The aim of career education is to support, accelerate and ameliorate this process.

Current provision in the UK

In the United Kingdom, career education has been commonly defined as having four aims. The first is self-awareness: awareness of the distinctive characteristics - interests, values, abilities, skills - that define the kind of person one is and the kind of person one wishes to become. The second is opportunity awareness: awareness of the range of possibilities that exist, the demands they make, and the rewards and satisfactions they can offer. The third is decision learning: awareness of the styles in which decisions are made, and acquisition of the skills that will help one to make decisions in a manner more satisfying to oneself. And the fourth is transition learning: acquisition of skills that will help one to implement decisions and manage the transitions that ensue (Law & Watts, 1977).

It was in the early 1970s that career education began to be incorporated into the school curriculum (Schools Council, 1972). With the advent of a National Curriculum in England and Wales in the early 1990s, careers education and guidance was defined as one of five "cross-curricular themes": the others were health education, economic and industrial understanding, environmental education, and citizenship. The official guidelines also identified five ways of organising careers education and guidance within the curriculum: as permeating the whole curriculum; as part of a separately timetabled personal and social education programme; as a separately timetabled subject in its own right; as part of a pastoral/tutorial programme; and through "long blocked timetabling" where the programme could run for a longer period of time outside the constraints of normal school timetabling (NCC, 1990). The cross-curricular themes, however, had no statutory force and were not formally assessed. Moreover, they came to be viewed by government ministers as a "dangerous distraction" from the academic subjects which form the mainstream of the curriculum (Graham & Tytler, 1993). The re-

sult was that they tended to be marginalised in many schools. A more recent survey by Ofsted (1998) reported that students aged 12—13 were allocated, on average, 9 hours of careers teaching, while those aged 13—16 received an average of 12 hours each. The report commented that "the very wide variation in content organisation, and time allocated for careers work is unacceptable".

In recent years, the most common form of delivery for career education has been as part of an integrated personal, social and health education (PSHE) programme. This is sometimes delivered by house or form tutors, as part of their pastoral role alongside their formal subject teaching role; and sometimes by semi-specialist teams. Within the newly revised National Curriculum, this has been formally recognised by incorporating careers education and guidance within the guidelines for PSHE. As the guidelines state: "PSHE is concerned with helping pupils prepare for the range of roles they will fulfil in life. Careers education and guidance (CEG) is concerned with helping pupils develop their role as learners and workers. In curriculum terms, therefore, CEG is a component of PSHE and cannot be considered in isolation from it" (QCA, 2000b). Moreover, while the main attention to career education occurs in the later years of secondary school, some attention is given in primary schools to "career-related learning" - "helping children to understand what happens in the community beyond school, the roles that people fulfil, and the relevance of learning to their future lives" (QCA, 2000a).

An important aspect of career education programmes is direct experience of work. Almost all pupils in the UK now have at least one week of work experience in their final year of compulsory schooling. These comprise programmes in which pupils experience work tasks in work environments, but without taking on the full identity of a worker. The programmes are often used to enhance academic subjects, or for personal and social education purposes, as well as for career education. In addition, some schools offer access to other experiences of work: through work simulations, in which pupils experience work tasks within school environments (e.g. business schemes, production simulations, work practice units); or through work shadowing, in which the pupil follows a particular worker for a peri-

od of time, observing all the tasks in which he or she engages, and doing so within the context of his or her total role. Each of these techniques has its distinctive strengths and weaknesses: shadowing, because of its focus on roles, has particular value for career education (Watts, 1996b). All, to be effective, require support from career education programmes, to provide the preparation and the reflective follow-up which help to convert experience into learning.

The current position regarding career education in England and Wales is complex one. PSHE remains non-statutory. It has however close links with citizenship, which has become a new subject within the National Curriculum. Moreover, its career education element is statutory: under the Education Act 1997, schools now have a statutory duty to provide a planned programme of career education in Years 9—11 (i.e. for pupils aged 13—16), though the nature of this programme is not specified. It remains to be seen whether this complicated set of arrangements results in a strengthening or a weakening of the position of career education within the curriculum.

Career education is not confined to schools. In further education, which provides alternatives to school at ages 16—19 as well as a wide variety of courses for adults, career education tends either to be part of tutorial group programmes or – particularly in the case of broad pre-vocational course like those leading to General National Vocational Qualifications (GNVQs) – embedded within integrated course structures (Sadler & Reisenberger, 1997). In higher education, three approaches tend to be adopted: as a separate career management module within a modular course structure; integrated into existing course components; or delivered outside the curriculum, either via technology or via non-credit-bearing special events – for example, one-off seminars on particular skills (e.g. self-presentation skills) or short residential courses (Hustler et al., 1998). There is also other career education provision for adults: for example, course provision for unemployed individuals, career development workshops conducted within large companies, access course for women returning to work after a break, and pre-retirement courses, all commonly contain strong elements of career education.

In higher education, a more recent survey of provision across Europe found that there were curriculum programmes in vocational orientation career planning and development of career management skills not only in the UK but also in Austria, France, Germany, Ireland, the Netherlands and Spain, as well as more specific programmes on self-presentation and other aspects of job search in Belgium, France and Sweden (Watts & Van Esbroec, 1998): this list may not have been exhaustive. In many of these cases, such provision was confined to a small number of institutions. In France, however modules were offered in over a third of universities: sometimes they were integrated into the course work, and sometimes they were offered by guidance psychologists independently of the study programme (Leray, 1998).

Issues

It seems clear, then, that formal career education programmes are now widespread across Europe. If such programmes are to become embedded and to be effective, we need to address our attention to a range of underlying issues. Six will be briefly addressed here: timing, content, method, models of delivery, progression, and assessment.

On timing, career education programmes have traditionally been concentrated around key career transition points. There is however a strong argument for starting such programmes much earlier. Perceptions of self and of work are formed early in primary school: if we want to intervene in this process, the interventions must start early too. This is also merit in starting before choices are imminent and "the subject has become emotionally charged" (Hill, 1969) – similar arguments have been advanced in relation to sex education. In the USA in the 1970s, the concept of career education was viewed as starting in kindergarten (Hoyt et al., 1974). In the UK, there has recently been a growth of interest in career-related learning in primary schools, recognising that most such schools attend to issues related to self and work, and that the concept of career-related learning can build upon and add value to such experiences (McGowan, 2000). Also, some of the key career management skills can be developed not only through curriculum programmes but also through curriculum processes: in particular, the process of recording achievement and action planning, in which pupils

periodically sit down with a tutor or teacher to record and review what they are learning, and to set short-term and longer term goals (Law, 1996b). These processes can start in primary school and continue throughout schooling and beyond.

On content, an important issue is the balance adopted between the different aims outlined earlier. Programmes of working life familiarisation and arbeitslehre, for example, clearly give prime attention to opportunity awareness and, perhaps, transition learning; other programmes give more attention to self-awareness and decision learning. Again, there may be important differences in the relative attention paid to objective data - both on the world of work and on self - and to subjective approaches designed to help students construct their own career narratives. This may be linked to other differences. What space is provided for emotion as well as cognitive processes? Is the underlying model one of rational progression towards occupational crystallisation, or development of skills, knowledge and attitudes in each of these areas for flexible and iterative usage? If at the end of such programmes some students have not crystallised a clear occupational preference, is this a mark of failure or of success?

Such issues regarding content are closely related to issues regarding method. How much attention in career education programmes should be given to didactic approaches in which the teacher transmits the information, to experiential learning using group processes, and to experience-based learning (e.g. work experience or work shadowing)? In current programmes, the balance between the three varies considerably. Each produces a very different range of outcomes, and has very different implications for the role of the teacher and for the training required to prepare them for their task.

The relative merits of different models of delivery need to be more carefully evaluated than hitherto. For students enrolled on educational courses, there would seem to be four broad alternatives: a specific enclosed model, in which career education is provided as a separate subject or module within the curriculum; an extended enclosed model, in which it is provided as part of a more broadly-based subject or module - for example, in the UK context, personal, social and health

education; an integrated model, in which it is integrated across the curriculum as a whole; and an extra-curricular model, in which it is provided as an additional element outside the boundaries of the formal curriculum.

The integrated model is attractive, but difficult to deliver. It seems to work best where the curriculum itself is built on a closely integrated basis – as in the case of General National Vocational Qualifications in England and Wales, for example. Where however the curriculum is based on a range of different subjects or modules, career education needs to be "infused", and this seems to be problematic. Certainly there are opportunities for such infusion in all subjects, but there are difficulties in persuading and equipping subject teachers to take advantage of these opportunities. Concentrated efforts to do so were made in the 1970s in countries including the USA (Hoyt et al., 1974) and West Germany, but proved problematic. In West Germany, attempts to ask teachers of traditional subjects to incorporate relevant occupational material were abandoned, on the grounds that "the knowledge-based nature of the material of these subjects, and the orientation of teacher training to the content of the disciplines, always prevail to such an extent that attempts at incidental occupational orientation remain ineffective" (Busshoff, 1977). Again, in the 1990s, an infusion approach was adopted in England and Wales whilst the notion of "cross-curricular themes" in the initial version of the National Curriculum legitimated a variety of approaches, it gave particular attention to infusion into mainstream academic subjects (NCC, 1990). Whitty, Rowe and Aggleton (1994), however, demonstrated the difficulties of infusing such themes into traditional subjects based on very different "recognition rules" – in other words, rules about what teachers and pupils regarded as legitimate discourse within particular lessons.

At the same time, there are clearly similar difficulties with the enclosed models, in introducing curriculum programmes based on different principles from the rest of the curriculum. In Greece, for instance, where a specific enclosed model for career education was adopted, Watts et al. (1994) reported that problems had arisen from the introduction into an inflexible school organisation of a new subject which lacked a specific body of knowledge that pupils had to "learn"

in order to be "examined" and "evaluated". This created difficulties with pupils who expected, from their experience elsewhere in the curriculum, that their active participation in the learning process would be rewarded with a "good mark". Another source of problems was the change in the role of the teacher, who needed to be the animator and coordinator of an active learning process, in contrast to academic subjects where students tended to be the passive recipients of knowledge from the teacher "expert". Yet the academic subjects tended to be considered by students as more important because of the utilitarian value of examination passes. This resulted in some careers teachers facing discipline problems, especially if they had received no specialist training.

A further problem with the specific enclosed model is that it is competing with other elements of the curriculum which are concerned with pupils' personal and social development. This leads to the argument for the extended enclosed model: that these elements should be brought together in a broadly based programme. This is the rationale for the currently dominant approach in schools in England and Wales: programmes of personal, social and health education which cover a broad range of topics including moral and religious education, personal relationships, and health issues including sex and drugs education, as well as career education. The range of such courses, however, poses problems for teacher training. Where teachers are expected to cove the full range of topics, they may feel more ill-equipped in some areas than others: some, for example, may feel ignorant about career opportunities and career management processes, and so reduce the attention they give to such topics. Accordingly, in some schools, a "carrousel" approach is used, with specialists rotating across groups: this however risks splintering the programme.

The fourth alternative, the extra-curricular model, has the advantage that it escapes the confines and constraints of the curriculum, and enables a fresh set of "recognition rules" to be established. The French approach, of an intensive programme delivered by guidance specialists over a series of half-days, has this merit. The danger, however, is that becomes marginalised and detached, separated from the mainstream of the school and of the learning process.

We urgently need a clearer analysis of the advantages and disadvantages of these various models. The range of different models evident across countries suggests that such a study could fruitfully be conducted on a transnational basis. It may that what we need is a mixture of two or more of the models, but with a clearer articulation of the distinctive contribution which each model can make, and ways in which they can be effectively combined – as, for example, in the comprehensive guidance programme developed by Gysbers and Henderson (1997) where the limitations of the infusion model delivered by teachers are in effect made good by "extended enclosed" elements delivered by guidance counsellors.

Within such an analysis, attention is also needed to the issue of progression. What needs to be learned when, and how does such learning need to be conducted so that it builds in a coherent way? A useful contribution to answering such questions is the career learning theory developed by Law (1996a) in which he suggests that career-development learning can be built in cycles, which develop progressively through four stages: a sensing stage, in which the individual is able to sense career-related information and impressions; a sifting stage, in which they are able to sift this material into recognisable patterns that can become the basis of action; a focusing stage, in which they are able to focus aspects which require attention and suggest enquiry; and an understanding stage, in which they are able to relate causes to effects and anticipate the consequences of actions. Law (1999) suggests that these processes provide a second dimension to set against the four aims of self awareness, opportunity awareness, decision learning and transition learning Efforts have been made in several countries to define the learning outcomes from career education programmes (e.g. QCA, 1999). Much learning in this area is however spiral in nature, as Law's model suggests. Moreover, the "compression" and "lift-off" points in such spirals are irregular and vary between individuals. The spiral nature of the learning also poses a semantic challenge: to find language which enables individuals to recognise the similarities with what they have done before, so that they can consciously build upon it; but which also seems fresh and not merely repetitive.

Learning outcomes are also relevant to the issue of assessment. Should

students' learning in relation to careers education be assessed and accredited? If so, how? Within educational institutions where value tends to be measured in terms of accredited outcomes, assessment and accreditation legitimise career education as a worthwhile activity. They accordingly add value and motivation for students, increase credibility for teaching staff, and make it easier to secure curriculum time and other resources. They can also add to the rigour of the activity. On the other hand, they tend to externalise the focus of concern: students become more concerned with impressing the assessor (self-presentation) than with engaging in honest reflection (self-disclosure). They may distort the aims of career education programmes, in favour of those which are easier to measure: they may, for example, lead to a greater emphasis on knowledge elements (e.g. opportunity awareness) and skills related to self-presentation (part of transition learning), and to less emphasis on more personal areas (e.g. self-awareness, decision learning). Also, the notion of "failing" on career management skills is problematic.

The key issue here is whether it is possible to find forms of assessment which are congruent with the aims of career education and which support the learning process. This is easier where the overall model of assessment being used within the curriculum as a whole is broad and flexible, permitting a variety of assessment methods, and attending to the assessment of skills as well as knowledge. In such cases, it may be possible to integrate the assessment of career education into the assessment of the broader curriculum. Where it is not the case, more difficult decisions will need to be made, between the tactical benefits of adopting such integrated assessment, and opting for differentiated forms of assessment which preserve the integrity of career education itself.

文章来源：

Watts A G. Career Education for Young People: Rationale and Provision in the UK and Other European Countries[J]. International Journal for Educational and Vocational Guidance, 2001, 1(3):209-222.

附录6

How Low-qualified Adults Enact their Career-Findings From a Narrative Study in German
（节选）

Career paths, career development and participation in adult learning are to a large extent dependent on learning experiences and labour-market entrance in early life stages. However, within the group of people with relative weak educational and vocational background variance was found in terms of how people perceive their situation and how they describe, plan and realise their career. Based on narrative interviews with low-qualified adults, the presented study describes individual circumstances and approaches to lifelong learning and career development. Based on the concept of enacted career, the article shows how the differences in the perceptions of career and learning can be understood as contextualised action. The article shows inner resources and external constraints have potential influence on the educational and career development in this group. The discussion focuses on consequences for career counselling and guidance.

1.Introduction and theoretical background

Linking both sides (subjective construction and constraints and opportunities from environment), one can argue that in postmodern societies career counsellors (and other professionals) need concrete knowledge about how people experience their education, work and career and how they enact their life and their career. Enactment in this sense is more than constructing an identity. This might be relevant for counselling of all kind of people in our diverse societies. The growing group of people who do not have those skills that are asked from high qualified jobs and career opportunities, who live in risk and precarious situations need special attention (Dörre, 2013, p. 33). To support and enrich the development of theory and practice, it could be useful to look closer into the perceptions these people have and the action people take when they enact their career or seek for decent work or 'livelihood' (Arulmani, 2014, p. 9). In this sense, looking closer into the group of low-skilled people and their perception of education and work is an approach to develop 'contextresonantinteractions' (McMahon, Watson, & Patton, 2014, p. 13).

2. Aims and method of the analysis

(1) Counselling theories describe the complexity of life contexts as relevant. What does this target group describe as influential for their career questions subjectively and what aspects can be reconstructed as relevant in the individual process of career and life enactment?

(2) Findings about low-qualified people and their educational attainment or career success are rather structural, sociological or individual and mostly based on aggregated data (Cedefop, in press). But can variance be identified in terms of subjective career interests and of how people shape and enact their career?

(3) Individual career is, on the one hand, an individual constructive process. On the other hand, we assume institutional opportunities and constraints to be relevant. To what extent are individual experiences and resources and institutional factors connected within the career process of the individuals?

(4) Assuming that the design of the individual careers is an active process that requires subjective meaning and reflection it can be asked if action schemes and reflection loops can be identified in the narratives from this group? How do such 'biographical action schemes' (Riemann & Schütze, 1991) look like?

3. Results from the analysis of the narratives

The process of coding alongside the given deductive code systems has produced data that mainly support the empirical knowledge about influence of different factors on low educational attainment in this group of people (see Cedefop, in press). The typical educational problems and the barriers for integration into labour market are supported as expected. For instance, also in these cases milieu and family background (i.e. social and cultural capital) are of high relevance for education and labour market entry. Early disadvantages and negative experiences in the educational path influence the educational attainment throughout the whole life. The second step of open coding and the interpretation of case-inherent dynamics has enabled us to explore patterns and variances between the cases and to develop a tentative typology of how individuals from this group enact their career.

4.Discussion of the research questions

The first research question asked for aspects relevant to the individual career action process. In accordance with this idea of the enacted career, they are the building blocks for individual action. The research can show that the process of enacting career is a long-term project and that these individuals experience long-lasting trajectories, sometimes with many attempts to reach a more stable career or education, sometimes with some success and some stability. With evidence from all cases, there search shows that career in this target group is connected not just to work and education, but to relevant other issues like family, leisure, culture, religion and others and that people try to connect to these different fields of life. People take action to make sense of the parallel aspects within their identity construction and they are working to gain coherence and try to actualize themselves on different levels (i.e. work, education, family).

With the second question, we asked if there is variance to be identified in terms of subjective career interests and of how people shape and enact their career. This seems to be important because sometimes groups (like so called low-qualified) are labelled and treated collectively. We have identified variation, for instance, in terms of the actual approach people show to enact own career. It is also visible that the narratives mirror these differences in terms of how people speak about education and work, in some cases referring to a more active approach, sometimes with notions of passivity and agony. For some, the search for alternatives to the work and career opportunities that are available seem to be very important.

With the third research question, we acknowledged that individual career is, on the one hand, a (psycho-social) constructive process; on the other hand, we

assumed institutional opportunities and constraints as relevant. The narratives show that the individual can be understood as the actor of an own career, but with very different resources. Aside the inner and biographical resources, it seems to be that institutional aspects have strong influence on the enactment of the individuals' careers. However, the individual educational experiences, the self-concept or the life-motives are today, they have faced and face structural constraints and sometimes opportunities that are important for how the individuals can (or cannot) enact their career.

With the fourth research question we try to link the narrative research to a theoretical reflection. We argue that individuals contextualise their career interaction in a two-fold way. On the one hand, they contextualise what they plan and do with their inner experiences and resources. On the other hand, they contextualise what they plan and do with their subjective view on their environment. The capacity to reflect and to plan one's own qualification and career path seems to be crucial to fulfil this task.

5. Conclusion

The presented research explores, based on a piece of narrative research, some questions that seem to be relevant for the discussion and further development of counselling practice and theory. At the same time it offers to take a glance at a special group of people having particularly problems to adapt to career and life opportunities. It seems to be interesting and important to discover the actual way these people enact their careers and life. Research and practice that allow an insight into subjective perceptions of life and career could be very relevant in times, when the pluralisation of life and identities are the dominant patterns and where collective support structures erode or change.

文章来源:

Peter C. Webera, Alexander J. Kochemb and Sylvie Weber-Hauserc. How low-qualified adults enact their career – findings from a narrative study in Germany[J]. British Journal of Guidance & Counselling, 2016, (44): 158 – 170.

附录 7

Using Participatory Action Research to Study the Implementation of Career Development Benchmarks at a New Zealand University
（节选）

In the New Zealand context, tertiary institutions are diverse in their structures and purposes. All tertiary institutions provide education beyond secondary school, yet the curricula, qualifications awarded, and institutional structures vary. Tertiary institutions include 18 polytechnics that focus on technical training, but these polytechnics also offer qualifications at the degree (bachelor) level, and some offer postgraduate qualifications up to the master level. There are also eight universities, which award qualifications up to the doctorate level. The tertiary sector also includes a number of private training organizations that usually have a "for profit" structure and award qualifications in skill, trade and technical areas.

Implementation the Secondary School Benchmarks received impetus from the New Zealand Ministry of Education's requirement that all secondary schools provide career services (Ministry of Education, 2012). However, no such mandate exists for career services in New Zealand tertiary institutions. The structure and extent of career development services in New Zealand tertiary institutions are therefore quite varied, ranging from no specific career development services to extensive and comprehensive services. The Tertiary Benchmarks provide guidance to all tertiary institutions to ascertain the quality and comprehensiveness of their career services and aspirational goals for career services in the New Zealand tertiary sector to be "world class."

Benchmarking

New Zealand is a small country and geographically isolated. Looking outward

to learn from the experiences of others when developing programs and practices is historically well established in New Zealand (Mann & Grigg, 2004). Various attempts to identify career management competencies for New Zealanders and to develop structures in New Zealand education to promote career competencies have been of great interest over the years (Vaughn, 2011), but it was not until the development of the Secondary School and Tertiary Benchmarks that national and systematic guides existed.

During the development of the Tertiary Benchmarks, Careers New Zealand reviewed a number of existing international standards for career services. Many of these standards for career development, however, focus on competencies for career practitioners rather than programmatic standards. For example, the European Centre for the Development of Vocational Training (Cedefop, 2009) published standards for European career practitioners. Among the professional associations that have developed standards or competencies for career practitioners are the International Association for Educational and Vocational Guidance (2003), the National Career Development Association (2009) in the US, and the National Steering Committee for Career Development Guidelines and Standards (2001) in Canada. More generically, Arthur (2008) and Zelloth (2014) have synthesized standards from international sources to propose global standards and training qualifications for career development practitioners.

In addition to competency statements for career practitioners, various agencies and professional associations have also developed guidelines to provide organizational standards for structure and functioning of career services in tertiary institutions. For example, in the United Kingdom, the Association of Graduate Career Advisory Services (AGCAS, 2011) published a matrix to define standards for tertiary career services. Australia has been active in developing, publishing, and promoting comprehensive career education standards (e.g., McMahon, 2007). The United States-based National Association for Colleges and Employers (NACE, 2013) similarly developed standards for four-year college and university career services (e.g., NACE, 2012), which focus on employer relationships and on-campus recruiting. Although defining services to link graduates

with employers are significant components of many career services in tertiary institutions, assisting graduates to make career decisions and ease the transition to employment or further education are also important goals (Hoover, Lenz, & Garis, 2013).

A number of definitions for benchmarking exist, but in general, benchmarking is understood to be activities that organizations undertake to compare their performance with others for the purposes of adapting practices that will improve performance (Stapenhust, 2009). According to Camp (1989), benchmarking can be thought of as the search for best practices that underpin enhanced performance. Professional practice is supported by the notion of quality and standards. Benchmarking enables career practitioners to assure stakeholders that the career education and development services are meeting international best practices. Stanbury (2005) characterized benchmarking for career development as reference points that are not fixed, but provide a shared understanding for discussing what is and what could be.

Richard's (2005) review of published journal articles that described exemplary career programs resulted in a framework for career program content, process and infrastructure. He concluded that there is great benefit for the improvement of career practice by discerning what has been seen to be effective in a range of contexts. However, the collection of ideas represented in the career literature was not constituted into formal benchmarks. Yet, more formal pronouncements about international best practices have been developed. Watts (2005) and Watts and Sultana (2004) described how investigations by the Organization of Economic Cooperation and Development (OECD), the World Bank, and the European Commission of the career guidance practices in 37 countries resulted in a synthesis of public policy about career guidance.

Recognized best practices have proven useful to appraise career services at the tertiary level. McCowan and McKenzie (2011) reported on the benchmarking of career services at the University of Technology Sydney (UTS) in Australia against principles for career development services formulated by the CICA (2007a). Specifically, they used eight Guiding Principles for Career

Development Services and fifteen Guiding Principles for Career Information Products that emerged from the Professional Standards for Australia Career Development Practitioners (CICA, 2007b) and the Australian Blueprint for Career Development (Ministerial Council on Education, Employment, Training and Youth Affairs, and the Department of Education, Employment, and Workplace Relations, 2010). In their procedure, the UTS career service staff first completed a self-assessment of the existing career services against each of the principles. Afterwards, an external consultant was employed to interview UTS students, the UTS career center staff, and other UTS staff in order to assess the degree to which career services complied with the Guiding Principles. Additional comparisons were made by the development of a rating instrument that employed the matrix standard developed by the Association of Graduate Career Advisory Services (2011) in the UK and the professional standards of the NACE (2013) in the US. McCowan and McKenzie (2011) concluded that the benchmarking process showed great promise for identifying which career services being offered by UTS were consistent with generally accepted professional standards and which services could be targeted for improvement. Further, the instrument developed during the benchmarking exercise at UTS was seen as appropriate for use at other Australian tertiary institutions for assessing the quality of their career services.

New Zealand Tertiary Career Development Benchmarks

The Tertiary Benchmarks drew from the international literature, but the developers of the benchmarks, i.e., Careers New Zealand, were cognizant of the unique environment in New Zealand. The resulting Tertiary Benchmarks are intended to provide standards without being prescriptive about how to achieve them.

While we recognize that the sector is hugely diverse, there are key facets to career development that apply to all students. These benchmarks allow each organization to reflect its own circumstances and contexts. It's a tool you can adapt to your own settings and contexts, a starting point for conversations about effective practice (Careers New Zealand, 2012).

The Tertiary Benchmarks were developed to assist tertiary career practitioners assess their services, and provide guidelines for bringing them to best practice standards. In this way, the Tertiary Benchmarks are intended to serve as a self-review tool rather than a compliance mechanism. The focus of the Tertiary Benchmarks is students' needs (not organizations' needs) and students' career competencies. It is recognized that achieving certain elements of the Tertiary Benchmarks may well take time, and the Tertiary Benchmarks are not proposed to be quick fixes. The Tertiary Benchmarks are intended to allow organizations to focus on areas of institutional career education priorities by recommending that each tertiary organization identify how to address each Benchmark over time (Careers New Zealand, 2012).

The overarching goal of the Tertiary Benchmarks is to assist students acquire career management competencies. Student career management competencies are the intended outcome of the career services provided, but they do not, in themselves, comprise a benchmark. To support the development of student career management competencies, the Tertiary Benchmarks are comprised of three dimensions: Employer and Industry Engagement is any contact between tertiary organizations and employers and industry that enables students to develop their career management competencies. Student Engagement is the way in which students connect with careers programs and services in order to develop their career management competencies.

Organization Engagement deals with how the tertiary organization as a whole enables its students to develop their career management competencies. (Careers New Zealand, 2012) Each dimension has a number of specific elements, with sub-categories under each element. The Employer and Industry Engagement dimension has two elements, the Student Engagement dimension has four elements and the Organization Engagement dimension has three elements. The Tertiary Benchmarks are envisioned to provide guidance to career services and organizations in all three dimensions, but recognize that implementation is an incremental process. Therefore, the elements within the dimensions of the Tertiary Benchmarks need to be prioritized for implementation, acknowledging that each institution may approach the benchmarks differently according to resources and context.

Participatory action research

The current study employed a participatory action research (PAR) methodology. PAR methodology was considered to be a useful and appropriate for studying implementation of the Tertiary Benchmarks. PAR is an approach for investigating social phenomenon by forming a team comprised of researchers and stakeholders who observe, act, and reflect on the phenomenon. In PAR, the researchers try to understand the phenomenon and also actively influence the course of the phenomenon. Kidd and Kral (2005) distilled the essence of PAR as getting "people who are affected by a problem together, [to] figure out what is going on in the group, and do something about it." They argued that the approach has the potential to make significant contributions to social science research.

Somekh (2006) identified the advantages of PAR. PAR integrates research and action holistically and incorporates evaluation of the processes developed during action. PAR is a collaborative partnership of participants and researchers. PAR develops knowledge and understanding from an "insiders" perspective. PAR is not value-neutral but incorporates the goal of "common good." PAR involves high levels of reflexivity and refection during the study. PAR engages with a wide range of existing knowledge. PAR results in learning by both the participants and the researchers. Finally, PAR locates the inquiry in a broader context rather than only in the immediate question. Hansen and Brady (2011) noted that there is no one research method associated with PAR. Often, a variety of data collection methods and analysis are employed. And, while PAR is typically associated with a specific issue, circumstance, and context, the outcome of PAR can provide important insights to others who may wish to pursue similar or related questions. Munford and Sanders (2003) provided the essentials of the PAR approach. Characteristic of this methodology is that each member of the research team has equal input into the research and the direction it will take. The members of the research team should have expertise and important knowledge to contribute. In PAR, the research is structured around cycles of action and reflection. Lastly, PAR adds value to the organization that is the focus. "Action research is about working towards practical outcomes and also about creating new forms of understanding, since action without reflection and understanding is blind, just as theory without action is meaningless" (Reason & Bradbury, 2008).

PAR differs from other research approaches with respect to the involvement of the researchers themselves. The researchers are immersed in the research as participants, rather than objectively observing and reporting on phenomenon. As a result, questions of validity in PAR may arise. Heikkinen, Huttunen, Syrjala, and Pesonen (2012) countered that validity is addressed in good PAR through five principles. The first of these is historical continuity. Understanding and taking account of the historical background contributes to validity of PAR by helping researchers understand and account for the possible causal relationships in the phenomenon under investigation. Second, the principle of reflexivity adds to validity in PAR. By understanding and accounting for the fact that the researcher creates the story/explanation of the events, the researcher is assisted to present results transparently. Iterative reflection further serves as momentum to trigger further actions. The third is the principle of dialectics. Dialectics consider how researchers' insights develop in dialogue with others. The voices and interpretations of others add richness to consideration of events and allow other possible explanations and courses of action to be considered. A fourth principle of PAR discusses workability and ethics. How realistic and "doable" are the actions developed during PAR? Do the actions developed encourage new practices that are supportive and complementary to the intended goals? What are ethical issues and how are these dealt with? The last principle of PAR expressed by Heikkinen et al. is the principle of evocativeness. This principle centers on the mental images, memories, and emotions related to the research topic. This principle is useful for supporting the researchers in constructing approaches that take advantage of their past personal experiences and to add to the current consideration of action and approaches the support the intended goal.

Purpose

The purpose of the current study was to employ the Tertiary Benchmarks during the establishment of a new career service in the Business and Law Faculty at a large New Zealand university. The impetus for the creation of new career service

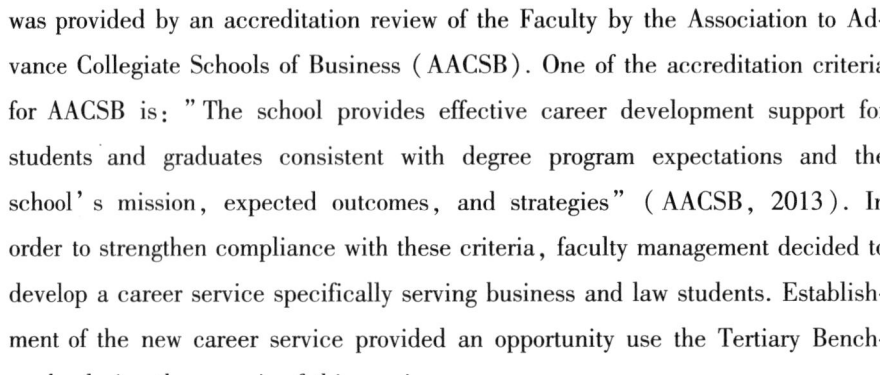

was provided by an accreditation review of the Faculty by the Association to Advance Collegiate Schools of Business (AACSB). One of the accreditation criteria for AACSB is: "The school provides effective career development support for students and graduates consistent with degree program expectations and the school's mission, expected outcomes, and strategies" (AACSB, 2013). In order to strengthen compliance with these criteria, faculty management decided to develop a career service specifically serving business and law students. Establishment of the new career service provided an opportunity use the Tertiary Benchmarks during the genesis of this service.

Research design

PAR was used to undertake the investigation. PAR was considered to be a useful approach as it allowed the input of the researchers who were investigating how the Tertiary Benchmarks were being used during the implementation of a new career service at a New Zealand university.

Participants

Three experienced career practitioners formed a reflective team to study the implementation of the Tertiary Benchmarks in the Faculty of Business and Law. Team members' backgrounds in career development were different; this was viewed as a strength because career development experiences and knowledge were mutually complementary. One of the team members (Trought, third author) had been recently employed by the Faculty of Business and Law as the Director of Careers and Employment and charged with establishing a career service specifically designed for students in the faculty. The Director was previously employed at a university in the UK before immigrating to New Zealand, when he was appointed as the Director of another large university's career service for business students and later as Director of Careers for the University. Following that, he was employed for a number of years as the Director of Career Development for an industrial trade organisation in New Zealand. The two other team members were academics who teach in career development qualifications at the university. One of the academic team members (Bailey, second author) had extensive experience teaching and supervising career development students. She also had been part of

the staff of the university's central career service. This team member also recently had responsibility for establishing a new career centre at a polytechnic institution in the Middle East. The other academic (Furbish, first author) had been the director of career services at a university in the United States. He led the development of the academic qualifications in career development at the university and oversaw the endorsement of the qualifications by New Zealand and international professional associations. Both academic members of the reflective team had participated in the development of the Tertiary Benchmarks as reviewers for Careers New Zealand.

Structure of the PAR

The agenda for the initial meeting of the reflective team focused on reviewing the principles of PAR and establishing a framework for the project. It was agreed that the reflective team would meet every 2 weeks during the 15-week Semester Two in 2013. Members agreed on ground rules based on the PAR tenets of planning, doing, and reflecting. Members established role expectations. The reflective team would meet as colleagues to monitor the implementation of the benchmarks in the development of the new career service in the faculty. However, it was clear that the Director had positional responsibility for the actual development of the service. Each member would take notes during meetings and distribute their notes to other team members via E-mail. Team members would be responsible for reviewing the summaries of the meetings and for preparing their reflections for the next meeting.

After establishing the PAR team, members immediately performed a SWOT analysis (i.e., strengths, weakness, opportunities, and threats) for the newly created Careers and Employment Office. The analysis identified strengths for the Careers and Employment Office as: support from the Faculty management, a history of contacts with employers who had hired graduates in the past, a number of student organisations and clubs that could be used to promote the Office, the incentive to comply with AACSB standards for career services, and a Faculty curriculum requirement that all students participate in co-operative education (i.e., work experience). Identified weaknesses were: students' expectations about the role of the Careers and Employment Office, minimal historic support for career development of Business and Law students, differential career development needs between domestic and international students, and no information management system within the faculty for career-related student data. Opportunities were perceived to be: the availability of the Tertiary Career Development Benchmarks to guide the Office, the possibility to engage all academics in the faculty in activities to enhance students' career development, the use of social media to communicate with students and develop professionally acceptable "profiles," and the opportunity to develop career development services for Business and Law students attending across multiple university campuses. Possible threats were: the relationship between the Business and Law Careers and Employment Office and the central career office in the University, which offered parallel services to all students of the University. There was concern that students and faculty could experience confusion owing to similar goals of the two services and that "turf" issues were possible between the two services. Other possible threats were gaining the involvement and support of academics in the faculty and managing the expectations of employers for "career ready" applicants.

The team reviewed the current status of career services for Business and Law students in light of the SWOT analysis and also in light of the Tertiary Benchmarks. The benchmarks provide sub-categories and descriptions of levels of effectiveness for each of the dimensional sub-categories. The levels of effectiveness range from ineffective to adequate, to consolidating effectiveness to highly effective. The benchmarks document suggests that tertiary institutions employing the benchmarks prioritise which dimension of the benchmarks should be addressed first, recognising that implementation of the benchmarks is an incremental procedure. The team concluded that the Organisation Engagement dimension was the foundation for programme development and therefore decided to focus on the three elements and sub-categories for that dimension. Sevicke-Jones (2014), who studied implemen-tation of the Secondary School Benchmarks, also concluded that giving priority to Organisational Engagement was important, that Organisation Engagement was essential, and should be given highest priority.

The research team met on a regular basis to reflect upon the outcomes of the events and to evaluate actions that were generated. Prioritization of the dimensions and elements of the benchmarks and strategies for implementing them were included in the actions. Because the Director of Careers and Employability was a member of the research team, important milestones were identifiable.

PAR employs the use of iterative cycles. The timetable for the proposed research, while relatively short, was adequate for the development of supplemental actions to refine the implementation of the selected dimensions and elements. The team's final agreed-upon task was to produce a written document that chronicled the period during which the PAR occurred. The document served as an audit trail and was a summative review of the process.

Results

PAR outcomes

Developing a strategy for implementing career programming and policy, which are sub-categories of Organization Engagement Benchmark, was the first action considered. The team recognised the benefits and the necessity of developing a well-articulated, strategic plan for the Career Development and Employability Office to conceptualise the mission and activities of the office. Further, a strategic plan was identified as useful for the Director to inform executive management faculty about the philosophy, intended activities, and resources needed. The Director developed a draft strategic plan that was reviewed by the team. The team was aware that multiple career services existed at the University, but these were fragmented and under-resourced.

Another sub-category under Organisational Engagement is organisation wide-approach. Although the focus was the implementation of career services specifically in the Faculty of Business and Law, the team recognised that strategies for linking with other career services were necessary elements for increasing the effectiveness of the faculty's service. While the majority of Business and Law students studied at the main campus, where the Director was located, some Business programmes were offered on other university campuses. The new service was not serving students on other campuses as well as the students on the main campus. The

team acknowledged that strategies to provide career services to these students were a necessary component of the strategic plan.

Equity is another sub-category under the Benchmark of Organisational Engagement. Specifically, equity calls for strategies to address career development needs of Maori (indigenous New Zealanders) and Pasifika students, who are targeted equity groups in New Zealand. In addition, the research team considered the special career development needs of international students, who comprise a significant segment of Faculty of Business and Law enrolment. The Director identified specific career development needs for students in each equity group with input from other team members. Another useful strategy was linking to other university offices with special resources and understanding of equity group students. Further, the team developed specific programmes and support to address the career development and employment of Ma ¯ ori, Pasifika and international students.

The Organisational Engagement Benchmark contains a number of sub- categories that target staff qualifications and leadership. Reflecting upon the degree to which these subcategories were met, the team concluded that this area was approaching the "highly effective" Benchmark standard. The academic qualifications and competencies of the Director and his positional membership in policy-making groups within the faculty were specific subcategories being met. Moreover, the Director's role was clearly defined by the Faculty Senior Management, meeting yet another of the sub-categories under the Organisational compliance Engagement Benchmark.

Another sub-category of Organisational Engagement focuses on career development information management and professional resources allocated to ensure that programmes and services meet the identified needs of all students. Information management was an aspect that the team considered inadequate as currently configured. The team recognised that information about the career plans and career needs of students in the Faculty were neither systematically gathered nor recorded. While information such as this can be difficult to obtain from university students, who are not in continuous contact with the Careers and Employment Centre, the team viewed that a centrally accessible database of student career plans would be desirable. Such a source of information would be beneficial both to the Careers and Employment Centre and to academic faculty when advising and developing co-operative education work experiences for students. The team tasked the Director with investigating how a career development information system could be developed and integrated into the faculty.

The final sub-category of the Organisational Engagement Benchmark states the need for research integrated into the career service. The team identified this sub-category of the Organisational Engagement Benchmark to be a strength within the Careers and Employment Centre. The team concluded that this Benchmark was being fulfilled as evidenced by the PAR project itself.

Iterative cycles

PAR calls for iterative cycles of action and reflection. The current research was time-bound within one university academic semester. Therefore, desirable review and refinement of actions taken were not fully realised because of this time limitation. However, PAR is an organic and ongoing approach of action implementation, setting the stage for subsequent actions that flow from completed actions. By the end of the semester, the team was able to reflect upon the actions that occurred in the Careers and Employment Office. Moreover, the team prioritised Employer and Industry Engagement as the next Benchmark standard to be addressed during the development of the service.

Discussion

The use of PAR for implementing the Tertiary Benchmarks had a number of advantages and generated positive outcomes. First and foremost, PAR provided a mechanism for systematically applying the Tertiary Benchmarks during the development of the Career and Employment Centre. As Baudouin et al. (2007) asserted, career services and programmes are not often held accountable. The use of PAR during the formative stages of a new service provided an opportunity to document to internal stakeholders and external accreditation agencies that the strategies and specific approaches taken were guided by identified standards. Although the development of the Career and Employment Centre is ongoing, the

PAR team contributed to the legitimacy and robustness of the action and strategic planning from the outset.

Beneficial outcomes

Formation the PAR team composed of career development practitioners and academics resulted in a number of positive outcomes. The Career and Employment Centre has no other staff other than the Director. Therefore, academics on the team provided collegial support to and acted as an external reference group for the Director during the early stage of the Centre as well as helping to develop operational strategies. In large organisations such as universities, staff, who have similar but complementary expertise, do not always have the opportunity to work together and to collaboratively use their expertise. PAR brought together the Director from the Faculty of Business and Law, and two academics who teach career development in the School of Education. PAR resulted in the cross-fertilisation of ideas and experience from participants who are not organisationally or physically proximal. Interactions among the team members resulted in the formation of a community of practice (Wenger, 1998) characterised by mutual engagement, joint enterprise, and shared repertoire across disparate roles at the university. The sharing of ideas and perspectives reassured the team that their thinking was comprehensive. The team generated multiple solutions to problems from which the best or most appropriate could be selected. All three members of the team had considerable practitioner experience in addition to management and academic experience, thereby promoting accountability by developing practices ground in theory and in experience.

Participation in PAR enhanced the perspectives of the academics about the benchmarks. Through being involved in the "real-world" implementation of the benchmarks, the academic team members gained insights that will be useful when teaching about the benchmarks in their career development class. As a matter of fact, the academics involved in the current research developed a new course focusing on the benchmarks. The experiences provided by participating in the research will enhance lectures in this course.

The benchmarks provided a useful structure for both developing and monitoring services. Employing the benchmarks in the early stages of creating a new service produced a framework that was logical and easy to follow for both the Director and for faculty managers and decision makers to whom he was accountable but who did not have a career development background. The benchmarks made the links between student career development and other student outcomes in the faculty more explicit, such as the graduate profile and co-operative education, and thus identified how career development can support wider faculty initiatives.

The process used during the creation of the Careers and Employment Centre in the Faculty of Business and Law has produced a model that other faculties in the university may consider. Resources for the university's central career development office have been reduced over the past few years. Consideration has been given to career development services located within each faculty. Although advantages and disadvantages exist for both centralised and de-centralised career development services within a university, the use of PAR in the initial stage of development of faculty-specific career services for Business and Law students provides documentation of the process that could be useful to other faculties that adopt the in-faculty model.

文章来源:

Dale S. Furbish, Robyn Bailey, David Trought. Using Participatory Action Research to Study the Implementation of Career Development Benchmarks at a New Zealand University[J]. International Journal for Educational and Vocational Guidance (2016) 16:153 - 167.

Career Development Courses and Educational Outcomes: Do Career Courses Make a Difference?
（节选）

Method

In order to outline the method of this study, we first identify the research design we used. Next, we discuss participants, comprising two groups (one experimental and one quasi control), and describe the setting in which this study took place, including the particulars of the career development course which acted as the independent variable of the study. Finally, we address both data collection and data analysis and identify appropriate statistical analyses for each of the five research questions.

Research Design

This study used an ex post facto design in which archival data were accessed and analyzed to answer the aforementioned research questions. The study included two samples of students from an 8-year span (2000–2007): (a) those who completed the career course during that time and (b) a statistically comparable sample of students who did not take the career course to act as the comparison group. The independent variable in this study was the career course. Those students who enrolled in and completed the class were included in the experimental or treatment condition. The dependent variables were persistence to graduation (measured by graduation in 6 years), graduation rate (time to graduation), credits taken to graduate, and the number of course withdrawals executed by students. A cohort of students who did not enroll in the career class served as the comparison group.

Participants

Both groups in our sample were comprised of students at a large private university during the years 2000–2007. One group included students who enrolled in and successfully passed the career development class (with a grade of C-minus or better), and the other group included students who did not take the career development class. The comparison, nonclass participant sample was initially drawn from the population in a mostly random fashion (the only constraint being that the student could never have taken a career course). This yielded a significantly unbalanced comparison sample in terms of year in school with freshmen and sophomores comprising 75.7% of the career course group and only 28.5% of the nonclass participant group. It was thus decided to pull the data again but to match the nonclass participant group to the career class group on the variable year in school. No additional demographic information was used to match the groups to allow for as random a draw as possible and with the intention to control for group differences in the main analysis should they appear.

Table 1 Descriptive Statistics Comparing the Categorical Variables of the Career Course and Noncourse Participant Groups.

Variable Class level	Course Participants ($n = 3,546$)	Noncourse Participants ($n = 3,510$)
Freshman	1,785 (50.3%)	1,760 (50.1%)
Sophomore	1,228 (34.6%)	1,220 (34.8%)
Junior	391 (11.0%)	390 (11.1%)
Senior	142 (4%)	140 (4.0%)
Gender		
Male	1,863 (52.5%)	1,763 (50.2%)
Female	1,683 (47.5%)	1,747 (49.8%)
Ethnicity		
White/Caucasian	3,126 (88.2%)	3,201 (91.2%)
Hispanic	161 (4.5%)	125 (3.6%)
Asian	104 (2.9%)	82 (2.3%)

Hawaiian/Pacific Islander	75 (2.1%)	50 (1.4%)
American Indian	32 (0.9%)	25 (0.7%)
Black	29 (0.8%)	17 (0.5%)
Other	19 (0.5%)	10 (0.3%)
Major		
Open major	1,582 (44.6%)	673 (19.2%)
Family, home, and social sciences	415 (11.7%)	521 (14.8%)
Fine arts and communications	335 (9.4%)	482 (13.7%)
Business	330 (9.3%)	382 (10.9%)
Life sciences	248 (7.0%)	403 (11.5%)
Engineering and Technology	187 (5.3%)	354 (10.1%)
Humanities	186 (5.2%)	239 (6.8%)
Physical and mathematical sciences	127 (3.6%)	224 (6.4%)
Education	77 (2.2%)	112 (3.2%)
Nursing	59 (1.7%)	120 (3.4%)

The combined total number of participants from the two groups was 7,056 undergraduates, 3,430 women (48.6%), and 3,626 men (51.4%). About 85% of the participants were classified as freshmen and sophomores and approximately 90% were White. Other ethnic groups represented included Hispanic (4.1%), Asian (2.6%), Hawaiian/Pacific Islander (1.8%), American Indian (0.8%), and Black (0.7%) with 29 participants listed as "other" (0.4%). About one third of participants ($n=2,255$, 32%) were listed as "open major," while the other two thirds (68%) had declared a major.

Group 1. The first group was comprised of 3,546 undergraduates who had enrolled in and successfully passed (with a grade of at least a C-minus or better) the career course from the year 2000 to 2007. This group, considered as the treatment group in the study, was referred to as the career course group, and students in this group were referred to as course participants. Categorical demographic information for this group (and the second group) is presented in Table 1.

Group 2. The second group of participants was comprised of 3,510 students who did not take the career course and were matched to the career course group on the variable year in school. This group was considered the quasi-control group of the study and is referred to as the comparison group; students in this group were referred to as noncourse participants. Demographic information representing continuous variables for this group (and the career course group) are presented in Table 2.

Table 2 Descriptive Statistics Comparing the Continuous Variables of the Career Course and Noncourse Participant Groups.

Varlable	Course Participants ($n=3,546$)		Noncourse Participants ($n=3,510$)	
	M	SD	M	SD
HS GPA	3.667	0.342	3.679	0.335
ACT score	25.96	3.737	26.55	3.474

Table 3 Descriptive Statistics Comparing the Dummy-Coded Variables of the Career Course and Noncourse Participant Groups.

Variable	Course Participants ($n=3,546$)	Noncourse Participants ($n=3,510$)
Major status		
Undeclared major	1,582 (44.6%)	673 (19.2%)
Declared major	1,964 (55.4%)	2,837 (80.8%)
Minority status		
Majority	3,126 (88.2%)	3,201 (91.2%)
Minority	420 (11.8%)	309 (8.8%)

Within the major variable, the largest proportion of students in both groups was "open major." To simplify the analysis, a new variable was dummy-coded in which open majors were coded as 0 and students who had a major were coded as 1. Similarly, within the ethnicity variable, the largest proportion of students in both groups was "White/Caucasian." Since no remarkable trend was noted other than the discrepancy between Whites and all other ethnicities, a new variable was created in which Whites/Caucasians, considered in this context to be students in the ethnic majority, were coded 0, and all other ethnicities (those in the ethnic minority) were coded 1. Table 3 depicts the frequencies in the two groups (career course and noncourse participants) of these collapsed variables.

Career exploration course. The career course examined in this study is typical of career development courses in postsecondary settings. The University Catalog provides the following description for the course: " Applying theories of individual, academic, and career development to the university student. Exploring university opportunities and college majors; graduation planning." In addition to this description, four learning outcomes for the course are identified thus:

1. Increase knowledge of college majors, career options, and additional world-of-work factors that influence career choice.

2. Develop greater awareness of personal qualities, interests, skills, and values that play a role in career-decision making.

3. Demonstrate increased confidence and ability to make decisions as well as progress toward making career decisions.

4. Display an awareness of and ability to access educational and career information resources.

This course is taught by many individuals, including professors, psychologists, career specialists, and graduate students. While a common curriculum unites the various sections, the teachers are fairly free to adapt the lessons to their interest and the needs of the class. All sections subscribed to the same learning outcomes, and we can reasonably assume that all students who completed the career class engaged in similar processes and content regardless of the section in which they were enrolled.

Data analysis. The first task of the data analysis was to test our two groups for similarity based on the identified comparison criteria (i.e., year in school, race, gender, high school GPA, and American College Testing [ACT] score). Following the methodological example of Folsom (2000) whose study we aimed to replicate, we used a x2 test of independence to compare between-group frequencies for the race, gender, and year in school variables since these data were categorical in nature. Independent ttests were used to compare group means when it came to high school GPA and ACT scores. The null hypothesis in each of these tests was that there was no significant difference between the two groups on each factor. In the event that significant differences between the groups were found, we treated those particular variables as covariates during the main data analysis.

For the first research question concerning whether students who take the career class graduate at a rate significantly different from those who do not, dummy-coding was employed to create a new variable that represented whether students graduated in 6 years or not. As Smith-Keller (2005) described, "students who persisted to graduation within six years of matriculation into university were coded '1' and those students who did not persist to graduation within the six-year time frame were coded '0'." A binary logistic regression was computed (since the dependent variable is categorical/dichotomous) to determine whether the career development course with covariates was a significant predictor (at the .05 level) of persistence to graduation.

The second research question (which asks about differences in time to graduation) was answered using multiple regression. For this research question, time was measured in terms of semesters (with a term being considered half a semester). Then, the multiple regression was able to assess whether the career development course significantly predicted (at the .05 level) students' time to graduation in the presence of other covariates.

The third research question, concerning credits to graduation, was answered by employing multiple regression. Doing so determined whether participation in the career development course was a significant predictor (at the .05 level) of students' total credits at graduation in the presence of the other covariates.

The fourth research question regarding course withdrawals was answered by calculating means and standard deviations using the total number of course withdrawals executed by those who did persist to graduation in the two groups. Using multiple regression, it was determined whether between-group differences (at the .05 level) in terms of number of course withdrawals were accurately predicted by the career development course.

The fifth and final research question concerning cumulative GPA was also answered using multiple regression to determine whether there were significant differences (at the .05 level) between the treatment and control groups. Specifically, the career course was examined to see whether it was a significant predictor of group differences in cumulative GPA.

Results

The purpose of this research was twofold: (a) to determine what impact college career development courses have on student outcome variables and (b) to contribute to a growing body of literature concerning the effectiveness of career courses at universities and colleges across the United States, in a way that is particularly needed (by examining outcome rather than output of the course). Specifically, we examined the long-term impacts of completing a credit-bearing career exploration course on student and institutional outcomes of specified interest including student retention, time taken to graduate (measured in terms of both semesters and credits), number of course withdrawals, and overall academic success (measured by total cumulative GPA at graduation). To examine the impact of the careerdevelopment course, a group of students who did not take the class was used as a comparison sample and assessed on all of the same outcome variables.

Results to each of the research questions will be detailed below. However, before addressing the five research questions, the results of the statistical analyses used to determine whether the two groups (the experimental or career course group and the quasi-control or comparison group) were reasonably matched will be presented.

Group Comparisons

Given that the quasi-control sample (the group of students who did not take the career course) was only matched to the experimental group (encompassing the group of students who did take the career course) on one criterion (year in school), the two groups were statistically compared on each of the other matching criteria (gender, ethnicity, major, high school GPA, and ACT score), in order to assess whether or not the groups were reasonably matched before proceeding to answer the main research questions. These six dimensions were identified from the Folsom (2000) and Smith-Keller (2005) studies and replicated here to maintain consistency and attempt to control for potentially confounding variables. Results to each of these six criteria-based comparisons will be discussed in turn.

Year in school. After initially pulling an unrestrained random sample of the students available who had not taken the career course, it was discovered that the two groups were significantly mismatched in terms of year in school, with the non-class participants being much more heavily weighted toward juniors and seniors (freshmen = 431, sophomores = 700, juniors = 846, seniors = 1,995), while the career course group contained (predictably) many more freshmen and sophomores proportionately (freshmen = 2,090, sophomores = 2,389, juniors = 1,094, seniors = 343). A w^2 test of independence was calculated comparing the class level of the career course participants and noncourse participants. A significant interaction was found, $x^2(3) = 2,945.908$, $p < .001$, indicating that there was a significant difference between the two groups in terms of year in school compared to what would be expected proportionately. In an effort to procure a comparison group that was reasonably similar to the career course group in terms of year in school, the data were pulled again, this time by using the year in school makeup of the career course group to match the quasi-control group. For example, for every x number of freshman students in a given year who passed the career course (with a C-minus or better), the registry was queried for that same number of freshman students in that year who did not take the career course (these students were also checked to ensure that they never enrolled in the course during their time at the university). With the new data set, after excluding students who were identified as visiting students or otherwise nontraditional students, another x^2 test of independence was computed, and no significant relationship was found, $w^2(3) = .034$, $p = .998$. It was thus concluded that there was no significant difference between the two groups in terms of class standing (freshman, sophomore, junior, or senior).

Gender. Considering that year in school was the only criterion used to match the two groups at the time of the data pull, the rest of the identified criteria were

used to statistically assess for group similarity between the two groups (course participants and noncourse participants). The next criterion used to compare the two groups for similarity was gender. A x^2 test of independence was calculated comparing the proportion of males to females in each of the two groups. No significant relationship was found, $x^2(1) = 3.768$, $p > .05$, and it was concluded that the two groups were reasonably matched in terms of gender. That is, both groups contained proportionately similar numbers of males and females.

Ethnicity. Ethnicity was initially coded into seven groups (White/Caucasian, American Indian, Asian, Black, Hawaiian/Pacific Islander, Hispanic, and other). To simplify the analysis, these groups were collapsed into two broader categories: students considered to be in the minority (American Indian, Asian, Black, Hawaiian/Pacific Islander, Hispanic, and other) and those in the majority (White/Caucasian). A x^2 test of independence was calculated comparing the proportion of students in the minority to those in the majority both in the career class group and in the quasi-control group. A significant interaction was found, $x^2(1) = 17.607$, $p < .001$, indicating that groups were significantly different in terms of ethnicity. Specifically, students in the minority were found in the career course participants more than what would be expected based on proportions. In light of this finding, ethnicity was treated as a covariate in the main analysis.

Major. Because the largest proportion of students in both the group of course participants and the noncourse participants had undeclared majors, participants were categorized as either undeclared major or declared major. A x^2 test of independence was calculated comparing the frequency of undeclared major students and declared major students in the career course and noncourse participants groups. A significant interaction was found, $x^2(1) = 524.996$, $p < .001$, indicating that the two groups were significantly different in terms of major status. There were fewer students with an undeclared major in the quasi-control group than was proportionately expected. Given this difference between groups, students' major status was treated as a covariate in the main statistical analysis.

ACT score. The final criterion used to compare the two groups was ACT score. An independent samples t-test comparing the mean ACT scores of the career course group and the quasi-control group found a significant difference between the means of the two groups, t(7016) = 6.925, p < .001. The mean ACT score of the career course group was significantly lower (M = 25.96, SD = 3.737) than the mean ACT score of the noncourse participants (M = 26.55, SD = 3.474). Since this criterion was found to be significantly different between the two groups, ACT score was added to the list of covariates to be controlled for in the main analysis.

Given that the quasi-control group was pulled in a mostly random fashion (matched only on the variable year in school), we are able to make some observations about the composition of these groups at the outset which would not be possible if the groups were made to be as similar as possible. For example, it is interesting (though perhaps unsurprising) to note that the major variable was a point of marked difference between the groups. It can thus be inferred that, in general, course participants have a much higher proportion of undecided students than noncourse participants. The same can be said for the other significant differences between groups, ethnicity, and entering ACT score: Overall, the career course generally contains higher than expected minority students, and the career course participants have lower ACT scores than noncourse participants. It bears repeating, however, that these differences, while interesting, were treated as covariates in the data analysis, and thus, their potentially confounding effects were controlled for statistically.

Research Questions

Having determined the degree to which the two groups (course participants and noncourse participants) were matched, the main research questions were addressed using the appropriate statistical analysis, treating major, ethnicity, and ACT score as covariates.

Retention to graduation in 6 years. A x^2 test of independence was calculated comparing the retention to graduation within 6 years in the two groups (the class cohort and nonclass cohort). No significant relationship was found, $x^2(1) = .691$, p = .423, indicating that there was no significant difference between the class cohort and nonclass cohort in terms of graduation within 6 years.

Table 4 Logistic Regression Predicting Graduation in 6 Years From Career Course, Major/Minority Status, and ACT Score.

Predictor	B	Wald x^2	p	Odds Ratio
Career course	.135	3.389	.066	1.145
Major	.130	2.809	.094	1.138
Minority	.232	4.666	.031	0.793
ACT	.075	57.264	.000	1.078

To control for the potential confounding effect of the covariates (ACT score, ethnicity, and major), a binary logistic regression was also computed to determine whether participation in the career class could significantly predict whether participants graduated within 6 years or not (a dichotomous variable) in the presence of the covariates. A test of the full model against a constant only model was statistically significant, indicating that the predictors (participation in the career class and the covariates, ACT score, ethnicity, and major) as a set reliably distinguished between those who did graduate within 6 years and those who did not ($x^2 = 73.907$, $p < .001$, with df = 4). Within the model, the career course variable was not a significant predictor of graduation. Table 4 shows the logistic regression coefficient, Wald test, and odds ratio for each of the predictors.

Employing a .05 criterion of statistical significance, minority status and ACT score had significant partial b weights. Participation in the career course was not a significant predictor of graduation within 6 years. It was thus concluded that there was no significant difference between the experimental and quasi-control groups in terms of retention to graduation (as measured by graduation in 6 years).

Time to graduation in semesters. The second research question asked whether students who complete the career course graduate in a different amount of time (measured in semesters) than those who do not take the course. A multiple linear regression was calculated predicting students' semesters to graduation based on being in the career course and the covariates (major status, minority status, and ACT score). A significant regression equation was found, $F(4, 7017) = 24.945$,

$p < .001$, with an R^2 of .014. However, the career course did not significantly predict differences in students' semesters taken to graduate ($\beta = .021$, $t = .411$, $p = .681$). It was thus concluded that there was no significant difference between the course and noncourse participants in terms of the amount of time (in semesters) it took for them to graduate.

Time to graduation in credits. The third research question had to do with whether students in the career class take a different amount of credits to graduate than those who do not take the course. A multiple linear regression was calculated to predict participants' total credits at graduation based on the career course and the covariates (major status, minority status, and ACT score). A significant regression equation was found, $F(4, 7017) = 153.050$, $p < .001$, with an R^2 of .080. Participants' predicted total credits are equal to $91.113 + 4.78$ (career course) $+ 3.828$ (minority) $+ 2.239$ (ACT), where career course is coded as $0 = $ no, $1 = $ yes; minority is coded as $0 = $ majority, $1 = $ minority; and ACT is a continuous score. Career course, minority, and ACT were all significant predictors. It was concluded that students who take the career course differ significantly from the noncourse participants in terms of total credits at graduation. Students who took the career course graduated with 4.78 more credits than those who do not take the class.

Number of course withdrawals. The fourth research question that was posed was whether students who take the career course withdraw from courses differently from those who do not. A multiple linear regression was calculated predicting students' number of withdraws based on being in the career course and the covariates (major status, minority status, and ACT score). A significant regression equation was found, $F(4, 7017) = 8.804$, $p < .001$, with an R^2 of .005. However, the career course did not significantly predict differences in students' number of withdraws ($\beta = -.055$, $t = -1.366$, $p = -.172$). It was thus concluded that there was no significant difference between the course and noncourse participants in terms of the number of withdrawals students incurred.

Total cumulative GPA at graduation. The fifth and final research question of this study asked whether students who took the career course had significantly dif-

ferent cumulative GPAs than students who did not take the course. A multiple linear regression was calculated to predict participants' total cumulative GPAs at graduation based on the career course and the covariates (major status, minority status, and ACT score). A significant regression equation was found, $F(4, 7017) = 350.411$, $p < .001$, with an R^2 of .167. Participants' predicted total GPA is equal to $2.357 + .035 (SD 117) 0.091 (minority) + .039 (ACT)$, where career course is coded as $0 = no$, $1 = yes$; Minority is coded as $0 = majority$, $1 = minority$, and ACT is a continuous score. Career course, minority, and ACT were all significant predictors. It was concluded that students who took the career course differed significantly from the noncourse participants in terms of total cumulative GPA at graduation. Students who took the career course graduated with cumulative GPAs 0.035 higher than students who did not take the course.

In conclusion, it was found that while the two groups (career course participants and noncourse participants) were similar in terms of gender and high school GPA, they significantly differed in terms of major, ethnicity, and entering ACT score. Controlling for the effects of the covariates, the career course was not a significant predictor of whether or not students graduated in 6 years, the number of semesters it took students to graduate, and the number of withdrawals students incurred. However, in the presence of the covariates, the career course did significantly predict the total number of credits (with course participants graduating with about five more credits than the noncourse participants) and cumulative GPA at graduation (with course participants graduating with higher GPAs than the comparison group).

Discussion

This study examined the impact of a university credit-bearing career exploration course on measures of academic outcomes (retention, time to graduation, and withdraws) and achievement (cumulative GPA). It was found that participation in the course did not make a significant difference in terms of retention, as measured by students' rates of graduation (within 6 years), time to graduation (in terms of semesters), and the number of withdraws. However, the course was found to significantly predict students' total credits at graduation and their overall academic performance (measured by cumulative GPA).

Each research question with its accompanying results will be discussed in turn below. This discussion will address how the findings from this study compare with previous research (particularly Folsom, 2000; Goodson, 1982; Smith-Keller, 2005).

Integration of Findings

Retention to graduation in 6 years. Results indicated no significant difference between the career course group and the noncourse participants in terms of graduation within 6 years. This finding mirrors that of Folsom (2000) who also found no significant difference. However, it differs from the results of Smith Keller (2005) who found that students who had taken the career course at that university persisted to graduation at a rate significantly higher than those who did not take the class. Although it is unclear whether Goodson (1982) was measuring retention to graduation, a significant difference was found between the students who took the career class and those who did not in terms of the percentage of students completing 4 years of college. It was reported that 67% of students who took the class completed 4 years of college at the time of the 10-year follow-up, compared to 57% of students who did not.

While the career course was not found to predict a significant difference in terms of students graduating within 6 years, it should be noted that the graduation rates in that time for both the course participants (86.6%) and the comparison group (85.7%) were much higher than the national average of 59% (U.S. Department of Education, Institute of Education Sciences, National Center for Education Statistics, 2015). Graduation rates are predictably different when one considers the type and acceptance rate of the institution—universities with less stringent admissions tend to have lower graduation rates, while those with higher admission standards tend to have higher graduation rates. Given that the site institution had an acceptance rate of 48.7% in Fall 2013 (U.S. News and World Report, 2015) and 55.0% in Fall 2014 (Brigham Young University Admissions, 2015), these numbers are also higher than the national average for nonprofit in-

stitutions that accept between 25.0% and 49.9% of applicants (77.5%) and these same institutions that accept between 50.0% and 74.9% of applicants (62.3%).

Time to graduation in semesters. Results indicated no significant difference between the career course group and the comparison group in terms of time to graduation (measured in semesters). Course participants on average graduated in 10.26 semesters, while students in the comparison group graduated in 10.15 semesters. This finding provided evidence that even in the presence of other covariates (major, ethnicity, and ACT score), participation in the career course did not significantly predict the time it took students to graduate (as measured by semesters). Similar to the results of the first research question, this finding again reflected Folsom's (2000) study, as he likewise found no significant difference between the two groups in his study on this variable (although time in that case was measured in months, not in semesters). However, Smith-Keller's (2005) study did show a significant difference on this variable of time to graduation reporting that "students who had not taken the career course took significantly less time to complete their degrees and graduate, compared to students who took the course."

Time to graduation in credits. Time to graduation measured in terms of credits was one of two outcome variables for which there was a significant finding. Results indicated that the two groups differed significantly in the total number of credits at graduation with the career course group graduating with 4.78 more credits than the comparison sample, in the presence of the covariates. While noncourse participants took 151.23 credits to graduate on average, students who took the career course graduated with 154.74 credits. Although this difference in means is 3.51, the multiple regression equation, which took into account the combined effects of the covariates, yielded a difference of 4.78 credits. This finding showed a trend similar to that found in Folsom (2000) who reported that "the adjusted mean number of credit hours taken to graduate by course participants was (M = 110.85)," and the "adjusted mean number of credit hours taken to graduate among non-participants was (M = 109.90)." In other words, in both studies, career course participants graduated with more credit hours than students who did not take a career course. Smith-Keller (2005), on the other hand, found that students who took the career course graduated with significantly less credit hours than those who did not.

While, taken alone, this finding may seem to suggest that career course participants took longer time to graduate, it is important to again note that there was no significant difference between the groups in terms of semesters taken to graduate. Taken together then, it appears to bode well that while the students who took career exploration may have taken a few more credits to graduate, they did so in the same amount of time (semesters) as their nonclass peers. It bears noting as well that although there was a difference of 4.78 credits between the course participants and the noncourse participants, the career exploration course itself accounted for two of those credits. Career courses are hypothesized by some (Folsom, 2000; Reardon, Folsom, Lee, & Clark, 2011; Smith-Keller, 2005) to serve an efficiency function—that is, that career courses help students determine what they want to major in and thus enable them to take courses more intentionally geared toward their major requirements from an earlier point in their education—it may also be that career courses empower students to use their courses as opportunities to explore different major and career options. This may explain in part why students who took career exploration graduated with more credits than noncourse participants.

Number of course withdrawals. Interest in this outcome variable stemmed in part from the desire to replicate Folsom (2000) and in part as an alternative to another variable of interest, the number of major changes to which we did not have access. The university does not have a central way of tracking if and how many times students change their majors. Folsom (2000) stated that the number of course withdraws was of interest in studies of this nature because "if career course participants gain a clearer career focus, then one possible outcome is less within-course starting and stopping and hence less course withdrawals executed in comparison with students who did not complete the career development course." Contrary to Folsom, results of this study indicated no significant differ-

ence between course participants and noncourse participants in the number of course withdrawals executed. This supported the conclusion that students who take career courses withdraw from classes at a rate similar to students who do not take the career course. Smith-Keller (2005) likewise found no significant difference between what she called the class cohort and nonclass cohort in terms of course drops.

Total cumulative GPA at graduation. The fifth and final outcome variable we examined was total cumulative GPA at graduation. Results indicated that the two groups were significantly different in terms of total GPA at graduation and that students in the career course group graduated with higher cumulative GPAs than the comparison group. While the difference in GPAs was marginal (.035), it remains a meaningful finding that even in the presence of the covariates (major, ethnicity, and ACT score), the career course significantly contributed to the outcome variable, cumulative GPA at graduation. That is, students who enrolled in and successfully completed the career class (with a grade of C-minus or better) graduated with a .035 higher cumulative GPA than students who did not take the class.

Limitations

This study is limited in its scope due to several factors that ultimately constrain the generalizability of the results. These factors include variability across the teachers of the course, data collection occurring entirely at one, somewhat unique university, differences between the quasi-experimental and the comparison groups, and the presence of nontraditional students in the sample.

Variability across teachers. The career course was taught by different teachers, who were generally free to adapt the course to their interests and style. While the stated learning outcomes of the course were consistent and did not vary by teacher, individual teacher's approaches to teaching did vary and this may have introduced variability.

One university. It should be noted that the scope of this study (and the generalizability of the results) is limited by the fact that it only examined one career course at one university. While the sample is large and this course seems to be similar in content and process to other career development courses at other universities, future research should examine the impact of various career courses at multiple sites.

Between-group differences. Although the effect of between-group differences was controlled for in the data analysis, there is one significant group difference that should be kept in mind as a potential confound. As was presented in Table 4, the quasi-experimental group and the comparison groups were significantly different in terms of major status. Specifically, nearly half of the students in the career exploration group were open majors (44.6%) compared to less than a fifth of students in the comparison group (19.2%)—meaning that over 80% of the comparison group had declared a major compared to only 55.4% of the career exploration group. While this difference was statistically controlled for in the analysis—this variable was treated as a covariate in the data analysis—it raises the question of whether having more similarly matched groups might have strengthened the study.

Nontraditional students in sample. Failure to collect the demographic variable of age of the students made it difficult to track which students might be nontraditional students. This can be seen as a potential confound in that nontraditional students take varied paths to graduation, and the research questions motivating this study were more focused on the traditional, entering first time freshmen and whether taking the career course made a difference to those students on certain outcome variables. Given that these students comprised less than 2% of the sample as a whole, it is not likely that they represented a significant confound in the study.

Implications for Future Research

This study has implications for future studies. First, this study and other studies like this (Folsom, 2000; Goodson, 1982; Smith-Keller, 2005) were each conducted at one university and examined the impact of one career development course. Future research should consider a multisite approach in which multiple, similarly structured career development courses are assessed simultaneously for these same outcome variables of interest. In addition, future research should

seek to compare one-credit career courses with two-credit and three-credit career courses. This study examined a two-credit hour course, Folsom's (2000) study examined a three-credit hour course, Smith-Keller (2005) reported on a one-credit hour course, and Goodson's (1982) study reported on a non-credit-bearing career course. These differences should be studied empirically to determine whether career courses of different credit configurations impact student outcomes differently.

In connection with one of this study's limitations, future research might look at only students who received a grade of B-minus or better in the career course (Folsom, 2000). As it can likely be assumed that career courses in general do not carry the same academic rigor as other classes, it may even be worthwhile to include only students who got an A grade or A-minus in the career course to more discriminately delineate between students who presumably benefited most from the class and those who did not meet learning objectives. In addition, the variability between the course teachers might be more effectively addressed by standardizing curriculum and/or investigating the outcomes of a course taught by a single individual.

Implications for Practitioners

The practitioners for whom this study is relevant are not only those in career counseling, and those who teach the course, but also personnel in higher education more generally and anyone who interacts with college students and can make recommendations to those students. It is not only helpful to know that a career development course is an option for undecided students; it is also validating to be able to show that this course has a significant impact on student outcomes (e.g., students who took the class graduated with significantly higher GPAs than those in the comparison group). Perhaps it makes little difference to students that those who pass the career development class tend to graduate with five more credits in the same amount of time (semesters) as students who do not take the course. But as we start to consider what those five credits represent—conceding that two of the credits account for the career development course itself—additional credits can be seen to represent not only additional coursework but the added knowledge and educational experience that coursework provides. What is more, these credits were accumulated in the same amount of semesters as the comparison group, which suggests that this additional coursework is being completed in an efficient manner that does not incur the unnecessary financial cost of extra semester(s) of tuition and living expenses.

In addition, it is worth noting that while this course seems to be drawing generally equally from men and women (recall that our two groups were not significantly different in terms of gender), there was a higher than expected proportion of minority students in the career development course, and this can be seen to have implications for those who work with ethnically diverse students. It appears that this class is being recommended to or pursued more by diverse students, which further justifies its continued implementation as it is reaching a historically marginalized and underserved population of students.

It also bears highlighting that the groups were originally found to be significantly different in terms of entering ACT score (with students in the career course having lower ACT scores than their noncourse participant peers). Given this between - group difference, it appears all the more noteworthy that course participants graduated with significantly higher cumulative GPAs than those in the comparison group. Put another way, assuming that ACT scores and GPAs measure some part of what they purport to measure, course participants who had a lower readiness for college to begin with (as measured by their ACT scores) graduated in the end with higher academic performance (as measured by total GPA at graduation) than noncourse participants. Extrapolating some, one could argue that although initially comprising a group of students, some might expect to underperform compared to their peers (whether that be considering their significantly different composition in terms of race or in terms of ACT score), students taking the career course ended up performing at equal or higher levels on multiple dimensions (i.e., comprising both significant findings of no difference and significant findings in which the career course group could be said to have outperformed the comparison group, this includes time to graduation measured in semesters, retention to graduation as measured by graduated in 6 years, the number of

course withdrawals incurred, and total cumulative GPA at graduation).

Conclusions

This study adds to the growing body of literature concerning the effectiveness of career courses at universities and colleges across the United States, in a way that is particularly needed (by examining outcome rather than output of the course). This was accomplished by replicating portions of Folsom's (2000) and Smith-Keller's (2005) studies in an attempt to provide needed clarity surrounding their conflicting findings. Specifically, a two-credit, career development course entitled was treated as the independent variable in the study, while the following outcome variables were identified as dependent variables of interest: retention to graduation (within 6 years), time to graduation (measured by semesters and credits), the number of course withdrawals, and overall academic success (measured by cumulative GPA at time of graduation). To try to isolate the impact of the course, a comparison group comprising students who did not take the class was likewise assessed on each outcome variable.

Results revealed no significant differences between the two groups in terms of retention to graduation (within 6 years), semesters to graduate, and the number of course withdrawals. However, results indicated statistically significant differences between the quasi-experimental group and the comparison group in terms of credits taken to graduate (with course participants graduating with more credits than noncourse participants) and cumulative GPA (with course participants graduating with higher cumulative GPAs than noncourse participants).

文章来源：

Jamie M. Hansen, Aaron P. Jackson, Tyler R. Pedersen. Career Development Courses and Educational Outcomes: Do Career Courses Make a Difference? [J]. Journal of Career Development, 2016:1-15.

后 记

　　2007年,教育部办公厅印发《大学生职业发展与就业指导课程教学要求》的通知指出,职业发展与就业指导课程建设是高校人才培养工作和毕业生就业工作的重要组成部分。从2008年起,提倡所有普通高校开设职业发展与就业指导课程,并作为公共课纳入教学计划,贯穿学生从入学到毕业的整个培养过程。2012年,教育部办公厅印发《普通本科学校创业教育教学基本要求(试行)》的通知指出,各高校应创造条件,面向全体学生单独开设"创业基础"必修课。《国家中长期教育改革和发展规划纲要(2010—2020)》和《教育部关于普通高中学业水平考试的实施意见》(教基二〔2014〕10号)均明确提出了"建立学生发展指导制度""加强学生生涯规划指导"的相关要求。进入新时代,随着基础教育、高等教育全面普及化的来临,人才的竞争越来越激烈。这些文件的相继出台,说明国家已经深刻意识到开展职业发展教育是提高教育质量的有效方法,说明构建大中小学职业发展教育体系的时机基本成熟。目前,我国对职业发展教育的关注度正在逐渐提高,高校都将职业发展与就业指导课纳入到必修或者选修,针对小学、初高中生的职业发展教育教材数量和类型逐渐增加,开设的学校不断增多。

　　不可否认的是,职业发展教育还存在形式化的问题,原因有观念上的、制度上的,还有专业人才培养滞后、师资队伍短缺、教材建设不到位、学科专业数量偏少等,需要学校、社会、企业、家庭、学生多方形成合力,完善职业发展教育相关理论,构建有效的职业发展教育实施体系,探索职业发展教育的实践模式,推动职业发展教育迈出新步伐。2019年10月,教育部在对十三届全国人大二次会议第1215号建议的答复中提出"要求高校加强学生职业生涯发展教育,对低年级学生着重进行职业生涯启蒙,对高年级学生着重提升职业素质和求职技能","推进职业发展教育相关学科建设。支持有条件的高校在教育学等一级学科下自主设置职业发展教育相关学科方向,促进高等教育职业发展教育良性发展,输送更多高层次博士硕士人才。"郑州大学教育学院2012年在全国率先设置了"职业发展教育"硕士点,随后其他高校也设立了类似硕士点、博士点,如2013年上海市教委发布《上海市学生职业(生涯)发展教育"十二五"行动计划》提出,依托上海师范大学创设职业生涯教育专业硕士点和博士点,培养学生职业(生涯)发展教育的高学历人才。构建一个学科十分不易,需要厚实的学科知识体系做支撑。"职业发展教育"是郑州大学的特色建设学科,在河南省委宣传部、河南省教育厅和郑州大学的支持下,我们组织编写了"职业发展教育"系列著作,《比较职业发展教育》就是其中的一本。

河南省宣传思想文化战线"四个一批"人才项目"生涯教育比较研究"、河南省高等学校哲学社会科学创新团队(2019-CXTD-09)、河南省高等教育教学改革与实践重点项目"基于三螺旋模型的创新创业人才培养体系探索与实践"(2017SJGLX013)和郑州大学教务处、教育学院为本书的写作和出版提供了大力支持。郑州大学出版社孙保营社长、崔青峰副总编辑给予了全力帮助,其他有关人员付出了辛勤汗水,这里一并感谢。

周　倩

2020年2月